DATE DUE

MR 1 2 '98			
MR 1 9 '98			
APR 8 9 1998			
NO 15 04			
Apr 21			
MR 3 1 '09			

DEMCO 38-296

HEAL ABUSE AND
TRAUMA THROUGH ART

ABOUT THE AUTHOR

Dr. Linda Bushell Spencer is an artist, researcher, and self-empowerment counselor. She is a graduate of The Institute of Transpersonal Psychology in Palo Alto, California. Born and raised in New York, she lives in Los Gatos, California with her husband of 16 years. She uses her own artwork to process the traumas of life by creating paintings of actual events that have caused her pain. She successfully used this method to heal residual childhood traumas, parental kidnapping, and divorce. Dr. Spencer believes that acknowledging our inate gifts helps to lead us to our truth, and that finding our individual truth helps remove creative blocks thereby enhancing creativity.

The author can be reached directly by writing to:

L. B. Spencer, Ph.D.
23494 Sunset Drive
Los Gatos, CA 95030

fax: 408-353-2167
e-mail: SpencerArts@worldnet.att.net

HEAL ABUSE AND TRAUMA THROUGH ART

Increasing Self-Worth, Healing of Initial Wounds, and Creating a Sense of Connectivity

By

LINDA BUSHELL SPENCER, Ph.D.

Personal Empowerment Coach
Los Gatos, California

CHARLES C THOMAS • PUBLISHER, LTD.
Springfield • Illinois • U.S.A.

Published and Distributed Throughout the World by

CHARLES C THOMAS • PUBLISHER, LTD.
2600 South First Street
Springfield, Illinois 62794-9265

© *1997 by* CHARLES C THOMAS • PUBLISHER, LTD.

ISBN 0-398-06729-5 (cloth)
ISBN 0-398-06730-9 (paper)

Library of Congress Catalog Card Number: 96-41715

With THOMAS BOOKS *careful attention is given to all details of manufacturing
and design. It is the Publisher's desire to present books that are satisfactory as to their
physical qualities and artistic possibilities and appropriate for their particular use.*
THOMAS BOOKS *will be true to those laws of quality that assure a good name
and good will.*

Printed in the United States of America
SC-R-3

Library of Congress Cataloging-in-Publication Data

Spencer, Linda Bushell.
    Heal abuse and trauma through art : increasing self-worth, healing
of initial wounds, and creating a sense of connectivity / Linda
Bushell Spencer.
        p.   cm.
    Includes bibliographical references and index.
    ISBN 0-398-06729-5 (cloth). — ISBN 0-398-06730-9 (paper)
    1. Art therapy—Case studies.   2. Women artists—Psychology—Case
studies.   3. Transpersonal psychology—Case studies.   I. Title.
RC489.A7S64   1997
616.89'1656—dc20
                                                                96-41715
                                                                CIP

FOREWORD

Throughout human history in all societies, art has been a powerful influence. It both reflects the culture from which it originated and communicates back to that culture. In the individualistic culture of today's Western world, art is more individualistic than in times past or in other cultures. It is still reflective of our society, but also of the individual artist. The finished piece communicates back to its creator as well as to the society that views it.

This reverberation between art and culture or individually between artist and viewer is both powerful and mysterious. We recognize that visual expressions can move us but the ways in which they do are difficult to understand and more difficult to articulate. Equally mysterious is the experience of the artist. We recognize that some are driven to create; some sacrifice almost everything else in their lives to do so. We retain our associations of independence and even eccentricities among artists. But what do we really know of the art-making process?

The healing potential of that process, for both individuals and for groups, is at the foundation of the relatively young field of art therapy. As director of an art therapy graduate program, I find that almost all applicants to the program whom I interview wish to enter the field as a result of the significance and solace their own art-making has brought to them. They wish to bring that experience to others. Many of those I interview are young people who at an early age have discovered the power in their own art. Some are middle-age. They are people who have established their art as a guide in their lives through its various stages. Most are women.

Western art has traditionally been a man's world. Only since the rise of feminism in recent decades have female artists of the past gained prominence. And only in recent times have women artists made a significant impact on the art world. There are strong connections between art-making and the tenants of feminism. With the recognition that "the personal is political," women artists tell their personal stories in their art.

Think of Frida Kahlo, for example. Prior to feminism, her reputation had been overshadowed by her more famous husband, the artist Diego Rivera. Although her highly imaginative, deeply personal/painful self-portraits pre-date feminism, it is the feminist movement that brought her to a wider audience in this country, particularly with the publication of her biography in 1983 by Hayden Herrera (*Frida, A Biography of Frida Kahlo,* NY, Harper & Row).

Linda Spencer, like Frida Kahlo and other women artists today, has pursued and found herself in her own art expression. This book, therefore, is rooted in her deeply felt experience rather than in the dispassionate observations of a more distant observer. She knows the territory, the questions to ask, the doors to open, in bringing us, the readers, into the intimate lives of the eight women art-makers with whom she has examined the healing properties of art-making.

A focus of this exploration is painful, personal experience. All the women here, including the author, have suffered considerably in their lives. This book looks at the mysterious processes by which creating art transforms that experience. It is not necessarily exactly the same for each woman, but there are common threads that weave their experiences together. The pain does not vanish, but it is transmuted.

Some of the artists appear to enter an altered state while creating. I have known that experience myself during creative activity where concentration is so focused that time and space disappear and all that exists for me is my evolving painting and the materials I am using to create it. The author compares this sort of altered state to meditation and in some instances to ecstasy. For some of the artists, it appears that in this state they can open themselves and let their images "come" to them, rather than directing them initially. This is the sort of receptivity that can allow one to be most deeply in touch with one's inner self.

But in a more particular sense, the artists here have also tackled their pain directly. To quote from the text, " . . . the artist can depict threatening images, conquer fears, and gain peace of mind through meeting adversaries on canvas rather than in real life."

Art-making is often a solitary pursuit. We retain the stereotypic image of the reclusive artist alone in a garret painting feverishly (and probably starving). The very act of creating through traveling deeply within is not usually a social process. But there is a paradox here, for often the inward journey brings us to the universal, the fundamentals of life that connect us to others. These connections are not necessarily shared, except as we view the art of others that speaks to us in some way. But the connection is between the viewer and the art. The artist is seldom personally present in the gallery.

In contrast, this study has provided a context in which these women have come to feel connected to one another through their stories and through their art. Linda Spencer has found in undertaking her exploration that she and the eight women with whom she met have all been changed by the exploration itself. Telling their stories to one another has extended their expression beyond the canvas. (This is the stuff of which art therapy is made.) The readers of this book, too, may become witness to the creative/healing processes of these women. We are invited to enter the healing creative community they have formed. As Linda Spencer discovered in interviewing the artists, we, too, may hear echoes of our own experience in their stories. The connection that these women felt validated their own experience. We, too, may find self-validation as their lives are opened to us in ways that may connect with our own.

Linda Spencer introduces this book stating: "I have found artistic expression the most powerful form of therapy I have ever experienced — far more healing than individual therapy, sandtray therapy, or group process work." That statement and this book that has grown out of it suggest powerful implications. The author and the women who speak through her are artists. But what about those of us who are not? Might not creative expression be important for all of us? Perhaps it should be encouraged far more than it is in our school systems so that our citizens will grow up learning to "heal" themselves with this safe, ever-available medicine. It's something to think about, perhaps to do something about. As a beginning, we might each try art for ourselves and our own children. Whether we choose to do so or not, the intense and intimate stories of this probing book will open our eyes to the healing power of art expression.

HARRIET WADESON, PH.D., A.T.R.–BC, HLM
Professor and Coordinator
Art Therapy Graduate Program
University of Illinois at Chicago
Author: *Art Psychotherapy, The Dynamics of Art Psychotherapy,*
Advances in Art Therapy, A Guide to Conducting Art
Therapy Research

PREFACE

There is something unique in the creative experience. People report that there is a point in art where it becomes a transcendental or even divine experience. In the creation of an artifact you draw from the wounds of life experience at the most intense level. If you draw from that resource, and you do it in a way that the creative is awake and active, something happens that enlarges the reality beyond it. When that happens you see the reality beyond the creativity and this allows the ego to take on a different perspective. The ego does not disappear, it just becomes less active. The artist begins to feel that there is something bigger. Ultimately when the artist accesses this feeling it is what seems to heal. They find in the creative act itself something that goes from ego to God. It transcends the ego.

The ego appears to be more active if you are wounded. It makes one more defensive. The ego gives the impulse to protect the physical organism, when we are hurt physically or emotionally. This gets translated by the ego into a hyper-watchful state. You have to live defensively. The ego says "you have to watch out." As Rank says, "We fluctuate between a fear of life and a fear of death." If my life is not being supported, it is being threatened.

In a life that has suffered much abuse, the ego has taken on a bigger part; more attention is used and less is left for the person to get connected to their spiritual essence. This is the case until such time as the person realizes that it cannot be done, one cannot protect themselves satisfactorily. With this realization something very different happens; either severe panic or a look toward the spiritual essence. In creating an artifact a person can go through the art experience into the imagery that comes out of it. Creativity and intuition literally connects them to the creative force of the universe. Once the wounded artist embraces the imagery that was once so threatening, it ceases to have the initial impact. The experience of connectivity to the universe is something that happens when you're putting your creativity, your wounding, and your imagery together in a most intense way.

ACKNOWLEDGMENTS

In the process of completing this work I have acquired my own voice. It has been a valuable and stimulating experience which expanded me technically and socially. I found my story within the stories of these other artists.

Karl Herbst, my husband has unwittingly taken this journey through psychological awareness with me and I want him to know I have appreciated his endurance and understanding. Our relationship has deepened as a result.

I want to acknowledge Jennifer Clements, whose practicality helped me clarify ideas and find my voice. Thank you Henry Wolgemuth, for helping me recognize the transpersonal in myself and in others. Thank you also Hal Bennett, Bob Frager, William Braud and Olga Luchakova for reading and commenting on the original work that led to this manuscript. Most of all, I want to thank my mother, for embracing me as I explored my emotional depths, which resulted in bringing up a myriad of conflicting emotions.

On the technical side: Thank you Pamela Sheets for lending your keen artistic eye to the process of photography, and for "being there" when patience was as important as professionalism. And I thank Rudy Haynal, my art agent, for figuring out how to combine two paintings to capture one idea for the cover of this book. That idea being, "When one surrenders to spirit, healing takes place."

CONTENTS

HEAL ABUSE AND
TRAUMA THROUGH ART

Chapter 1

INTRODUCTION

*Art is the province of every human being. When the artist is
alive in any person, regardless of genre, that person becomes an
inventive, searching, daring, self-expressing creature. (Henri,
1923)*

This book explores the healing aspects of artistic expression in the
lives of eight women. It isn't a "How To" book. This work takes us
into the creative experience itself through the eyes and words of women
who have lived it, experienced it, and have grown through the painful
memories of abuse and trauma in the process. Through their art, these
artists experience personal growth and increased self-worth. They have
learned how to be the star in their own life play rather than a bit player
in someone else's.

In transpersonally oriented therapy, it is usually considered important
for the client to experience an altered state of consciousness because the
positive healing shifts happen in the psyche when such states are activated.
This altered state can be activated through artistic expression, hypnosis,
breathwork or many other types of selective awareness. Childhood
memories can become activated through artwork allowing one to get in
touch with the bodily and emotional component of early memories.
Painting provides a safe place where feelings are released in much the
same way as they are in a therapeutic situation.

In this work I have used an approach that incorporates elements of the
sacred, transformative, and transpersonal. I take the reader inside the
mind and heart of the women whose stories are shared. Questions and
observations were used in lieu of statistics. When feminist researchers
ask questions, the responses are usually in the form of stories because
reading a personal story makes history less remote. By using an open-
ended interview technique, a complete set of themes emerged from the
data collected. From this data, commonalties of experience reveal the
actual experience that takes place through creative expression.

Those artists' who had abusive childhoods found art expression helped to dissolve painful memories even when those memories and life events remained unresolved. In other words, they didn't have to try over and over to get their abuser to admit to and apologize for their abusive behavior in order to come to terms with their past. Producing, viewing, and even dialoguing with their artwork afforded personal insights which allowed the artists' pain to diminish. When one interacts with one's art, it is as if the charge is removed from painful memories. The memories don't disappear, they just don't produce the same charge as they used to.

My interest in this subject stems from personal curiosity because I have observed extraordinary connections between releasing my creative energy and experiencing spiritual growth. My creative work is a self-exercise in intimacy, a way to face painful feelings that have been inaccessible for many years.

I have noticed a clear connection between past pain, trauma, and my own artwork. Personally, my painting has been an emotional release system, engaging my unconscious as well as my conscious mind, and that interactive flow is unifying. I have found artistic expression the most powerful form of therapy I have ever experienced—far more healing than individual therapy, sandtray therapy, or group process work. Painting has been the very essence of my healing.

As I paint, I feel a transformation happening, a shift into an alternate dimension. As I painted a dream that occurred to me 30 years ago, I reexperienced the childhood asthma that devastated my youth. My throat constricted, and I interrupted the painting process many times to regain my breath. I could not get enough air: My lungs clamped shut. I tried, to no avail, to draw a breath. I was suffocating and terrified. I felt as if deep, primal emotions were being released—as if I were choking them out. Releasing color to the canvas seemed to pull my rib cage open, allowing air to enter. I was mentally and physically drained. Unbelievably, I was reliving the identical suffocating feelings of so many years before. It was a process of making conscious the unconscious, releasing the pent-up trauma, being both "in" the work and "beyond" it simultaneously. I was able to tolerate my feelings; this time I was in control.

I was quite ill as a child and the only one in my family to have nearly died many times. Also, I was quite artistic—the only one with a creative flair. Since neither my parents nor grandparents were artistic, I have often wondered from whence my talent came.

When I was ill or depressed, I would have a strong urge to draw or paint. The more upset or depressed I became, the better my artwork became. When I met the artist, Mary Chabiel, whose art changed following the death of her son, my curiosity in how art parallels life germinated. Writings by Kenneth Ring (1992) further piqued my interest. Ring discusses the role of dissociation in opening people up to alternate realities which predispose one to experiences such as Unidentified Flying Object (UFO) sightings and near death experiences (NDEs).

I wondered if this type of dissociative state may also be a causative or influencing factor in opening the door to activating our creative side through an unconscious attempt at self-healing. I spoke with other artists and was amazed by how many had traumatic lives. I was also fascinated that many artists have had NDEs, or have seen or felt the presence of angels.

I believe true creativity may lead a person out of despair. When I create on canvas, my creation mirrors my inner world: It confronts me. Confrontation can happen intentionally or unintentionally, consciously or unconsciously. When this occurs, the healing process begins. Confrontation allows one to move from using art as isolated moments of crisis release to art as maintenance.

Whatever the style of the age, in each stage of Western art history, there has always been a group of successful artists whose artwork reflected the acceptable standards of their society. There was yet another group, whose art survives today, who did not fit into the cultural conventions of their peers, but whose artwork came from the deepest recesses of their being. Most of these artists had an unusually high instance of trauma in their lives, such as the loss of a parent, which dynamically altered their creative potentials. Could creativity be the gift of a difficult upbringing?

This book focuses on both the artist and their work in order that we may come to better understand the process by which art can be used to connect with the creative gifts in our lives. One need not be an artist to experience this process. A crayon or pencil combined with a piece of office typing paper can serve the same purpose. The women's stories in this book help identify issues or problems that exist for women in general and I encourage you to try it without being judgmental about what you produce. Your work need not end up in a museum. It is just as effective taped to your bathroom mirror.

Art may be used to dissolve life issues such as dealing with anger, and with self-esteem. Here I detail the process by which art may be used as a vehicle toward greater transpersonal wholeness and transformation. New ways of knowing are made possible by art and creativity, and new sources of information and strength become possible. I believe that "shadow" aspects of oneself are made more accessible through the symbolism in art. Through the womens' stories we observe how greater assimilations and integrations of our darker side are possible. Art puts one in touch with other aspects of one's self and with other aspects of nature. Symbols, images, and nonverbal processes have been reviewed. These help us access ways of knowing and expressing through means other than words. Symbols help us understand what it is that is being expressed and how.

Illustrative Example of The Healing Power of Art

Maxine Junge (1987) tells the story of a young woman who used her art as therapy. Yvonne, the oldest of three children, was nine years old when her father suffered a nervous breakdown and died in his sleep. The death was not discussed in the family.

Yvonne became allergic to everything; and when she became allergic to her favorite dog, it was euthanized. Yvonne became depressed, stopped eating, was often ill, and spent a lot of time alone.

When she was 14, her mother was operated on for open-heart surgery, lapsed into a coma, and died. Yvonne then lived in a series of foster homes. Her depression continued; she drank, used drugs, and was sexually promiscuous. During this time she began to draw. She remembers: "I started to draw these little people with things happening to them. They're all about a lot of pain. The images would just come. I would sit down with a pen and I'd feel better."

The earliest drawings Yvonne speaks of are of little people floating in air. They appear passive, are circular, and lack fingers, toes, or sexual characteristics. The eyes appear frightened, and the mouths are tiny.

Her drawings evolved into desolate landscapes. One has a large figure of a girl, her head hanging by strings to her body, and dead trees. This symbolized her feelings of disconnectedness.

When she came of age, an inheritance from her mother allowed Yvonne to buy a cabin in the woods. She loved it, and it became her protective shelter. She said: "As a kid I always felt very connected to nature and the earth. I spent a lot of time alone there. When I was up in the mountains after my mother died, I started to go out alone and walked the land a lot to find solace, and the nurturance I needed there. I moved into the mountains because I had to go. I found my mother in the earth."

One drawing shows her cabin and land. In a corner of the picture, an encapsulated city represents the split she felt between the hostile city and the supportive rural landscape. Junge writes:

> This treatment of the cabin echoes the theme of the tree detached from its root system and could be construed as both a reflection of Yvonne's sense of separateness from her "roots," the ground, and also as a defensive mechanism and self-protection. Yvonne's artwork was therapeutic. It provided a safe container for her thoughts, feelings, and questions. Her artwork gave her a visual, permanent record confirming that she existed in what had become an all-too-impermanent world.

Through her art, Yvonne could express and work through her childhood memories and the death of her parents. She could grieve. Themes of loss and death coexist with creativity. She used imagery in her search for self. At 29, Yvonne underwent this therapeutic process alone, and is a professional artist and writer. Her story is illustrative of others in this book. Not all the artists in the stories herein have been cognizant of their own healing process and yet healing still took place. They were only aware of their emotional and physical pain. They coped well with the pain; they didn't suppress it, or deny it. They contained it; they learned how to hold the pain. This is very healthy psychologically because it helped them love themselves as memories were brought into awareness in spite of the horror of the events themselves.

In addition to painting, I urge you to talk with your work after it has been spontaneously painted. Jean, whose story you will find in this book, created a series of paintings which she dialogued with directly. This method of interactive communication with artwork can have an extremely powerful effect on one's psyche. It can bring insights and the release of early, wounding pain.

The benefits of art are not limited to the painter. It was found in this study that as the woman's self esteem grew and her "self" image increased, there was less psychological pressure on the spouse. The artists' personal life purpose became connected to creativity rather than dependence on the husband. There was less space for projection and therefore their capacity to respect and relate to each other as real human beings was increased. A sense of security and trust emerges out of seeing your life as "making sense."

Chapter 2

A BRIEF HISTORY OF ART AS THERAPY

Cherish your own emotions and never undervalue them. We
are not here to do what has already been done. (Henri, 1923)

Using artistic expression as a form of healing is nothing new. Artistic
work functions as a means of expressing pain and tension rather
than keeping those stressors within the body-mind. A review of the
literature explores various theories regarding the origin of creativity and
the correlation between trauma and creativity. The fact is that trauma
may act as an antecedent to creativity.

With an emphasis on life review narrative which can lead to healing,
spiritual growth, and personal transformation, Ettling (1994) describes
personal transformation as "the process of growing in the consciousness
of the oneness of all things. It means living more and more in the reality
of that unity, feeling less divided within myself or separated from anyone
else."

Self-Actualization

Arnheim (1969) believes that art is an indispensable tool in dealing
with the tasks of life and that artistic expression provides a balance for
feelings, thoughts, and experiences. He notes that painting provides a
safe place for difficult thoughts, feelings, questions, and a means of
communication, clarification, and expression for the artist.

"By capturing an experience, owning it, and by portraying it well, he
has lifted that experience out of the tangled morass of misunderstanding
into the beauty of language by rendering it into art" (Wakefield, 1995).
Artistic expression, facilitates this untangling through projecting one's
innermost feelings in symbolic representation onto canvas. I believe this
process may lead to personal transformation and self-actualization.

Painting gives a visual, permanent record of a person's existence in an
unstable and impermanent world. In artwork, themes of loss and death

can coexist with creativity as the artist uses imagery in his/her development of the search for self. Carl Gustav Jung (1960), one of the greatest philosophers of our time, refers to this process of self-actualization as "individuation" and describes the process as an attempt toward achieving selfhood. This refers to an integrated state of psychological development.

Maslow (1971), a psychologist famous for studying the highest forms of human behavior, describes self-actualization as an organism's intrinsic growth and notes that development proceeds from within the organism; and, the highest motive is to behave purely expressively. Because self-actualization is growth—motivated rather than deficiency—motivated at the highest levels of human development, the distinction between coping and expression is resolved.

Artistic Expression

Jung (1964) proposed that there are distinctly two different types of artistic expression: the sensory style artist, and the imaginative style artist. The former possesses what Maslow calls special talent creativeness; this artist paints objects or scenes things of nature in a directly representational style. This style is usually referred to as "realistic."

On the other hand, the imaginative style artist paints in an abstract, dreamlike, fantasy, or otherwise non-figurative style. In discussing non-figurative art, Jung (1960) writes:

Nothing in works of non-figurative art reminds the spectator of his own world—no objects in their own everyday surroundings, no human being or animal that speaks a familiar language. And yet, without any question, there is a human bond. It may be even more intense than in works of sensory art, which make a direct appeal to feeling and empathy. . . . At present, non-figurative art seems to me to offer the one opportunity for the painter to approach the inward reality of himself and to grasp the consciousness of his essential self, or even his being. . . . I believe that the painter will be able, in the time to come, to return slowly to himself, to rediscover his own weight and so to strengthen it that it can even reach the outward reality of the world.

The sensory-style artists in this study say that their subjects beckon to be painted. The imaginative artists, those who paint memories, also state that they likewise surrender choosing subjects and describe an even more passive state in which internal images emerge to paint. A kind of active passivity seems to be the most desirable state for beginning a work of art for both sensory and imaginative artists. Both groups describe their absolute trust in allowing themselves to be stimulated to paint. Rosenberg and Epstein (1991) remarked, "As the final decision is made, many artists describe giving themselves over to a mutual need, the need of the subject to be painted and the artist to paint it."

In art the artist opens her/himself to the preconscious; then, it is possible to access the unconscious—both the personal and collective. At the latter level, mind expands and joins with the unifying psychological and spiritual forces that underlie the human race. These forces appear as primordial symbols that have been meaningful for all times and all people, as witnessed by their appearance in the art of all cultures. Assagioli (1971) describes 14 categories of symbols: introversion, descent, ascent, expansion, awakening, illumination, fire, development, intensification, love, path, transmutation, rebirth, and liberation. Symbols point to something not easily defined and, therefore, not fully known.

The most significant symbols of interest in this study will be those transpersonal symbols that emerge repeatedly in human consciousness and are considered to have archetypal origins. Archetypes are patterns of energy within the creative field (Vargiu, 1977).

> By deliberately visualizing such a symbol, we form in our mind a pattern that is in tune with the creative field, and therefore can be brought to reverberate with it, and thus draw energy from it. We establish such a reverberation by concentrating on the visualized image and its deeper meaning with sufficient mental tension. The symbolic pattern within our mind thus absorbs a portion of energy from the field. It then transforms this energy, steps it down, and lets it flow to nearby mental elements, and eventually to our feelings. The particular kind of symbol or pattern chosen will determine the mode of the reverberation and thus the particular quality of energy absorbed and the corresponding feeling evoked. (Vargiu, 1977)

We can observe the creative field through the effects it produces: we can observe creative phenomena most easily through a study of symbols. From the perspective of Jungian psychology, art reflects archetypes. Different archetypes emerge at various times in different ways for every person; symbols are vehicles for an artist's intuition, an artist's feelings. Artwork may portray the "archetypal stage" of a painter's development.

Jung (1972) considered that the archetype of the mandala (a circular form) comes from the collective unconscious, the residence of all symbols and images. He (1964) explains the collective unconscious as the biological and unconscious development of early humanity—humanity still close to the animal. If Jung (1964) was right about the existence of a collective unconscious then some of our image-making and responding may be inherited, presumably genetically . . . again, an internal physical source. Drawings of mandalas suggest that being "centered" may have a biological as well as a psychological source (Rubin, 1985).

Jung believed that art is more than random pictures; that pictures of a patient varied widely depending on the stage of the patient's psychological process. Certain motifs accompanied certain stages, and the mandala, a circular art form, most often appeared in connection with chaos, disorientation, or panic within the artist. The process of creating a mandala has a healing effect on the artist. Jung (1964) believed the circle, a frequent shape in artwork, symbolizes the self, and he felt that meditating on a mandala could put one in touch with the "self" because the circle expresses the totality of the psyche, including the relationship between man and nature.

According to Hagood (1987), "Integration of the conscious and unconscious was to be attained and the creation of the mandala was believed to facilitate such a process."

Hagood (1987) noted that archetypal figures often appear in mandalas and that they indicate a struggle within the person between opposite parts of his or her personality. When these opposites are brought together, healing takes place and the person becomes whole.

According to Bear (1985) the ability to create images—which represent the primordial substance of our picture of the world—in the mind's eye, is a key element of all perceptual and attitudinal change; consequently, visualization can be instrumental in every phase of rehabilitation.

We think in images and in art react to them, work with them, know them, and somewhat control them with our choices of composition, color, and style. Rubin (1985) writes: "It is not a simple matter of an image arising to the surface from the unconscious to concrete conscious form. Externalizing an idea or feeling in an image often allows the artist to become aware of something not previously conscious, that is to have an insight."

An artist engages actively in the concretization of an image. Rosenberg (1987) comments that artists depend "upon their mental imagery in three essential phases of art-making: collecting and storing images, art-making itself, and response to completed paintings. Of particular interest are the ways in which artists work to match their internal images to external product through skillful manipulation of art elements and use of artistic principles."

Most of the artists in this study used symbols to access "higher" aspects of themselves. What Csikszentmihalyi (1990) calls "flow" and Maslow names "peak experience," I define as "a state of unity." In this state, one feels as if one is connected to something bigger than oneself; something is flowing through you. Csikszentmihalyi (1990) describes the "flow" as the state in "which people are so involved in an activity that nothing else seems to matter; the experience itself is so enjoyable that people will do it even at great cost, for the sheer sake of doing it."

Maslow (1987) describes "peak experience" as "integration within the person and therefore between the person and the world. In these states of being, the person becomes unified; for the time being, the splits, polarities, and dissociations within him tend to be resolved; the civil war within is neither won nor lost but transcended. In such a state, the person becomes far more open to experience and far more spontaneous and fully functioning."

Maslow's observations suggest that the release of energies fulfills a need for pleasureful experiences and is, as well, a deeply embedded drive toward personal wholeness through the integration of mind and body. The integration of body and mind through body-image projection is a highly important aspect of pictorial expression. According to Uhlin (1972), when a person draws a human figure, house, or tree he projects his personal body image with all of its somatic and psychical meanings onto the paper.

Maslow (1987) distinguishes "special talent creativeness" from "self-actualizing creativeness" and explains that the latter springs much more directly from the personality. Furthermore, self-actualizing creativeness " . . . seemed to be made up largely of "innocent" freedom of perception, and "innocent," uninhibited spontaneity and expressiveness." The innocence inherent at birth is lost or buried as a person becomes enculturated and sophisticated (Maslow, 1987).

Creativity

There is little agreement on what inspires creativity, and definitions of creativity vary. Freud defined creativity as "sublimated sexual energy." Both sexual energy and creative energy create powerful drives in the human body. Eastern traditions have studied these energy forces for thousands of years and distinguish different types and functions of energies in our lives. One of these subtle energies of the life force is termed Kundalini and is often associated with energy movement within the body and/or paranormal experience. "The pain and upheavals of Kundalini awakening are similar to those of individuation, where the former persona and false selves are abdicating their role in favor of the unification of personality around the deeper self" (Greenwell, 1990). She continues, "In addition to these unconventional activities many people report awakened creativity, and begin to write or produce art, at least as a temporary stage of the process. This seems to serve a healing and integrative function in their lives."

Torrance and Hall (1980) theorized that creativity is a combination of ability, skills, and motivation and thus is teachable. Piaget's (1962) theory of cognitive development relates directly to creativity in that Piaget concludes that children reintegrate "creative imagination" as they age: Creative imagination increases along with intelligence during the developmental process.

Some definitions require socially valuable products if the act or person is to be called creative (Barron, 1968; Dudek, 1968), while others (Cooperstein, 1979; Chambers, 1969), see creativity itself as being intrinsically valuable—nothing of demonstrable social value need be produced. Ford and Harris (1992) feel creativity is the actualizing of our potential and states that creativity generates possibilities and allows the creative person to choose among them.

Maslow (1987) views creativity as the self-actualizing state in which one engages one's full capacities; concentration and total absorption characterize immersion in this state. Maslow noted when people were at their best, they felt more whole and integrated than usual. At those times, they were using all of their capacities to the fullest extent in an effortlessness way. They were self-determined, fearless, and free of criticism. They were spontaneous and responsive; and they felt creative in a harmonious way. These people were keenly present in the moment and felt complete. In summation, these people were playful, delightful, and joyful and felt fortunate that their lives were so wonderful. For Maslow, "peak experiences," or moments of ecstasy, are transient moments of self-actualization. Art, whether created or merely viewed, can be a vehicle of entry to this state.

Of particular interest to me was Maslow's (1987) comment that "creativeness in self-actualizing people was in many respects like the creativeness of all happy and secure children. It was spontaneous, effortless, innocent, easy, a kind of freedom from stereotypes and clichés. It seemed to be made up largely of "innocent" freedom of perception and "innocent," uninhibited spontaneity and expressiveness."

He noted that these people's innocence was combined with sophisticated minds and that he felt these characteristics were inherent at birth and lost or buried as one became enculturated. As artists' such as Conqueror, Mari, and Saille are able to access these states through their art, this same effortless kind of freedom envelops them, affording them a sense of happiness and security.

Vargiu (1977) notes a connection between energy fields and creativity. He believes that there is both a creative field and an emotional field which interact with mental elements and tend to organize these mental elements into configurations corresponding to their specific energy patterns. "The interaction between fields may yield either harmonious or discordant feelings. In the instance of an emotional catharsis, mental images and visual memories may appear which lend insight regarding the original trauma."

By working with mental images and symbols, blocked emotional energy may be transformed and released. "When one's emotional field and creative field resonate, a person may experience a state of deep inner harmony similar to those peak moments when a life-changing illumination has changed the course of a person's life" (Vargiu, 1977).

Jung (1972) defines creativity as an "an innate drive which seizes a human being and makes him its instrument." The artist is a person who allows art to flow through him or herself.

In Adler's (1936) opinion, an individual produces art to compensate for personal inadequacies or defects. On the other hand, May (1975) disagrees with Adler's compensatory theory of creativity. I agree with Rollo May (1975) who writes: "it [compensatory theory] does not deal with the creative process as such. Compensatory trends in an individual will influence the forms his or her creating will take, but they do not explain the process of creativity itself."

Although Gardner (1983) writes about intelligence rather than stages of creativity, his concepts aid in understanding why some people are musically or linguistically creatively inclined, and other people exhibit their creativity in other endeavors. Gardner's descriptions of intelligence types supports the contention that creativity manifests in myriad ways.

The dancer, musician, mathematician, mime, and businessman are all creative.

Otto Rank (1932) and Robert Henri (1923) agree that whatever we do in life becomes our artistic contribution to society—as human beings, art is our lives. Rank feels that a certain dynamic tension builds between the artist and society because, at one level, the creative artist must violate society's norms. If the artist is successful, another set of problems emerge from this encounter. Society moves to embrace this genius by paying money for the artist's work. Many artists are seduced by the monetary rewards and slide into a role of pleasing their audience.

Bruner (1962) hypothesizes that disengaging oneself from conventional ideas is a necessary condition for creativity. Perhaps this ability facilitates violating social norms. In some instances, disengagement may entail dissociation, a behavior often acquired in childhood as a pain defense.

Rank (1964) defined three stages or phases of realizing one's creative potential as types of people: the adapted type, the neurotic type, and the creative type. The adaptive type identifies with his/her parents and feels no urge to separate from them. The adaptive type fits easily into society; hence, he/she is called average or normal. "This person lacks a strong drive toward individuation and does not experience conflict concerning social norms. Consequently, although the adaptive type endures less conflict, that person enjoys fewer creative possibilities."

The next move toward individuality and creativity is stimulated by interpersonal conflict and is referred to as the neurotic stage. Most creative people reach this stage wherein one sets one's own goals and standards rather than conforming to those set by society. "Growth possibilities emerge that were not present at the adaptive level. If these possibilities are realized, the person enters the realm of creativity; if the possibilities are not realized and conflicts go unresolved, feelings of guilt and inferiority ensue" (Rank, 1964).

Rank describes the third type of development as "the will, the counter-will, and the ideal formation born from the conflict between them which itself has become a goal-setting, goal-seeking force."

Nydes (1962) writes:

The creative person differs from the highly disturbed person in having the capacity to tolerate and override anxiety, to integrate and admit into awareness an unusual depth and intensity of conflicting feeling without being overwhelmed by panic and losing touch with reality. Their ego strength, if you will, can accommodate the chaos of emerging inner experience and be further nurtured by the ability to discover a larger order even in paradox and emotional turmoil. For the truly creative his or her work may serve to resolve inner turmoil.

As a person moves through life from the trauma of birth to the trauma of death, the personality is shaped and determined by the interaction and strengths of two basic fears: the fear of life and the fear of death. Rank (1964) believes that the fear of life (fear of separation) drives a person backward to earlier states of union with the mother, as well as to later stages of dependence on other persons more powerful than the self. The fear of life encompasses being alone, standing out from the crowd, of living one's life, of independence, and of being oneself.

Psychic Tension

Although there is abundant literature that focuses on ways in which tension affects performance, our interest here relates to whether the energy involved in tension is taken in or released during the act of painting. Neumann (1974) believes that psychic tension is present in the creative person from birth; such a person has a kind of alertness which sensitizes that person to the environment.

Eissler (1963) addresses psychic tension, seeing it as "the back and forth movement of as yet unbound energy which is in the process of being formed into the pre-stages of creative actions. Bringing to the canvas a strong emotion such as anger, pain or grief will relieve the artist of some tension and can transform the personality, by offering personal insights to the artist as he/she is in the act of painting."

Tension and relaxation ebb and flow throughout the creative experience. While some therapists speculate that creative activity resolves tension, others think that creative activity produces tension. Some evidence suggests that artists purposefully seek and use tension in the creation of their work. Eissler (1963) describes this phenomenon in her reference to Schiller, a friend of Goethe's. During a time of tragic destitution, Schiller received housing and money from a friend; however, Schiller could not endure favorable conditions for longer than a year. He wrote to his benefactor: "My heart is contracted and the lights of my imagination are extinguished. I am in need of a crisis. Nature brings about a destruction in order to bring forth anew. It may well be that you do not understand me, but I understand myself all right" (Eissler, 1963).

According to Eissler, Goethe also preferred tension and thus refrained from "dissipating his feelings of guilt, which evidently provided momentum towards creation" (1963). She refers to Goethe's failure to write or visit his sister when she was gravely ill.

Sometimes, I must paint a series of paintings before my inner tension is relieved. The constant wave of desire to paint and the release from the desire to paint correspond to the mounting and releasing of tension in my body. However, I do not believe that lessening tension diminishes the quality of the artwork: only the desire, the craving to paint declines. The ability does not. It is my impression that those artists I would refer to as "special talent" artists accumulate a tension build-up in the body during the painting process which is only relieved upon completion of the painting. The "self-actualizing" artists, on the other hand, appear to have a cathartic release of tension during their painting process. Thus, we have two types of artists and these types show a clear difference in how the energy involved in tension affects their body.

Trauma

Trauma may act as an antecedent to creativity. Several authors have discussed the incidence of trauma (e.g., abandonment, loss, severe illness) in lives of great writers and philosophers such as Dante, Hugo, Rousseau, Camus, and Sartre (Anzieu, 1975; Assael & Wacks, 1989; Jaimison, 1984; Pollock, 1961; Rentchnick, 1975). "The impact of a traumatic environment is felt from the very beginning of life" (Giovacchini, 1994). Miller (1990), who, from an analytic perspective, researched Pablo Picasso's life, explains that traces of childhood events are always present in a person's creative work. Miller thinks that Picasso's theme of the distorted human body was imprinted on his psyche when he, as a three-year-old, witnessed his mother giving birth to his sister only a few days after Picasso's town was shocked by an earthquake, which sent hundreds of people running for safety.

Ring (1992) postulates that trauma does indeed affect creativity and notes that age five is particularly pivotal, an observation borne out in all of the pilot studies in my research. Ring was first to notice that trauma happening at this age seems to devastate a child more than if the same trauma happened at any other age. May (1975) also accepts the idea that trauma can change the nature of the artwork produced.

Like Picasso, Austrian Expressionist artist Egon Schiele (1890–1918) was affected by childhood trauma including his father's death from syphilis and the deaths of his four siblings. Schiele's self-portraits depict him in a mutilated state; his painting was the way in which he dealt with the hopelessness of his life. "Schiele perceived himself and depicted himself according to his inner emotional state . . . " (Knafo, 1991).

The artistic process is an empowering process when one is overwhelmed by the lack of hope and the helplessness often present in grief. Unresolved grief manifests in various ways such as in the ability to form trusting relationships, poor self-esteem, depression, alcoholism, and psychosis. When a child confronts loss in a healthy manner as through artwork, the child gains skills which can assist that child with future trauma. McIntyre (1990) concludes that intervention is crucial for bereaved children because unresolved grief often results in pathology. Wylie and Wylie (1987) believe that the creative process gets to the core of grief; furthermore, visual art can express multiple feelings in a single image.

Frida Kahlo (1907–1954), afflicted as a child by polio, was injured at the age of 18 in an accident that she claimed "destroyed" her by fracturing her spine, shattering her pelvis, and crushing her foot. Her vagina was impaled by a steel handrail that eventually resulted in her inability to bear children. Despite plaster casts, corsets, and more than 30 operations, Kahlo was incapacitated and bedridden during long periods of her life. Kahlo's self-portraits enabled her to deal concretely with her pain while concurrently feeding her narcissism, which had been injured along with her body (Knafo, 1991).

Both Schiele and Kahlo used self-portraiture to deal with trauma. For Schiele, painting dealt solely with psychic pain; however, Kahlo painted to cope with physical injury and psychic trauma. Kahlo said, "Painting completed my life. I lost three children. Painting substituted for all of this" (Harrera, 1983). By giving birth to her art, Kahlo gave birth to herself.

Creating artwork may restore equilibrium in the psyche after the experience of loss by replacing the lost person or object. Thus, creative activity attempts to resolve separation anxiety. Through their creations, artists convert passive grief and helplessness into active mastery (Knafo, 1991). By observing a time span of artists' work, we can "observe the relationship of the psychology and traumatic stress to the artistic personality as it unfolds" (Junge, 1987).

Crisis can provide a turning point in one's life (Barron, 1968). Sometimes, a crisis can pressure a person to discriminate and choose consciously. Often, an emotional breakdown generates a breakthrough.

However, during a crisis, we may suffer from physical illness which masks the predicament. Kast (1991) writes: "The crisis, the factors that precipitated it, its meaning and the developmental possibilities lying within it, can only be reached with difficulty. Therefore one must get into real inner contact with their crisis. This can be the time in the life of the artist that break-throughs happen, the style may change or the favored media may be discarded in favor of something else."

My experience supports Kast's observation. When I began to process my personal history, my paintings changed from small, detailed oil paintings to fast-drying, large, acrylic canvasses. Furthermore, the content shifted from realistic depictions of external scenes to symbolic representations of my inner world. Mary, a participant in this study, had the same experience years earlier. Her paintings changed after the death of her son.

Without enough trauma, creativity may lie dormant; however, with too much trauma, an artist may become dysfunctional. Munch's depression became so deep that he was unable to paint. However, "When Munch was cured of his illness—and of his tensions, paroxysms, and hallucinations, he was also cured of his genius" (Wylie & Wiley, 1987). Munch's history suggests that some distance from the anxiety of an artist's trauma may allow creativity to flow better. Fortunately, medical intervention enabled Munch to regain enough ego strength to access to his creativity. Munch's case, in my opinion, points to a "window of creativity" which narrowly defines the creative process. Without enough trauma creativity may lie dormant, and with too much the artist may become dysfunctional.

Dissociation

Dissociation is an adaptive response to acute trauma (Putnam, 1989). In Ring's (1992) opinion, a child can temporarily feel safe by dissociating despite what is happening to the child. He writes: "A child who is exposed to either the threat or actuality of physical violence, sexual abuse, or other severe traumas, will be strongly motivated selectively to "tune out" those aspects of his physical and social world that are likely to harm him by splitting himself off from the sources of those threats, by dissociating."

However, Springer (1994), who views dissociation as "a kind of separation of certain aspects of our conscious minds," believes that dissociation occurs more than commonly acknowledged and can either be useful or dysfunctional. She contrasts dissociation to association, " . . . a state within which a person's thoughts, feelings, and memories are related to each other, presumably coexist, and are accessible" (Springer, 1994).

Weismann (1967) suggests that the dissociative function may be responsible for creativity. In my study at least two of the artists have dissociated on occasions. The degree of dissociation was so intense that they repressed memories of their abuse for years. Today, while these artists are in a dissociative frame of mind, images or symbols of the trauma that induced the initial dissociation appear. All is still linked. Artists in my study who experienced sexual, physical, or verbal abuse were more apt to have dissociated than those artists who experienced either physical illness or handicaps.

Certain core characteristics mark creative people. Such qualities include attraction to complexity, intuition, ability to tolerate paradox, high energy, broad interests, autonomy, flexibility, spontaneity, awareness of reality, a sense of self as creative, ability to solve problems, and a sense of personal creativity (Barron, 1981; Klein, 1971; Torrance & Hall, 1980).

Creating a piece of art invites, if not demands, using all of one's senses; and, in so doing stimulates development in other areas of intelligence (Swenson, 1991). Furthermore, "Links exist between physiological stimulation and the development of intelligence and also emotional and mental well-being because touching, seeing, hearing, smelling, and tasting involve active participation by the individual" (Swenson, 1991). The activity of creating art may engender a sense of personal discovery through stimulating access to heretofore unconscious sources (Melanson, 1985). Repressed emotions may surface and help us to identify intrapsychic conflicts.

Because art stimulates access to aspects of the unconscious, art facilitates the exploration of an individual's inner world. In successful art and meditation the question "Who am I?" is answered. Maslow (1987) focused on self-actualizing creativeness as something that can penetrate all of life. I believe the ultimate value of creativity is not the value of the piece of art but, rather, is the self-actualization, personal integrity and contentedness that leads to a wholeness of experience within the artist.

Wakefield (1995) reminds us "that incomparable joy comes from expressing ourselves in a creative medium. This joy is the key factor in the creative experience." I agree with him; I feel that we are most connected to our highest self through expressive mediums. In Wakefield's opinion, life is more fulfilling when seen as a creation. With that view, we move from being the passive victim toward being an active creator. One takes charge of one's world. A strength accompanies participating in one's life.

Historically, psychology has focused on pathology and its causes in the unconscious. I feel the unconscious also contains a beautiful spiritual essence with intrinsic wisdom as teacher and healer. Kubie (1958) was one of the first psychoanalysts to view creativity as a healthy process when he insisted that the preconscious rather than the unconscious was responsible for creativity.

According to Kubie (1958), the flexibility of symbolic imagery results from free, continuous, and concurrent action of preconscious processes." Just as dreams reveal unconscious material through the language of symbols so does art (Kris, 1952). As an art therapist, Wadeson (1980) agrees that art expression is part of a healthy process and notes:

A significant question for me is: "What is it that makes the creative experience so satisfying?" I believe that is a particular sort of paradox. On the one hand, there is a getting out of oneself, the sort of transcendence Koestler discusses in "The Act of Creation" (1964), a feeling of touching and being part of a more universal experience than the unique conditions of one's own life. For me, there is illumination and possible alleviation of pain in this sort of occurrence. On the other hand, the stuff of which the creation is made is deeply personal, often putting one more profoundly in touch with oneself. It is here understanding is achieved. Integration is probably the result of the interface of the personal and the universal. Finally, there is the pleasure. I as creator can look at my creation and admire it, and realize that I am looking at myself.

The symbol contains both conscious and unconscious elements. Art clarifies our own myths and symbols. Hieronimus (1985) points out: "If the self is a product of its symbolization, and no contemporary symbol system exists, experiencing the self would prove to be problematic and could result in both alienation and fragmentation of the personality." We can only become aware of certain dimensions within us, such as understanding, through symbols. Our personal myths and symbols lead us to wholeness, healing and the mending of our spirits. Symbol and myth bring primitive psychic content into our awareness but also bring us new meaning, a new external reality. Singer (1973) notes, "That goal is wholeness, which is integration of the parts of his personality into a functioning totality. Here conscious and unconscious are united around the symbols of the self."

Maslow (1971) noticed that people were happiest when they felt more whole and integrated than usual; at those times, they were using all of their capacities to the fullest in an effortlessness way. They were self-determined, fearless, and free of self-criticism. They were spontaneous and responsive; and, they felt creative in a harmonious way. These people were keenly present in the moment and felt complete; they were playful, delightful, joyful, and felt fortunate that their lives were so wonderful.

Artists expand human consciousness by participating in the continuous creation of the world. If the creative process is to be explored as representing the highest degree of emotional health rather than as the product of sickness, the creative process must be seen as the expression of normal people actualizing themselves.

Spitz (1989) writes: "Even brief encounters with art objects can magically, temporarily, heal narcissistic wounds and splits. . . . Makers and beholders alike can, in intense relations with art media or works of art, achieve through identification and projection a sense of the imaginary ideal, a momentary experience of an unfragmented, unconflicted self."

Art and Healing

Art's power to evoke emotion reveals art's healing properties. Bringing forth our images—regardless of their ability to unnerve us—and trusting that the process will allow us to transcend the mundane visually connects us with our inner core, a place of wholeness that remains intact. Furthermore, any person can reap the benefits of art; the content or quality of the product is secondary to the feelings and insights obtained through the processes of self-expression or through visual observation.

Art is a natural process for learning transformational thinking. The artist begins with some medium and creates something. As the artist works the image, he or she transforms it by adding to it or subtracting from it.

Artistic expression is a way of taming the impulsive drives and promoting the development of higher ego functions. Expressing feelings onto paper, canvas or clay vents feelings symbolically and negates the necessity to act out hostile emotions; the symbol gives conscious expression to unconscious mental content. Also, art therapy is an effective treatment modality because falsification is difficult (Bradshaw, 1988; Hammer, 1958; Johnson, 1990). Subject matter an artist may have difficulty confronting often appears in their artwork disguised in symbolic form. For instance, one of the artists discussed herein uses her artwork to confront childhood sexual abuse issues. When she began this process her symbolism was disguised, now it is blatant! As her acceptance of the past grows, the need for disguised symbolism diminishes. Art therapy can also be less frightening than talk therapy.

Hagman (1986) discusses the work of Mary Huntoon, a pioneering art therapist, and writes:

> Although many patients did not show any insights into what they had painted, their improved behavior indicated that they had worked out an unconscious conflict through their art production. Patients can enter the therapeutic process by observing and attempting to understand the forms and subjects of their own creations. However, patients who profited most directly from art therapy were those whose doctors followed each step in the art-making process and promoted the integration of psychic content expressed in the art products.

Margaret Naumburg (1987), the pioneer of the professional use of art therapy, felt that healing is activated through the creative transformation of pain and conflict. An artist projects one's subjective state onto one's work. According to Maxine Junge (1987), Erikson "believed that an individual search for identity is the essential and continuing theme of life." Erikson (1968) viewed the question of "Who am I?" as underlying the process of human development. Being able to "see" who you are in the moment and actually having that ability come from yourself (as in the creative art process) is empowering.

Artistic activity offers an arena in which to cope with problems. The artist can depict threatening images, conquer fears and gain peace of mind through meeting these adversaries on canvas rather than in real life. The artist's particular way of perceiving and shaping human experience is a necessary and important part of every creative endeavor; there are as many different ways of describing the same experience artistically as there are styles of painting. McNiff (1981) writes:

> Art provides a structure for being, for confronting what Keats called Negative Capability, the acceptance of uncertainties, mysteries, doubts, without any irritable reaching after fact and reason. If art cannot physically eliminate the struggles of our lives, it can give significance and new meaning and a sense of active participation in the life process. This is offered as an alternative to passive resignation to self-fulfilling forms of emotional "illness," which will ultimately cripple the strongest personality.

Bear (1985) contends that the art experience is a valuable coping tool for individuals, particularly those deprived of ordinary health. Persons with debilitating and irreversible physical conditions have many experiences which are beyond the boundaries of verbal description. Thus, nonverbal methods enable these persons to express an array of thoughts and feelings. An artist is rarely too incapacitated to paint; there is an association of mouth-and foot-painting paraplegic artists who, through their artwork, earn their livelihood.

Creating some degree of sensual contact with the environment is requisite in art. Consequently, drawing allows an artist to experience his/her feelings (Bear, 1985). Feelings of stress, fear, guilt, anger and despair can be released through creative expression; and, once the artist sees his/her artwork, he/she may be better able to cope with the stressor. Huntoon (1949) observed that patients' behavior improved after they participated in producing artwork; he believed that, despite the lack of insights, patients resolved unconscious conflict.

Painting can also relieve stress by resolving issues that are yet unconscious. Art connects us consciously to soul's light and shadow. McIntyre (1990) noticed that eating and sleeping disorders, dependence, regression, restlessness, inability to concentrate, and withdrawal occurred when children could not express their sadness or anger. No matter one's age, art can help one accept the conditions of ones life by enabling the person to experience a sense of control and integration manifested through their own artistic symbolism. Shapiro (1985) encourages artistic expression for "the cultivation of self-esteem" and sees artwork as a way to ease the emotional strain associated with chronic pain.

A brief glance at a piece of art may trigger an unconscious wound, and healing may begin because of the awareness brought about by the artwork. Thus, all symptoms contain genuinely creative aspects (Spitz, 1965). Symbols present in the artwork may provide insight regarding the underlying roots of depression; spontaneous creative activity may be a self-healing process to "ward off" depression (Assael, 1989).

According to Maslow (1987):

> To adjust well to the world of reality means a splitting of the person. It means that the person turns his back on much in himself because it is dangerous. But it is now clear that by doing so, he loses a great deal, too, for these depths are also the source of all his joys, his ability to play, to love, to laugh, and, most important for us, to be creative. By protecting himself against the hell within himself, he also cuts himself off from the heaven within. In the extreme instance, we have the obsessional person, flat, tight, rigid, frozen, controlled, cautious, who can't laugh or play or live or be silly or trusting or childish. His imagination, his intuitions, his softness, his emotionality tend to be strangulated or distorted.

Jung (1973) observed that mandalas frequently appeared in the creations of individuals undergoing states of psychic disorientation and chaos; he believed that the mandalas expressed " . . . order, balance, and wholeness. Patients themselves often emphasize the beneficial or soothing effect of such pictures." Artistic expression plays an important role in healing for "whenever illness is associated with loss of soul, the arts emerge spontaneously as remedies, soul medicine" (McNiff, 1992).

Creating artwork allows affective release and permits psychic material to emerge more concretely, making it more accessible to the observing ego (Avstreih & Brown, 1979). Primitive affects may be expressed in symbolic form.

Neurosis and Creativity

Many people believe that psychotherapeutic treatment interferes with creativity by short-circuiting the artist's connection to the essence of his work. However, not all theorists agree that creativity is dependent upon neurosis. Fenichel (1945) writes, "Experience shows that neurotic inhibitions of creation are removed by analysis much more frequently than creativeness." Hatterer (1965) notes, "It is becoming increasingly apparent that the creative process cannot be interpreted simply . . . as an attempt by the artist to rid himself of anxiety, rage or guilt or to balance his alternate depressions." Furthermore, Kubie (1958) writes: "Neurosis erupts, mars, distorts and blocks creativeness in every field. No one need fear that getting well will cause an atrophy of his creative drive. This illusory fear rests on the erroneous assumption that it is that which is unconscious in us which makes us creative, whereas in fact the unconscious is our straitjacket, rendering us as stereotyped and as sterile and as repetitive as is the neurosis itself."

Psychological Aspects of Creativity

Freud believed conflict was the genesis of both neurosis and conflict and that the creative act derived from the creative person's capacity to sublimate conflict—to divert and transform the sexual energy to higher, socially acceptable aims (Klein, 1971). I think Freud's theory has merit although it may not contain the entire picture. In modern society, a different cultural setting is changing the face of this sexuality/creativity theory. Perhaps the opposite of what Freud says is true—that is, is sexuality sublimated creativity? Victorian Austria did not have therapy groups dealing with sexual addictions; presently it seems that we spend more energy along sexual avenues than we do in creating great works of art. Indeed, there may be a connection between sex and art; but, in my experience, that connection is not unidirectional.

Dudek (1968) believes humanity's need to relate to the world is the primary motivation for creative experience. Dudek thinks that artwork is a function of constructive activity—not a function of regression. Creative experience entails the ability to experience deeply and then describe that experience with some detachment.

Nydes (1962) views creativity as a way of resolving inner conflict. Eissler (1963) concurs with the latter but adds an exception to this rule: the creative genius. Eissler focuses on the product rather than the artist. Consequently, she does not acknowledge the need of the artist for health and wholeness. Eissler's omission is particularly noteworthy because she is a psychologist doing an analytic study of Goethe. Many researchers observe that creative individuals reflect health rather than pathology (Barron, 1980; Torrance & Hall, 1980). Klein (1971) notes: "The creative person is able to remain flexible, spontaneous, imaginative, open to new experience and awareness, appropriately aware of the demands of reality and the problems with which he is grappling, and able to evaluate successfully his productions in terms which are not inappropriately restrictive."

Torrance and Hall (1980) state that highly creative people are more able to integrate opposites into their personalities and thinking than most other people. They believes creative people have an inexplicable ability to solve problems, and are, paradoxically, both more independent and dependent, serious and playful, timid and bold, and certain and uncertain. People who can tolerate the tension of opposites, that is, live in states of paradox, are considered healthier than individuals characterized by polarity thinking. Barron (1968) wonders:

> Could it not be that individuals of unusual sensibility and symbolic scope are more prone to despair, disgust, forlornness, and rage? That they are at the same time more capable of transcending these universal human bonds through metaphor and through identification with natural processes? Whatever is neurotic in them then becomes a part of the content, symbolically expressed, of their creative activity, and not simply a part of themselves that inhibits construction. We see frequently in creative individuals such an ability to transcend the ordinary boundaries of structures of consciousness; indeed, more than an ability, an actual desire to break through the regularities of perception, to shatter what is stable or constant in consciousness, to go beyond the given world to find that something more or that something different that intuitions says is there.

Spiritual Dimension

Both art and meditation entail focusing the mind. Such concentration engenders tranquillity. The mind stills. Then, insight may emerge. According to Vargiu (1977), "The classical stages of meditation [reflective meditation, receptive meditation, contemplation and discrimination] parallel the stages [preparation, incubation, and illumination] of the creative process." Engaging in artistic activity supports the development of the mental and emotional attitudes which are " . . . associated with life changes and personal transformation toward spiritual goals" (Vargiu, 1977). Vargiu reminds us that " . . . the attitude of serene attention has been emphasized by the spiritual teachers of all ages" (1977).

Fox (1983) notes that engaging in art as meditation, wherein the values lies in the process rather than the product, may stimulate spiritual expansion and self-expression. On this path, which Fox calls the Via Creativa, we find great artwork. Here, artists are co-creators with God. Art serves as a meditation, a centering, a return to the source. The artist's trust of images is a sort of faith. Our lives, as works of art, propel beauty back into the world. Fox (1983) describes the case of Hildegarde of Bingen, who healed by using art as meditation. From her sickbed, she produced a series of mandala drawings as well as writings. Her deep healing highlights the role spirituality plays in creative expression.

In creative expression, many artists, including ones in this study, speak of reaching a moment of compassion; at that time, they feel great joy and contentment. Fox (1983) remarks, "The creation-centered spiritual tradition considers compassion rather than contemplation as the fulfillment of the spiritual journey that takes one back to one's origins in renewed ways."

According to Fox (1983), "The single largest obstacle in teaching adults to meditate by means of art is getting them to let go of judgmental attitudes toward their self-expression." This important observation relates directly to the healing process because if fear of criticism prohibits our creativity, healing must find an alternate route (Fox, 1983).

We must learn to trust our own images even if they bring confusion and pain to us, because the pain of the image can be a renewing pain, a healing pain that brings with it new relationships with people, places and things, that ultimately leads to transcendence (Fox, 1983). Fox asks, "Who knows what lies behind and beyond our images until we trust them enough to ride them fully, even into the darkness and into the depths like a seed in the soil?"

Beauty is recognized when measured against the pain and evolves out of it. In this study, the concept that beauty can emerge from pain is operative in the life of one artist, who looks for the beauty and the message in her illness and contracts with God to share her gift with others in return for her ability to continue painting.

Griffin (1990) speculates that constructive or reconstructive art would assist in propelling us toward a re-enchanted world. Such art would be deeply ecumenical, portraying those elements that all cultures have in common, while equally celebrating our diversities with which we can enrich each other. "Such art would recognize our creativity as awesome, with both divine and demonic potential, while recognizing that art continuous with the creativity found throughout nature."

Creative transformation is a total process in which the creative principle manifests as a power related to the self, the center of the whole personality (Neumann, 1974). "New constellations of the unconscious and of consciousness interact with new productions and new transformative phases of the personality" (Neumann, 1974). These transformative phases happening on massive individual levels will affect the world community as a whole. Possibly, the effect will be that of growth towards wholeness and health. Wakefield's (1995) idea that the true spirit of creation—the spirit that is in us—waits to be evoked and enjoyed is very much an idea that I believe and hope to bring awareness to through this process of self-discovery.

Self-realization means adjustment to change by using one's potential, being flexible, and looking for other and new ways of being oneself, becoming one's potential: this is the creative attitude. "The more creative the attitude of a person, the more one actualizes one's potential" (Landau & Moaz, 1978).

As a person begins to self-actualize, one becomes compassionate. Matthew Fox (1978) writes:

> The whole idea of compassion is based on a keen awareness of the interdependence of all living beings, which are all part of one another and all involved in one another. . . . We need to turn to the arts once again not as an elitist thing but in order to recover the artist that is in each person. Every artist may not be a special kind of person but every person is a special kind of artist. Who can deny the experience of interrelatedness that one learns and therefore the compassion one learns from music, dance, laughter, cooking and carpentry.

"Each person has his or her own experiences, and each viewer experiences a piece of art uniquely. Each individual creates one's own mythos by stringing one's life experiences together in a meaningful way" (Hall & Nordby, 1972). I realize that we contain a vast variety of remembered experiences: both exciting and traumatic events such as births, weddings, funerals, earthquakes, fires, hurricanes, accidents, crowds, and family reunions. Some memories make us happy, and others sadden us.

Memory stimulates art; and, art stimulates memory. The sensual experience of working with color, texture, paint smells, clay, and other media enhances creativity. Also, the actual involvement with movement and sight stimulates the artist. Even the sound of the paintbrush swishing in water stimulates the memory.

In Jung's (1972) estimation, the creative urge expressed in art is irrational and will in the end mock all our rationalistic undertakings. "Whereas all conscious psychic processes may well be causally explicable, the creative act, being rooted in the immensity of the unconscious, will forever elude our attempts at understanding" (Jung, 1972).

Understanding the creative process is particularly important because it can assist in the management of rapid changes in our lives. The creative process *is* the process of change, of development, of evolution. Creativity is an extension of life.

We see frequently in creative individuals such an ability to transcend the ordinary boundaries of structures of consciousness; indeed, more than an ability, an actual desire to break through the regularities of perception, to shatter what is stable or constant in consciousness, to go beyond the given world to find that something more or that something different that intuition says is there (Barron, 1968).

Chapter 3

FEMINIST LIFE REVIEW RESEARCH

And remember always that you are unique. And all that you
have to do is let people see that you are you.
(Erickson & Lustig, 1975)

Combining life reviews with feminist methodology and an organic orientation emphasizes the sacred, the transformational, and transpersonal aspects of the individual. Presented in the following pages are descriptions of each of these approaches.

The Life Review

This work focuses on the lives of 8 artists—not simply on their productions. It was grounded in each artist's verbal descriptions of their art as well as their lives. With regard to the life review method of obtaining information about participants in a study, Bergman (1993) wrote: "The self-story is not a fixed entity. It first emerges in recognizable form in late adolescence. At that age people begin the activity of self-biography that continues for the rest of life. The process begins with development of a set of repudiations and assimilation's of childhood identifications into a configuration that includes plot, character, settings, scenes, and themes. The initial story is continually reworked . . . the meanings of the pieces change as new patterns are found."

Feminist Methodology

According to Reinharz (1992) and Kvale (1988), there is clearly no single "feminist way" to do research. There is room for individual creativity and variety. The connection between the research project and the researcher frequently takes the form of "starting with one's own experience," particularly when that experience is potentially disturbing. Feminists often start with a personal issue. Because there is widespread acceptance of the personal starting point for feminist research, there is an expectancy there would be a link between the personal experience of the researcher and the research project in which she is engaged. Reinharz (1992) feels personal experience is more than an asset, it is a necessity or a source of legitimacy. However, she also acknowledges that starting from one's own experience has its limitations, particularly the potential for solipsism or projection (Reinharz, 1992). For that reason, feminist researchers are careful to differentiate their own experience from the experiences of other women.

Organic Research

Clements (1994) described Organic Research as:

Sacred

This work emerges from a sense of responsibility, reverence and respect for the earth and all her inhabitants. We share the belief that competition and dominance will not give the necessary healing and we honor our own growth as individuals as well as that of each of the people we include in our studies. We are aware of the presence and support of the sacred and we strive to stay conscious as we are creative in our work.

Inclusive

Organic research is not aimed at proving anything. It exists to broaden knowledge rather than to focus it. Traditional research may be seen as a triangle with its point at the top. It begins at the bottom with a broad array of data and, through analysis, narrows the focus to a single idea, that which is proved or disproved.

Organic research, however, turns the triangle so that the point is at the bottom. One begins at the point with an interest, an idea, and by using interviews to gather human experience, the idea is expanded. Our research ends with more questions than it begins with. We do not feel it is necessary to gather the results into a single conclusion.

Subjective

The attitudes of the researcher are an integral part of the data. Traditional research aims at making the researcher a non-involved observer. Recently, the scientific community has acknowledged that an object is changed by its observer. Organic research not only embraces that idea but sees the need for the researcher to be a part of the data. The story of the researcher is even more important than that of those interviewed. It is not possible for the researcher to simply identify his or her biases and then move on. The interviews, the analysis, the results, even the literature review is presented as an ongoing dialogue between the researcher and the subject.

Experiential and Contextual

The data in organic research comes from people's experiences. Rather than tests or questionnaires, the researcher uses face-to-face interviews to gather data. In these interviews, the researcher encourages persons to tell their stories including all the details. We find that this story telling is a teaching tool which bypasses the analyzing part of the brain and affects the whole person deeply. Unlike traditional research, the significance of the data in organic research lies in the context of the whole story and cannot be abstracted. The flavor of the story is important as well as the facts. Feelings are as important as thoughts and in reporting and analyzing the data it is important to keep the essence of the story. The study is likely to be written in the first person.

My past experience, the context of the interviews, the stories of those who are interviewed, events which occur during the period of the research which are related, my reflections on similarities or differences from previous interviews, even the ongoing literature review is kept in context by the fact that the information is all in chronological order. An added bonus is that the study reads like a novel.

Transformative

The researcher, those who are interviewed, and the readers of the resulting study are changed by the work. To truly listen to anothers story involves the willingness to be altered by it. Having one's story completely heard changes one. It has been our experience that both we and our subjects feel that our involvement in the work is a part of our personal growth. We are changed by telling and listening to each others stories. There is a relational quality to organic research which both requires and offers transformation in the process.

Transpersonal

It has been said that transpersonal work includes the study of all human experience. With that in mind, organic research includes data and methods and a state of mind which honor ways of knowing and working like; intuition, non-ordinary states of consciousness, tacit knowing, creative expression, meditation, journaling, imaging, use of psychic gifts and ritual.

Individual

Organic research does not lend itself to abstract results. Each story is different and while similarities and differences can be noticed through the filter of the researcher's own experience, percentages and averages will not be found. The reductionistic quality of some traditional research is absent here. . . . The researcher will have opinions and intuitive responses but so will the reader and neither is more correct than the other. Results emerge from the stories of those interviewed as well as from the story of the researcher's experience of doing the study.

Understandable

Organic research is written to be read by anyone interested in the subject, not just the scholars in the field. We find ourselves annoyed by technical writing which uses exclusive language. The point of doing this work is to communicate what we have learned so it may teach and heal, so the writing should be easy to read. It should read like a story. It invites the reader to identify with the subject and come to the level of attention that allows personal growth. Since this type of research is in it's formative stages and is in flux, it requires the researcher to invent the method as she or he reviews the data.

The uniqueness of this research was that: the participant's acted as co-researchers, and the artists exchanged stories with each other and commented on that experience. This provided an organic element that helped to facilitate personal insights for each of the participants and myself.

Design

Demographics

There were no age requirements. These women ranged in age from 31–78 years.

This researcher is female. Artists needed only to self-identify as artists for inclusion in this study—not to show or sell their work. No effort was made to divide the group by age, race, ethnicity or artistic ability. Two important factors in the decision to include an artist were the proliferation and duration of her artwork. These factors allowed comparative analysis of the effect of trauma on artwork over time and the healing process of art.

Six participants live in California, one in Washington, and one in

Arizona. All but two were born in the United States. Myrtle and Dorothy, the sisters, moved to this country from Canada. Mary, a Latina, is the only non-Caucasian. Of the eight women, seven are married.

The Participants

Jean is 53, works while attending graduate school and has two grown children. She leads a very busy life and when she paints, it is in a frenzy of production. One Monday morning she said to me, "I painted 20 paintings this weekend." Jean suffered sexual, physical, and emotional abuse as a child at the hands of her parents and a teacher. Her childhood was violent and in adulthood she has suffered many accidents. She uses her art cathartically. Her artistic expression has opened a connection to God and her anger has been transmuted into compassion for all living beings, especially children. Mari has just turned 42, has two children, and is also a prolific painter. Mari also suffered emotional and physical abuse at the hands of her father and emotional abuse from her mother. All this began with the death of her grandmother when Mari was five years old. Her art has enabled her to release pent up anger and rage. Her supportive husband, who is in the computer business, has put her art on the Internet. Her art is also shown in galleries.

Helen is 46, married, with one adopted child. As a child she felt unloved and unwanted. Her mother began giving her diet pills at age 11 because she felt Helen was getting chubby. Helen suffers from severe depression and has used medication to alleviate its symptoms since high school. Art has given Helen a new identity, that of artist rather than victim. Art has enabled Helen to synthesize the fragmented parts of her self. Through a suicidal attempt and its resultant hospitalization she became aware of her emotions and no longer denies them.

Saille at 53, is a successful sculptor and watercolorist who sells most of her work to large corporations. Some of her sculpture is on the new Princess cruise ship. Her Irish father died when Saille was five years old thus beginning her great interest in Irish history and pagan cultures. She was raised by a somewhat emotionally imbalanced mother and uses her art to "stay sane." In Saille's words, "If I didn't have my art I'd either die or go crazy."

Mary at 78, is becoming more prolific as she ages. She tells stories about her artwork that would be wonderful made into children's books. Mary is retired and lives locally with her adoring husband. Mary's calm oil landscapes changed practically overnight into wild abstract acrylic Mesoamerican gods after the death of her only son in an automobile accident.

Myrtle is 73, and is making up for lost time, time she spent being ill. She still suffers the spinal scoliosis she incurred as a child. Myrtle has also survived breast cancer and two strokes not to mention a myriad of other illness over the years. She paints portraits of people and animals. Myrtle is active in many clubs and organizations and teaches handicapped people to paint. She gives lectures such as, "No matter how bad off you are there is still something you can do to contribute to the world." Artistic talent provides her with a sense of feeling equal to others.

Dorothy, at 72 is Myrtle's younger sister. She grew up in the shadow of an older sister who needed more attention than she did from their parents. She struggled in a co-dependent relationship with an alcoholic husband for many years. Her art provided a quiet island on a stormy sea. Dorothy is very in touch with nature and becomes one with it as she paints.

Mia just turned 31. She lives in Seattle and is the only single woman in this study. She is a musician as well as an artist. In fact, Mia has tried to deny her artistic ability as long as she can remember. She prefers any identity other than that of artist. Mia was born with facial defects and only one ear. She looks different. Art is part of who she is and sometimes she'd rather be someone else. Her music provides her with the ability to connect with the depths of her soul and to cry out her pain.

Kvale (1983) states that interviewing is more of an art than a science. He writes, "There exist only a few simple rules of technique which can be communicated, analogous to the laws of perspective and of color mixture within the art of painting." These rules are centered on the interviewee's life world and focus on themes which are interesting to both interviewer and interviewee. In this study the main theme was art and the interviewees interaction with it. I sought to understand the meaning of these themes in a person's life, and it was my goal to register and interpret what was said. Kvale (1983) states: "It is here necessary to listen to the directly expressed descriptions and meanings as well as what is said between the lines, and then seek to formulate the 'implicit message' and send it back to the interviewee." By doing this the interviewer receives feedback immediately from the interviewee as to whether she has correctly interpreted what has been said.

During the interviews with each artist, I was struck by how similar parts of each of their stories matched parts of my own story and, as the process continued, how similar they were to each other. I experienced a healing on a deep level as I read each story. The little details of a person's life matched what I previously thought of as insignificant details of my own life. The amount of "aha's" increased as each story unfolded. For instance, I noticed that fire came up in the stories where abuse had been in the artist's history. I got goose pimples remembering the autumn, when as a young child, I set the back meadow on fire. In her book on Sandplay therapy, Dora Kalff (1971) noted that when a child was ready to tell his or her secret, they would use fire in the sand or in other areas of their life. I began to wonder what secret I may have yet to unfold.

Interview

The following are representative of the questions used:

1. Please tell me about your life beginning in childhood.
2. Please tell me what part art played in your life.
3. How was your art received by those important to you?
4. I'd like to hear about those events that were catalysts in connection with your ability or desire to paint.

As the interviews went on I found myself wishing that Saille could read Jean's story and vice versa. I thought the exchange of stories may benefit both of them. When I initially approached the artists and asked them if they were curious to share their own story and to read the other artists stories, all said unhesitatingly, "Yes, I'd love to."

As interviewees described her life world, most made connections and saw new relationships between her life and her art. As the interview proceeded I condensed and interpreted back to the interviewee according to Kvale's model (1983) what she was describing. This method facilitated a story-like flow rather than scattered segments of life events. This "feeding back" also facilitated constant monitoring by the interviewee to confirm or disconfirm the information as it was being interpreted. Kvale (1983) refers to it as "on-line interpretation" and comments this type of interviewing is self-correcting with its "on-the-spot" verification. This technique proved invaluable as a few times when I interpreted back what I thought was said, I was corrected immediately.

Verification by participant:

After the interviews were completed, tapes were transcribed and transcripts were sent back to artists for corrections, additions and deletions. Participants were also asked to comment on their experience as co-researchers in this study. Often an artist added new thoughts or long forgotten details that came to mind after the interview.

Correspondence:

No attempt was made to limit correspondence by mail or telephone with any participant. My goal was to compile a complete history of each artist. I realized the initial interview did not always produce as much information as possible so I made follow-up phone calls. I also returned to the participants at times during the data analysis seeking further descriptions of her/his experience.

Story exchange

All stories were photocopied, and a complete set of all stories was sent to each participant. Participants were requested to comment on their experience of reading other artists' stories.

Extracting Themes

Words and phrases that pertain to the topic of this study: Trauma, art and healing were extracted from the text. By extracting significant statements themes emerged. Next, these statements were grouped into themes and sub-themes. In addition to this, I condensed each life story into a one page essence statement and wrote it like a poem.

Responses From Artists

I mailed the essence statements to the artists and requested a response. Seeing her life condensed onto a single page provided an overview of her life that had a profound affect on most artists.

Verification of Findings

I mailed a copy of the findings to each participant and requested a response. Communication with participants for validation of the findings was completed via mail or telephone.

About the Stories

The stories are a compilation of data that I received from each participant. They include personal material from interviews and subsequent information they shared with me which filled in some of the gaps in their transcribed stories. In addition, various additional material has also been added. This includes information gleaned from video tapes of their work, descriptions of each piece of artwork as it was given me by each artist, and general information I received from reading bits of information about them from other sources. For example, Mary is listed in, "Who's Who of California Artists," and Myrtle's story has been mentioned in a few books that I found in the Santa Clara library.

Since my own story acted as the filter for the stories, it seemed necessary that the reader be familiar with my story. I use the word "filter" because as data are received it is the researcher who has to choose what is retained and what is ignored. It is a process of "filtering out" data that seems superfluous, redundant, or in some other way unnecessary for the presentation of each artist's story. I am not implying that information was selectively chosen to reflect my biases, what I am saying is that I chose to include only that type of information that directly related to artwork, and/or health. Also, it may be noted, what has been chosen for discussion may be different from what another writer may have chosen to focus on. It is my personal experience as writer and interviewer that is brought to this study.

I also believe that art is a healing force. That bringing to the canvas a strong emotion such as anger, pain, or grief somehow relieves the artist of some tension which according to Bear (1985) ultimately leads to a profound sense of calm. I also believe that art can transform the personality, by offering personal insights to the artist as he or she is in the act of painting.

Chapter 4

THE STORIES

I have little interest in teaching you what I know. I wish to
stimulate you to tell me what "you" know. (Henri, 1923)

Although these eight women self-identify as artists, their stories were not chosen because of their artwork. In fact, their artwork is incidental to this process. It is not necessary that one be a great artist in order to heal life's wounding through artistic expression. Rather, it is only necessary that one be willing to put brush to canvas, or a pencil to paper. The creative process also works for those more inclined toward dance or music or, for that matter, any other form of artistic expression. The reason I have chosen to present healing primarily through painting is that a visual representation can have long lasting effect on both the artist and the viewer. Art can effect us in different ways on different days. In other words, it speaks to us in the language we need in the moment we view it.

The stories that follow describe the life of each artist and how art played a part in their lives and their healing. We begin with my story because it is through my eyes that the other stories are seen.

LINDA'S STORY

I have been married to Karl H. since 1980. We each have grown children from previous marriages. My daughter Lori, together with her husband and three children live in Orlando, Florida. I am 53 years old. Most of my story will be told through the art pieces that represent each event as it unfolded during a time of deep introspection. As part of my own psychological growth I decided it may be a good idea to release to canvas any negative feelings I had surrounding past life events.

As I stated in the introduction to this paper I was the oldest of three children and the only one who was artistic in the family. Although both my siblings had the usual childhood illnesses, I would usually get severely ill with each one of them while my sister and brother would recover in a week. From ages two through about seventeen, I suffered from asthma. I remember many a night gasping for air and not being able to get enough. My mother would frantically call the doctor when I appeared to be turning blue. He would show up about midnight and save the day, or night, by giving me a shot.

I didn't play with dolls growing up. My love of coloring, drawing and making things seemed to predominate my time. I liked the idea of seeing the results of playing. Mother bought me "Paint By Numbers" and I remember blending the little lines together so they didn't look like, "Paint By Numbers" paintings.

There was always a lot of fighting and arguing in the household and I think, in retrospect, my art was my way to "tune out" the family. My nerves would calm down when I could enmesh myself in art or crafts. Of course, at the time, I didn't realize I was using art as a coping mechanism. I doodled, and drew pictures of glamorous women, fantasizing that one day, perhaps, I'd become a fashion designer. This led me, with the help of my mother, to design some of the clothes I wore. My mother is an excellent seamstress and she showed me how to combine different patterns to create new fashions. I never did learn how to actually draw the pattern pieces but I became quite an expert in modifying existing pieces.

During my working life, which is often intense and hectic, I always try to maintain my sanity by doing something creative. The few hours I spend cooking or painting are just what I need to relieve the tension buildup that occurs in the natural course of trying to fit too much into one lifetime.

A painting I call *"Breaking Wave"* was done in the early 1980s. After it was finished, I remember looking at it and wondering how I ever did it. It did not seem possible that I could paint such a picture. Art has been a real self-esteem booster for me.

"Daffodils," (1983) was a picture I really enjoyed doing. Capturing the softness of the petals was a challenge and I feel that mine ended up looking more like porcelain than flower petals but that too was OK. I loved the vibrancy of the yellow background and chose to use yellow in the flowers as well. This picture reminds me of springtime and it helps me to warm up when I stare at it in cold weather.

"Portrait of Karl," done in (1984) is a painting of my husband. The neighbor of a friend decided to become a professional photographer and wanted practice photographing people he didn't know well. Thus, Karl and I were photographed. It was such a memorable day. When we arrived at the photographer's home we were both uncomfortable and nervous. He gave us a glass of wine and talked with us for half an hour. Then he took the pictures. I thought they turned out very flattering and I hung them all over the house. After staring at one of Karl, I wondered if I could paint it. I'd never done an oil portrait before. It just seemed to flow out without any problem. I was amazed. I had captured Karl's likeness and didn't even know I could do it. It was a huge boost to my self-esteem. His comment when he saw it was, "That is really great, I see you gave me thicker hair than I really have." I had to laugh because I had not realized I was doing that. But I was more surprised that he didn't seem surprised I could paint it. I felt like saying, "Don't you get it, I just painted this great portrait of you and I didn't know I could do it." I can't remember if I said anything, or more likely, just stood there stunned that he thought me capable of such wonderful feats.

"The Snow Scene," when I look at it now, this one has neither been signed nor dated. Hum! I remember painting it because when I chose this subject matter it made me feel cold. I've never been a fan of cold weather but my mother likes snow scenes so I painted it with her in mind. In fact, I remember doing two and giving her one. Karl also likes snow very much and we have this painting hanging in our bedroom. As I write these words, insights too personal to print, are coming fast and furious, and I may move that picture. It was pointed out to me that in describing this painting I used the passive voice as if I didn't know who

painted it. And further, that it may be possible I was "in" my mothers mind rather than just "with her in mind." Amazing!

During the summer of 1988, I was recovering not only from an appendectomy but also from post-traumatic stress syndrome that I sustained after the October 17, 1987 Loma Prieta 7.1 earthquake in California. Our home is on the San Andreas fault line less than five miles from the epicenter of the quake, and it experienced 90 percent damage. We moved out of the house for over a year while it was being rebuilt. During this time I had difficulty making decisions and focusing on details. In this condition I made all the choices necessary to rebuild the interior of our home. Karl took charge of the exterior rebuilding project and the grounds. Since decision making was so stressful, the research that went into each choice was enormous. By the time decisions had to be made, they were well thought out and the end results made us both proud.

While our house was being rebuilt, we lived in a neighbor's house whose tenant had vacated immediately after the quake. We were lucky. Within two weeks of moving back into our home, the post-traumatic stress began to subside. Redecorating was quite expensive so rather than buy artwork, I decided to paint something for the living room wall. I knew it needed to be something my husband would like so I painted an *"Austrian Countryside."* He was raised in Austria. It was my first experiment painting a large canvas and all I cared about was adding a lot of color to the room. I jumped right in and tackled a five by six foot canvas. It was one of the most freeing experiences I have ever had. I could feel my lungs opening up. I created the task for myself of making the lines soft since my husband likes soft romantic paintings. I also wanted to see if I could soften my personality by painting a soft looking picture. It was the hardest thing I have ever painted. My natural tendency is to paint crisp clear lines. At the end of each day I had to go back and blur all the edges. During the painting process, the edges kept retreating to sharp delineation. Finally, I had to say, "This is finished." As I look at this painting now, I see the tree in the lower right hand corner represents the feeling of being "blown away" by the entire experience. The houses nestled in the trees, are very representative of my neighborhood here on the Summit in the Santa Cruz mountains. The church steeple looks just like the one on the church I attend regularly. It is interesting to me that I thought I was painting an Austrian countryside and all the while I was painting my "home," the home that no longer existed.

During a course of study at the Institute of Transpersonal Psychology, my conservatism took a turn to a more expansive, even open, way of looking at life, even my own. I took part in a collage making activity. *"Love At Different Speeds"* was the result of that exercise. I remember making a very Victorian heart with pictures from a magazine. I cut out only those images that were pink or red and had women or children on them. Then I assembled them in a heart shape. It appeared finished but when I got it home I did not like it. Somehow, it felt unfinished. I got up the next day and added a background, some lace doilies on the top, and turned a Victorian heart into a modern day "teddy." This change of feeling is something that happens to me often from day to day, even moment to moment. Different sub-personalities seem to emerge on different days. I can never be sure which one will show up when I do my art work. The first day I felt sort of prim and proper and the second day, when I did the finish work, I was feeling more vampish. Thus, the title, *"Love At Different Speeds"* summed up my feelings. When I took the finished piece back, the instructor just stared at it and then at me. I got the distinct feeling she was processing a lot of information about me that she was not saying. It was unnerving.

When it came time to do the internship process for my doctorate degree, I was granted permission to do it on canvas. I created a series of paintings that described my psychological process as it unfolded at I.T.P.

The process of preparation began on a flight to Bermuda to celebrate my big "five–0." There was no way I was going to be in the country and subject to any more black balloons with "Over the Hill" written on them. I asked Karl for a trip to Bermuda for my birthday. I was lucky, he agreed. A tiny image caught my attention from a page in the in-flight magazine. It was a *"Vulture."* I saw the image and turned the page. But it wouldn't let go. I must have gone back to looking at that image five times before I just said, "Oh, I'll tear it out and take it home." It sat in my purse for a few weeks and then I was called to paint it. I realized if I did a series of oil paintings, the school year would be over before some of them were dry. I got the idea to paint with acrylic paints. I had never used them before so I went and bought some. I knew I had to do this series in a quick-drying paint in order that they could be transported and dis-played within the year.

It took only one day and the following afternoon to paint the vulture. He just flowed out of me. I had the intention to get the canvas covered and then to go back in with the details. When I went back in for the details I didn't want to add anything; thus, he stayed the way he was when he first hit the canvas. When I painted this bird I did not realize it was a vulture. It was my husband who came home and named it for me. He said, "What inspired you to paint a baby vulture?" My therapist also recognized it as a vulture. I was fascinated by these remarks. If I had known the bird was a vulture, I don't think I would have painted it. Vultures have a negative meaning for me. They remind me of death and "picking the bones" clean. In fact, it is exactly what the vulture represents that is so pertinent to my story. I was yet unaware of it but, I was about to "pick clean, the bones of my past." According to Erich Neumann, in his article entitled *Art and the Creative Unconscious:* "Birds in general are symbols of the spirit and soul. The vulture goddess Nekhbet was worshipped as a "form of the primeval abyss which brought forth the light." It is the symbol of the uroboric Great Mother, the Archetypal Feminine as the creative source of life, which is alive in the unconscious of every human being. As the devourer of corpses, the vulture is also the Terrible Mother, who takes the dead back into herself." I was about to begin picking away at the bones of my past.

The next painting came from a sandtray I made in a therapy session. It was my first tray and the theory among sandtray experts is that your first tray tells, "What is happening for you in your life, right now." It is referred to as the diagnostic tray. Sandtray is a process whereby the client looks over many shelves with miniature representations of life on them and chooses a few that strike his or her interest. For instance, some of the figures may be people, trucks, planes, trees, fences, bridges, dinosaurs, churches and so on.

I chose to put panda bears in a ring with people of different types looking on. Each of these people represent one of my sub-personalities. I call this painting *"Pandas."* I am very attached to it. Changes spontaneously took place during the painting process. Bamboo trees were added along with a shadow of the angel. A butterfly, which is usually considered a transformational symbol, was added to the foreground. After creating the painting I went to the symbol books to try to learn something about what I was doing. It surprised me to learn that the bear is one of the oldest verifiable sacred animals, and is the symbol of resurrection, new life in spring and also of initiation and inspiration. I was blown away!

The bamboo plant is thought to bring good fortune. It is frequently the object of meditative painting; the joints, individual segments, and straight growth of the bamboo symbolize the path and individual steps of spiritual development.

In the butterfly we again see symbolism representing rebirth and resurrection. It represents the soul leaving the body at death. The personal transformation which has been taking place in me does in fact seem like a rebirth.

A guardian angel was a personal Shakti who watched over a man and took him into her ecstatic embrace at the moment of death. Needless to say, after reading these symbolic descriptions I began to have more respect for archetypal imagery. The thought that my own artwork may be tapping into some universal consciousness seemed overwhelming to me, not to mention fascinating.

Then I painted *"My Elephant Dream."* It was the result of not only a sandtray, but of a dream I had 35 years earlier. In the introduction to this paper I referred to a painting that invoked my asthma. This was it. I made both the sandtray and the painting from my memory of the dream. The dream went like this:

> I was a young woman out for a walk. I found myself walking on a narrow path with tropical-type growth on either side of me. The growth was so high that I could not see over it. I was not afraid. As I pushed the bushes aside, I came upon a little pond. I noticed a tiny fish swimming back and forth in the pond and when I looked at the fish it looked back at me, and then continued its business of swimming. I stood at the edge of the pond and noticed that all around the pond was a two-foot wide path of sand. I realized that I could walk all the way around the pond, and wondered if I should. Then after deciding that I would, I wondered whether to start out to the left or to the right. As soon as I chose the "right" direction, I heard a loud sound coming from behind me. As I turned to look, I saw a huge elephant coming toward me. I jumped into the greenery so that I would not be seen. I marveled at the grace and delicacy with which this huge animal moved along the path. He went past me and hesitated at the pond. In a flash he turned to the right and began to take the walk that I was going to take. As he went along the path, I noticed that the bushes were not being damaged. The elephant saw the fish and the fish saw the elephant. The elephant looked worried and when he got about three-fourths of the way around the pond he hesitated. As soon as he hesitated, the fish, without ever having its tail leave the water, got bigger and bigger as it went toward the elephant. Its mouth went from tiny to huge. It gobbled the elephant up and then got small again as it receded back into the water. I was shocked and amazed. "That fish just ate the elephant, I exclaimed in my dream." Then I woke up.

My waking reaction was that I had just had a big dream. The making of the sandtray and the painting was an effort toward understanding.

It seems to me that this is more than a painting, it is somehow my life myth. I have discovered so many levels of understanding about it over the last three years. Krippner (1984) described personal myth as a pattern of thinking and feeling that gives meaning to one's past. I think it relates to my decision to follow in my mother's footsteps and make what she considered to be the "right" decisions for my life. Of course, I have come to realize they were right decisions for her and wrong decisions for me. I think another level of understanding this dream relates to is my first sexual experience. And another to my pregnancy. The path around the pond represents the embryonic lining of the uterus. The elephant, a fetus. These dream images continue to intrigue me.

The next painting in the series is entitled *"Shame."* It expresses the feelings I had when I realized that my first sexual experience resulted in pregnancy. This painting also symbolizes the shame that is culturally doled out to all of us in the course of our lives. Shame is an emotional experience that is regarded by many psychologists as the preeminent cause of emotional distress in our time.

The next painting *"Fear,"* completed immediately following "Shame," expresses the feelings of a young girl learning she is pregnant. "What am I going to do?" The swirling color reflects a peek into my mind. Thoughts were racing around with nowhere to go. It was a time of high energy mixed with a feeling of helplessness. I remember excitement and panic rolled into one.

As I began to come to grips with some of the sadness, I started to realize that out of that anguish and sadness came some of the greatest joys of my life, my daughter. The painting *"Emotional Fences,"* relates to how I used to interact with men. The clock depicts my daughter Lori as the light of my life. This painting was inspired by a sandtray created in therapy. The tray depicts me in the persona of a Barbie doll and evolves into me, as an adult "real person." The persona drops away as the painting is in progress. Also pictured is a man, "a good sport," going around in circles trying to get close to me. No matter how close he gets there will always be a fence between me and the people closest to me. When I finished it, I put in the time on the clock sort of arbitrarily. Then I stood back and said to myself, "That was interesting, why did I choose that time"? About three weeks later, while telling the story to a friend, she said: "Well, what happened at that time?" As she finished that statement, I got goose pimples, and out of my mouth came, "Lori was born." Of course then I took a second look at the picture with new eyes and saw the rays of the sun coming out from behind the clock and realized that she is the light of my life. Even writing this is bringing tears.

Life was not always rosy. I married Lori's father but the marriage did not last. We were divorced when she was three and one-half. When Lori was about 13, I was promoted from "manager" of a weight reduction clinic to "supervisor of the greater south bay area" and my hours got longer. This happened just at a time when the school she was attending went on split session, making her day shorter. The result, of course, was that there were more hours that she was home alone. She got lonely, and unbeknownst to me, was calling her father collect. One day I came home to find a note on the front door that read "YOUR DAUGHTER IS ALIVE AND WELL IN NEW YORK WITH HER FATHER." I felt devastated, angry and helpless.

During my internship process I felt committed to work through all of the painful memories from my past, thus I tackled the issue of parental kidnapping. The next painting in this series is called *"The Door,"* and is my old front door—the one that had the note on it. This painting of the door appears just as I remember it. It was difficult to paint. It brought back the feelings of rage, sadness, anger and pain. As I painted it, the brush stroked a thousand tears onto the canvas. I waited, I screamed, I painted. I tried to integrate the door into my present life and looked up what doors generally mean metaphorically.

I found that the door is also a symbol of transition from one realm into a new one. The closed door often points to a hidden secret, but also to prohibition and futility. The door is beginning to open; the secret is out. The guilt and shame of being helpless in the face of parental kidnapping has been released.

Once I began to heal from these old wounds a transition started to happen. I started to look at the different facets of myself—my sub-personalities, if you will. *"Persona,"* a variety of masks, represents my sub-personalities. I was noticing all the faces I wear as I go through my life. I am student, mother, daughter, bag-lady, queen, wife, friend, business woman, counselor, and trustee for the church to mention only a few. These masks make up what Jung called the persona, a system of relations between the individual and society, designed on the one hand to make an impression upon others, and, on the other, to conceal the true nature of oneself.

"The Birth Mandala" felt very healing to paint. It symbolizes a new beginning. This mandala depicts life at its start; the sperm entering the egg. Then fertilization takes place and the gametes doubles and re-doubles until finally, an embryo is formed. I feel like this embryo is the beginning of my life without old baggage. Once this mandala was completed I felt the need to go back and paint with oils. The need to quickly move through this work was tempered by the need to create something lasting, something from history.

I remembered seeing a Christmas card of two little angels and thought it was lovely. It was *"The Cherubs"* that I painted in response to that card. In my version the two children/angels represent the anima and the animus in each of us. The female (anima) on the left is honoring herself in the mirror. She is also being adored by the male (animus) on the right. These aspects, male and female, do not need to be in conflict. At the same time, in the wing of the animus, there is a profile of a woman with long, streaming hair. This is the joining of anima and animus in the adult, in my case, woman.

We balance these aspects, male and female, in a never ending cyclical pattern. The cherubs are looking into a mirror. The ancients attributed mystic powers to any reflective surface, because the reflection was considered part of the soul. Taboos were laid on the act of disturbing water into which a person was gazing, because shattering the image meant danger to the soul. This is where we get the taboo on breaking a mirror comes from. It is said to bring seven years' bad luck.

At about this time during my internship I was feeling quite new and rejuvenated. I thought it may be a good time to tackle some of my anger. I painted *"The Mermaid"* in response to that urge. I cannot begin to tell you how good it felt to get some anger out. I was raging for all the women of the world, including myself. The image of the little mermaid came up for me at once. A woman who could not stand on her own two feet. A woman who was willing to give up her mobility, even her voice, for the love of a man. I was mad at my mother for teaching me that I had to get married in order to be happy; I was mad at male bosses I've had over the years who made passes at me; I was mad at being thought of as "not presidential material;" and I was mad just because I was mad at being mad.

In my painting, the mermaid has her arm and hand out-stretched. Her fingers are on a heart. This is the heart of man. An image of a man is behind this heart. She is saying "No, no more. I will no longer give up my voice in the world in exchange for love." Most 90s women are no longer willing to make such a huge sacrifice. And they are concerned that their daughters are not sold the same myths. They are no longer willing to trade their sexuality in exchange for financial support. We women are no longer willing to give up our voices in the world in exchange for anything.

The "Mermaid" was such a powerful painting that allowed me to get in touch with so much of my anger that it actually shut down my painting process for a while. It was as if this huge weight had been lifted and a breath of fresh air came rushing in. I was reminded of my asthma and wondered where all my air has been. Could it have been taken away from me on some unconscious level?

I was getting braver. The next few paintings that flowed out were those of men. *"Caesar Chavez"* was one, *"A Doctor and His Patient"* another. Then out popped two more paintings of men and bingo! I realized that I'd been painting out past relationships of various types. Caesar Chavez indirectly kept me from marrying the wrong man. The Doctor and His Patient reminded me of my father and the other two men are two I'd dated when I first arrived in California. I was painting my past out of my body and rendering it to canvas where I could let it go, sell it, burn it or do whatever felt good. I haven't done anything with them yet. I am still contemplating this wonder. My inclination is to sell them cheap because they did not mean much to me. Ha! What a wonderful idea.

It is difficult to speak about ones own artistic style. I can see that my style became looser when I was working on my "issues." The paintings have more expression but perhaps less technical merit. I've always thought of myself as "someone who had a little artistic talent," but never as "an artist." When the process of writing this book is finished, I think I will focus a bit more on claiming that sub-personality. Yes, I will become "Linda, the artist." Change that, I *am becoming* "Linda, the artist."

Since it is also difficult to comment on the psychological aspects to one's own art, I write the words a friend said about it: "It is interesting, in this discussion, how often you slip into a passive voice, detaching from something you did, created or felt. It most often happens when you are describing your own creativity. It sounds as if there is an artist part of you who does not want you to be able to claim responsibility for her creations. Note, I'm not saying you are denying your creativity; rather, I'm saying your creative self is denying that *you* should take credit."

This thoughtful comment hit the nail on the head. There is definitely a part of me that is very artistic and creative and not willing for L. B. Spencer, the businesswoman; Dr. Spencer, the counselor; mom, the mother, or Linda, the wife; to take credit for my work. My creative part wants to be recognized as an individual, distinct from the mundane and the ordinary. Perhaps I'll paint under my maiden name since it was in childhood that Linda, the artist was created.

JEAN'S STORY

Jean is a doctoral student working on a degree in psychology. Her artwork is abstract; focusing on themes that are both personal and political. Her approach to painting is a wonderful example of how one is able to survive in the face of all three types of childhood abuse; physical, emotional and sexual.

Jean has not only survived her ordeal but has risen above it and become a spiritual being who feels a direct connection with god. She is a wounded healer, compassionate and understanding.

Born in 1943, the third of six children, she grew up on a farm in a very rural area. She has a sister who was born in 1946, on Jean's birthday. At the time of her sister's birth, their mother was diagnosed with rheumatic fever, and did not return home for about 6 months. During that time, while her father worked, the children were taken care of by several different housekeepers. There were lots of memories of chaos and confusion. She comments: "In my pre-verbal recollection, the sexual abuse began at that time."

Her closest, younger sister was mentally ill and had bouts of rheumatic fever. Even so, they were best friends. Jean recalls: "We would tie string on bushes, creating rooms, and then play school and house in them." Even at an early age Jean loved to create things "like pretend" and objects made out of mud.

In 1948, her next younger sister was born, and that is when they moved from a lovely city house to a large, old and ugly, rickety house. It was on a 75-acre farm in a rural neighborhood. That is where she started "Beginners," as kindergarten was called at the country school. The whole school only had 25 students, and in her class there were two boys and herself. Six of the school children were from her family alone. She says: "I wasn't a happy child because so many beatings were going on in the house. My father was unpredictable! When he'd get upset he'd hit us behind the head, clout your ear. It was always a surprise, because you never knew it was coming. I used to hide under the buffet when I knew he was really mad. He'd try to kick me with his boot. This type of abuse was always there, it seems that there was no beginning or end to it."

Her mother was none too passive either. Jean notes: "My mother had a wash stick and had us bend over a stream to hit us. I got so angry at this I would grit my teeth. I was stubborn. It was so unfair. I'd do the other kids work so they wouldn't get hit. I was the peacemaker in the family. It was chaotic. I thought it was normal."

Her mother put her hands over her ears when Jean would sing saying: "I'll get you a shovel to carry that tune." Needless to say Jean got little support from her mother. According to Jacquelyn Small (1991) "Sometimes parents' feelings were so explosive and dangerous there was physical abuse, and the children were not allowed to feel at all. They simply had to shut down in order to survive."

There was no relief at school for Jean either. She remembers: "The only teacher in the school was Mrs. Summerhill, a large, fat, old, and mean woman. She wanted control and was mean and sarcastic with the younger kids. Once I commented to the teacher that things weren't fair and she got upset. She swung and I ducked. She hit her hand hard against the door. I got home and told mother; who laughed. I had to carry water to the school house for a month after that." Jean remained in that school until seventh grade. She read all the books on the school shelves. In her home she did not have books, music, art supplies or TV until she was about 15 years old. She entertained herself through her imagination and in the woods.

There was no one for her to go to for respite, so in times of fear or anxiety she would hide in the doghouse for hours. Other times, she'd climb the highest trees to escape the violence. One day the physical education teacher came to the house to discuss something her older sister had said to her in class. It was about being abused by her father. Jean heard it and then saw her mother throw the woman out. The message was clear. She shouldn't mention her own abuse. She, too, was being abused but thought she was the only one. Between 1952–1961, she was often sick with kidney and bladder infections.

Her father told her if she would submit he would leave her sisters alone. I guess he told them all the same thing. All of these memories are now very clear in Jean's mind. There were years when they were repressed. In trying to discover her inner child she made a collage entitled *"Discovering My Inner Child"* She describes the process of creating it:

I spent about three hours finding pictures of woman and men with my kind of energy in magazines. I cut out phrases that inspired me. I cut some of the pictures with heads, but most of them without faces. I put my actual face above most of the bodies. Next, I found some photos of me at special moments: When my daughter was 30 minutes old, when I was first engaged, and when my second child was christened.

I asked my mother for pictures of me during childhood and cut them out with pinking sheers. I cut off parts of photos I did not like and blended them into the collage. I felt as if I let go of painful parts of my past. I left them with memories of past lives on the old country farm; rediscovered roots I liked, and left the rest.

Most of the childhood photos were sad; we all looked like orphans, but I got a kick out of blending them into my current mind-set. I am inspired when I look at my collage with phrases like: "Go For It," "Renewal," "What Every Woman Wants," "Dreams," and "She's got Theater Legs."

It wasn't until the year her father died that all of Jean's sexual abuse memories came flooding back to her. She recalls:

My father died in 1988. At that time, I was teaching in a district I'd been in for 20 years. A counselor was saying nasty things about me that were not true. I felt violated and went to see an attorney about it because I felt in danger of losing my job. I had to write down what happened, and every time I would write the word violation it triggered something in me that made the memories start to come.

I went to see a therapist and said something is wrong. The therapist said to sit with it for a month. During that time I went with my husband to a play about a dirty old man making passes at young girls. I thought I'd faint. I went white. My husband had to take me out. I went catatonic.

In therapy I sank down in the chair and felt like I couldn't move. In my mind, I saw bars and me being choked. I couldn't breathe. I realized my mother's hands were on my throat. In the next session I killed her with a gun and stabbed her many times metaphorically. She was dead.

In the next session paralysis occurred. The therapist asked me if I wanted to lie down. I took one look at the futon and remembered being attacked.

While in therapy I started journaling everything that was coming to consciousness into my computer. I wrote 10 to 15 hours a day. I ended up writing a book. It took me two years to edit it, but eventually I wrote myself well. During that time I went to the Fisher Hoffman course. We spent time studying our relationships; first our mothers, then our fathers. We had to write about all the incidents of our childhood. I connected everything. It was very healing.

The trauma in Jean's early life was due to mental, physical and sexual abuse and later from an unexpected pregnancy. As she tells it:

I was 22, and in grad school, when I got pregnant. I was so afraid to tell my mother and father that I went to a priest. He told me about a home in Ohio that would take me when I was six months along. I made up a story about going to work in California and left home. My parents never questioned me. I went to California to be far enough away that nobody would see me. I took my little car and no money. I just went. I slept in the back of the car on the way and got a job and a cottage when I got there. I worked graveyard shift.

Something happened with the hot plate in the cottage and I almost burned my kitchen down. Finally, I called a friend in Michigan. I went to stay with her for two months. I became the baby-sitter for their new baby. That was hard because I knew I was going to give my own baby away as soon as it was born. When I got to the home all I did was stay in my room. They didn't like that so they made me the social chairman. I had a boy and he got adopted. It was heartbreaking.

Within three months after giving up the baby for adoption, Jean had an accident in which she fell off of a horse and was hospitalized for seven months. Jean said:

I landed on my back and crushed my five lower vertebrae. I was back in school but couldn't attend so the professors sent the books to the hospital. It was a traumatic time for me. I got my M.A. in English by the end of that year.

She also remembered a dream experience:

Awakening from a powerful dream after a short, Sunday afternoon nap, I heard the lyrics of the old song, "I'm Looking Over a Four Leaf Clover," playing inside my head. Although I don't recall the specific details of the dream, I felt its emotion and compelling message: "Paint something! Never having painted anything—except for playful watercolor sessions with my friends two children, I faced an "edge" of consciousness inside my mind. At once, my inner critic screamed: "No way!" At the same time an inner dream character began looking for a surface on which to paint. Finding an old frame with glass in a storage room behind the house, I was unable to remove the glass from the frame; so I painted over it.

Having more experience with collage than painting, I immediately began ripping up earlier watercolor paintings and arranged the colored pieces on the surface of the glass. Humming the tune from "I'm Looking

Over a Four Leaf Clover," a remarkable thing happened; the details of my unconscious spilled onto the glass.

My mother had visited me from Los Angeles that weekend and she seemed different. For the first time ever, I believed (or chose to believe) that she liked me. The images and symbols, or what I nicknamed "symagery," from the dream inspired forgiveness, a shift in perspective, a new way of being with myself. My mother's favorite song (sung over a cradle in the dream) became my first painting. You must understand that singing is rare for my mother. The piece inspired this Haiku:

I come up roses;
The faces of forgiveness
I often call love.

Soon after Jean finished *"I'm Looking Over a Four Leaf Clover"* she awakened one morning to a dark dream character in her psyche that wouldn't go away. She remembers:

I felt heavy and awful and began drawing the figure in my dream notebook with this description below: Dream, struggling to be heard, can't express myself, ugly woman with wild hair, woman looking for a way.

I went back to my art room and put the first canvass I ever purchased on the table. Without thinking, I took down the photo that hung over the table, (a funny clown juggling colored red hearts with the saying: "The Power of Laughter and Play" on it). I glued it to the center of the canvas.

Painting colors around the photo, I was suddenly hungry and went outside to pick oranges from our tree. As I peeled one, I realized that the leaves and orange peels might complete the juggling scene. I placed them above the photo.

Suddenly I began painting a black figure. Out came a heavy, black dream character holding a magic wand; it reminds me of the "Fool" in the Tarot Deck. Suddenly the dream image shifted into a feeling of magic.

As I painted, I experienced the figure as balancing things and standing on the edge of a cliff. Immediately spying the cover of my alumni magazine that I have push-pinned to the wall, I took my pinking shears and cut out large white hands, stars, and the words: *"Discover the Magic."* Placing them over the black figure, she transformed into a wild, magic creature.

I realized I painted over my original clown photo. Deciding to cover it over with hand cream to stretch my paint supply; I covered my mistake and discovered a new glow coming into the piece.

Completely absorbed in the process, I experienced the formation of new images, letting go of former symbols. Potent "symagery" popped up without being censored; I allowed it to live—just as it appeared.

When I finished this piece I wrote this Haiku:

Up she popped
The power of laughter and play
With paint brush in hand.

Earlier in her life Jean also fell off a horse who then put his front paw on her chest and held her down. She also remembers falling out of a lot of trees and having rough fights with her siblings. For instance, she was hit over the head with a two by four board that had nails sticking out of it. Her brother threw a rusty license plate at her which hit her arm cutting her down to the elbow. Her sister pulled clumps of hair out of Jean's head in another fight. There was indeed a lot of violence in her childhood, the worst of which was her sexual abuse at the hands of her father.

Jean was raised Catholic but has been delving into a variety of religious experiences such as Indian meditation and "The Course in Miracles." She says: "The most significant part of my healing process was my discovery of the spirit within me. It is inside myself, not outside. I have connected with God."

She has a special affinity for angels. She experienced the numinous through angels and they appear in much of her artwork. One evening she returned home and was about to put her foot on the brake to stop the car in her carport. For some reason she hit the gas instead and went reeling through the back wall of the carport off a hill. She could see the brick wall in front of her and knew she was headed right for it. In that instant, she felt the car being lifted in the air by an angel, turned at a 45 degree angle, and set down gently on the ground. She was unhurt and felt very protected and unafraid. She had seen the numinous.

Jean has two masters degrees, one in English and one in Transpersonal Psychology. She has worked as a teacher for many years. During her lifetime she has worked in many different capacities. She has been married for 14 years and has two grown children. She has also had her share of surgeries, including back surgery, fibrous tumors of the uterus and foot surgery, which disabled her for a year. Two months of which she spent in a wheel chair. In the last few years Jean's healing and personal growth work have predominated her life rather than accident and illness. She has grown in her personal exploration, and has even had one-woman art shows. It is wonderful for me to witness this incredible woman's healing process in action. Jean not only paints but afterwards tries to dialogue with her art to gain further insight into the meaning of the images she has spontaneously expressed.

Her interactive artistic process as it unfolded was recorded as follows:

I have laid out in front of me my paintings. I am dialoging with them for the first time. My art, dreams and journaling all help me figure out what happened to me in the past and is now happening in my life. I feel that some important answers are portrayed in this sequence of paintings.

My colleague was fired on June 7th, which brought up very deep feelings of sadness. I believe it triggered abuse issues for me. I felt very angry and took off from work, because I felt her pain. Then I did a painting entitled *"Speaking Out."* I really got into the colors streaming out of this person's mouth which I had put on canvas. I felt there were bumps and light coming into my head giving me a headache so I needed to get all that energy in my head "out" somehow.

I'd spoken out that week for my friend, who was fired, and I was in shock that I was able to speak out for the first time in my life with such clear directness in my feelings and voice. This situation was both positive and negative for me and was very stressful. I instinctively felt that I needed light energy so I painted a lot of white and the words "Take your child on an extraordinary adventures." I used plural and singular at once. Reflecting on the images of the mother and father figures together with the big cross, I realized that this painting just popped right out of me. It seemed to portray a lot of memories for me about the relationship between my mother, father, and the Church. There was some connection there. Above those images was a ghostly death skull, the grim reaper combined with images at the bottom of all the bodies, skulls and atrocities done in El Salvador. What jumped out into my painting was what I remembered seeing on the cover of the New Yorker, in December, 1993, about El Salvador. It seemed I was trying to get in touch with old memories that I'd buried pretty deeply and was now ready to speak out about. The only balance that relieved all the darkness of these memories was all the white light shining on things on this canvas. I then realized I was starting to cut through a lot of stuff. I'd spoken out for my friend with lots of energy, and now on canvas, with lots of color. If I were to dialogue with, to ask the big blue face why it was here, it would answer: "To face things; to see things; to be seen, and to be able to stand up and verbalize things even though they are painful." I sure do like the colors coming out of the mouth, they're pretty exciting.

In my second painting, *"Secrets Seeping Out of the Trunk,"* I painted an old trunk that I dragged into my studio. It humored me that I tried to paint it so realistically, but I was really fascinated by the locks on this trunk. I seem to have this image running through my life of secrets, and things being locked up and hidden away. I have this sense of wanting to find the key to this trunk and get on with my life and not hold myself back with these kinds of memory scripts. While painting this, three figures suddenly appeared, a man and woman of the same height and a big gun jumping out of the trunk exploding in their faces. I used a lot of red depicting a lot of rage, and a lot of blood, and a lot of pain. There is raging and not even knowing where to rage. The word "FREE" is imaged in giant, huge letters. Below I wrote, "Free the children anytime, anyplace, anywhere." This is a goal for me, to help small children in the world, as well as the child inside of me. Free ourselves, anytime, anywhere, anyplace. It is much too painful to keep this stuff locked up. It's just NOT OK. to keep this buried secret history.

It is freedom to be spontaneous to deal with your history and move on, to survive and not get stuck with a hand in the trunk. This may be why this piece of work is not really finished. The image I made of this big "gray-something" above the trunk is wonderful to me. It speaks to me of fogginess. Like the feeling of experiencing amnesia. There is only a vague cloudy glimpse of something off in the distance, and then it fades with no remembrance of the former life experience. It feels like there are gaps in the time-line of my childhood memories that I can't recall. Maybe they will come back clearer someday. I guess, for me, the cloud is telling me there is hope because when you have a cloud you can have blue sky behind it, and light. Maybe there will be something I'll paint in that cloud later, and maybe not.

I'm still trying to be receptive to what I see, and feel, and sense, and listen to the gifts for me in this. I'm starting to dialogue with my paintings. I write questions with my right hand and answer with my left. It is a wonderful experience even though it is difficult to read the left-handed writing.

My third painting called *"Wow,'* knocks my socks off! It is bright blue and red, like lots of blood. I threw red paint, like blood, all over the canvas. It was very painful, very oppressive to paint this one. There are brown lines in the background which represent bars of a crib. A little child is down in there scared shitless with her hair standing on end and her mouth screaming. She didn't get heard. And here is the giant penis coming in on her. Above that is this little head, of this little kid screaming, "No! No! No!" I feel I was sort of the kid and almost the giant adult standing over the crib at the same time. I guess my overwhelming feeling was: "God, did that really come out of me?"

Last night I had a very unusual experience. I suddenly started to weep, going into a space where I was two or three years old. I was calling out for help and all my cries seemed to go out to the wolves. My father used to say that the only way to keep "wolves from the door" was for him to keep working and making money. Somehow I had a picture that there were wolves out there that are ready to break down my door and come in at anytime. It was a very scary image for me. In a way my father was like a wolf. It seemed like he was always stalking me, and he scared me a lot. I thought the wolf was outside, was inside the house, was in my head, I thought wolves were everywhere. After I started crying and felt like I would never be rescued, I closed my mouth, and there were no more tears. I gave up crying and got resigned to all the abuse.

With regards to this painting, *"Wow,"* I'm still reticent to dialogue with its images. But I'm trying to see that because this is so difficult, I probably need to do this. If the little girl in the crib were to tell me why she was here, she would probably say she was here to give me a voice and verbalize what has never been said, as well as grieve over me, and get in touch with how much I hurt; acknowledging that being a baby was not easy, and never minimize what has happened.

The first time I imaged bars in front of me at the age of two was in a therapy session, in 1988. I had an experience of being choked by my mother because I was telling her in a two-year-old manner, what things were happening to me. She tried to keep me quiet by choking me, by cutting off my voice. When I look at this big face at the top of this painting, with the big eyes and the huge "No!" coming out of the mouth, I realize I've finally got my voice back, and I don't need to choke off the memories and feelings anymore. And I don't want to be, or need to be, in a crib looking out at bars ever again. I can grow up and be my age, 51, the age I want to be.

The other image is of a big penis and balls coming right in on me as a child. This image says: "I am here so that you remember the abuse, and you don't ever allow yourself, or anyone else, to be abused if you can help it." Acknowledge it, name it, so it many save others from abuse. By facing your stuff, you can help others face theirs. This is what is so empowering about this painting. The other side of it's scariness is it's empowerment. Angie Arrien says: "No, is a complete sentence." This painting states a definite "No!" After I painted the first three, I was exhausted so I decided to take a trip to Elk, overlooking the cove where I did my first series of paintings.

"Openings" was done from the balcony overlooking magnificent rocks and openings in Elk. It's not finished; I worked very hard on getting the horizon even, but it keeps shifting. I guess it depends on your point of view. I did not have the colors I needed so the water came out very blue. I asked the ocean: "What are you here for?" And heard an answer: "I am rushing through openings, the unconscious." When I think of healing, I immediately go to the ocean. I have a lot of healing to do, healing from these paintings, a bunch of healing to do from the memories.

"The Penis From Behind" was done on June 26, 1994. I had a relaxing, healing time in Mendecino. The next day I found out my husband had skin cancer. I decided to paint. Just saying this title is hard for me. I painted it outside under the oak tree. My studio was all ripped up at the time. This tree came into the painting. As a child the woods were a place of safety. I would always be in, or with the trees often high up in the trees. I could go a mile without ever being on the ground. So this tree in my yard, a four hundred year old oak with giant limbs, is a very comforting tree, a tree that provides strength for me.

The white image in the painting came in as an angel saying, "I'm here, never gone. I'm the guardian angel you saw in childhood saying to you "I'm still here, even bigger, and you are bigger now, too." There is also the image of a giant man with a giant red penis, who has me by the arms, holding me, abusing me from behind. This is all so unpleasant to look at now. The giant penis is up in the sky, not even on the ground, and all this black is coming from behind, all around my father, the perpetrator. It is all this raping and darkness that he is coming from. All through my childhood I had this frightening dream that my father was always hiding behind a tree and was going to jump out and get me. In therapy, and bodywork in 1978, I first got in touch with that image and was able to diffuse it. When I drove the highway, I used to look off to the left and wonder if he was hiding in the trees. Now I don't feel afraid like that anymore, not about physical places. Maybe there is still something lurking in my memories and shadows but I am not afraid of being in the woods chased by him. I often feel helpless about these memories which still jump out and try to take over my psyche, but it's easier when I see them on my canvas. When I showed the paintings to my therapist, I did not hide or dissociate. But afterwards I was a basket case. Again, friends, helped me, and I felt so blessed to have them ground me and bring me back to the present.

"Pulled By Illusions of Ego" is telling me that I have to let go of my ego and surrender to God. I was in a state of being pulled by my ego and I was

getting nowhere. When I let go and asked the holy spirit into my life, I felt a sense of connection and comfort.

"Taking Off The Blindfold" was so intense for me because I didn't want to let go of it. It kept getting bigger and bigger, growing and growing. Facing things is up for me so I began with a "face" up in the left hand corner, a deep dark blue face. The colors pink, salmon and copper were also popping into my head. I felt like blinders were coming off and didn't like what I was seeing, but I knew blinders were coming off. I also drew two hands and two knives right beside my ear in the picture. I became obsessed with the O.J. Simpson case, and the knives continued to get to me. I became fascinated with a Buck knife I own and put it beside me to paint. Everything was coming up violent. There was also a mirror beside me on the table. I'd imagine back to when I was a child in a certain room staring out the window which I hated because everything seemed broken up by them. I tried to lift them up so all wouldn't seem so broken. Below the window are two hands saying they are tied with rope, tortured, unable to get free. Down at the bottom right is a little girl with laser guns, and star wars "light rods" trying to put light on the scene. Shadows behind a mirror off to the left are shadow figures of the other kids in the family knowing what was going on, but everything stayed bloody and broken behind the window blinds. I threw red paint all over this, and that was very upsetting. I finished it off. Then all of a sudden, I realized I needed help. There were two hands in surgical gloves reminding me of my therapist's help with my heart. The little heart was like my son's heart he made me with "I love You" on it. I remembered the regard and love my therapist has for me and realized this painting was tapping into so many levels. This was a breakthrough for me because I knew then I was going to look at these things coming up and get better. I knew I could do it.

"Burying Monsters And Ghosts" was done on Independence Day. I was a big white bear with monsters after me, but I was so big and so tall I could take care of myself. I painted the bear, who was supposed to be the empowered me, under my tree. I put a dismembered hand in. I chopped it to pieces before I asked it why it was there. The answer had to do with losing my strength, losing my hands, getting dismembered. It had to do with the things I would like to do with cruelty to try to get even. I made a coffin and buried a person in it with some fingers over it. The hand broke when I did this so I'll have to glue it. The barbarian quality is what I was getting in touch with. I realized then that what had happened to me was barbaric, brutal, and cruel. This person in the coffin is probably my father and I wanted to bury the ghost of his brutality. This is harder to

talk about than some of my other work as my mind is still trying to bury all this sometimes.

"Black Tears Or My Popcorn Sky Lost Its Star" was also very difficult to do. I painted it outside. I started thinking "blue sky" while eating popcorn. When I was a child we grew popcorn on our farm to sell to the Popeye Company. We had it everywhere and made it for every occasion. So the image of a childhood sky was a blue sky with popcorn in it. I found a star and thought back to the childhood time when I believed I was a special star in my father's eye. He was my star too. Suddenly the star I held fell on the cement and shattered into pieces. I started to cry. My first impulse being to quit painting. But instead, I glued the broken star into the canvas sky and realized that no longer was the ideal hope of childhood. It all ended. The sadness of the abuse and pain all of us suffered came back. All that time I thought I could protect them if I complied, I thought I could save her with my story. So here is this little child in the painting with black tears. The grief hit me hard while working, and I cried very hard; the black marks are my tears. My hair is also standing straight up because I am terrified. Down on the right side, there is a figure like an ape. Because my father worked with hay. I'll always have an image of him with a pitch fork. The image was first a man, then an ape; the pitchfork turned into the devil, and it all got very confusing. I circled all this with a big red circle depicting, "No more of this! No more pretending or denial, no more hurting myself! No more fantasies of a star in the sky, or ideals that are no more." Ideals are shattered. I was so upset doing this painting that I tried to recover by throwing red paint on it. At this time in my life one day was running into the next.

"Blown Away And Still Solid" is one of the paintings I really like. I started with a yellow figure and hair everywhere because I felt blown away. Then I painted my face in. There came a sense of a center of me which is the image down at the bottom of a circle, a mandala inside me. This is what I am like at my core. I could not get the circle right so I found an old frame to do it with. This core is steady; it goes up all the way through me; it is gold, green earth, growing with health. Coral went in to represent that this is what I have always been, and this is what we all are from. We are pure and whole from antiquity. We just got blown away because we forgot who we are. The two hands are very interesting because I felt I had to hold this piece out in front of me so I could really see it. Even though doing this work is disorienting there is a part of me that is healthy and whole, and healing and solid, and will not be blown away by what I am discovering. The big purple magenta wave behind me is trying to knock me over; yet it isn't getting anywhere. This is so exciting, so

empowering to see this. I love the title because of all this. When I shared this painting with my mentor, she saw so many levels in it which helped me see the progress I was making. I felt very affirmed and started to believe in myself again, treating my own images as honored guests.

"Facing It On Many Levels" was painted when I woke one morning very disturbed. I'd been having difficulties with a man at work, and the situation was pushing brother/father issues. I was also having some complex dreams involving men I knew and liked. I wanted to get on top of all this, but realized I was being pulled by the ego. To face this fact was difficult. Because there are many levels, there are three different faces in this painting. The first on the left is a little pink child face, representing that child space I didn't know how to get out of. The second face is much clearer, like me actually seeing I was in a child space trying to understand things. Then the big huge face is me as an adult, the part of me I now want to get in touch with. I was starting to need to move on from just child memories and old projections and stuff that doesn't do anyone any good any more. Because I was feeling "stepped-on" in my work, and feeling "stepped-on" by myself, I needed to not be in "a stepped-on place" any more. I step all over this painting while calling on the Holy Spirit, three figures in one, the Trinity. They came onto the canvas as the light. Five egos with blindfolds and an innocent little child take up the bottom. The egos could be my five siblings. I cut through the ego so I could face things straight on realistically deciding not to hang onto old stuff, or projecting it onto others. A feeling of strength, solidness, freedom came over me which made me feel more comfortable; wonderful. And I loved the color blue I used again.

"Longing" was done after not painting for a whole month. Passion and purple have always been a big thing for me as I was raised a Catholic with mass and the purple vestments. I was surrounding myself with this cross when it got so explosive. I knew I was cutting away, getting to the real part of me, of who I am. Much of this work was learning to own my own mother and father parts of me; not projecting them out, but giving it to myself. It felt like all of this growing edge was coming from my heart and the only way it could come further would be in the intense longing and hunger for God. I wanted to be in that place as much as I could be. I was feeling my Spiritual Self surge all through me, my own essence.

It feels delightful having all of these paintings sitting out here in my garden in the midst of all my flowers. I painted the fence to make it complete. It is a real *"Goddess Fence"* now. She has power and she is fueled by the sun. I am just amazed how beautiful this is. I have to say I am enormously proud that I was able to do this. I was feeling some stress about doing it but it feels freeing and I'm delighted.

This Author's Initial Reaction to Jean's Story

My first thought upon leaving the interview was, "How on earth did this girl survive with such a sense of spiritual connectedness?" I felt it would have been more normal for her to be angry, full of rage and hatred, and to have a more volatile personality.

Jean has used art as the epitome of healing. She has taken her creations and acknowledged their power to heal her. She has a history of horrific abuse, and yet she has evolved into an incredibly spiritual person. Speaking with her, one senses that she has a wonderful connection to the Divine. No anger emanates from beneath her calm demeanor.

She has used art as an avenue of expression and more—as a path to God. I wanted to show the reader how she uses her artwork as a personal processing tool; consequently, I included her series of interactive paintings.

The artistic process has been of great help to her in learning about herself from her own images and the process of working with art imagery in a healing modality. She says, "I have shifted into a very hopeful stage of my life. I am even considering sharing my healing process with 'Imagination and the Arts: Gateways to the Soul' in a presentation this summer."

This artist was sexually, emotionally, and physically abused. Most abuse survivors have not experienced all three types of abuse. Little by little, Jean has dealt with these traumatic issues. While experiencing the traumatic memories, she has pasted, painted, and smeared paint and various objects onto canvas board. Externalizing her uncomfortable feelings has been cathartic; she has felt a dissolving of the issues although they were never resolved with her father in his lifetime. She affirms that, "Moving through these issues with excitement, good health, and gusto are important steps in my ongoing process of healing." I am amazed that Jean is sane at all, much less as spiritually-centered as she is. She says: "The most significant part of my healing process was my discovery of the spirit within me. It is inside myself, not outside. I have connected with God."

From Jean's story I learned that a sense of unfairness is a theme for abuse victims. It appears to lead to a numbing of feelings. From this story I recognize that crises may be somatized and when one is vulnerable, without control, the chances of being ill or having accidents may increase. Also, I learned from this story more than any other the power of artwork as a healing modality.

The Transpersonal Dimensions of Jean's Story

After her father died, painful memories arose in Jean's awareness. She said, "My abuse memories surfaced in 1988. I recalled that mother tried to choke me and I had a terrible time trying to speak. I still have a thing about being choked."

Jean began intensive therapy to heal her childhood abuse pain. She said, "I did the Fisher Hoffman 13-week course. I connected everything. I had a big closure with my parents."

Jean used art and poetry to begin to heal. "I began doing art in a creative expression class, and I started writing poetry to keep the pain away." When she opened to the expressive arts, her deeper self began to emerge through bringing old pain into consciousness.

She began to heal the outer relationship with her mother: "I sent her a letter telling her about my book and that I forgive her. She visited me and was nice. Something shifted for me. I felt I had forgiven and had understood my mother."

Once this happened, Jean was able to begin healing her inner relationship with the Divine Mother. "I dreamt I sang the song she sung to me as a child. I began painting. It was my first painting and it was a combination of black and white. I call it *Spider.*"

Jean's deep heart opens through the healing of her mother/father wounds. Her art was a healing modality that facilitated the release of stored pain. She remarked, "I get irritable when I can't paint. I feel lost if I can't paint. There's nothing to look forward to."

In my opinion, Jean has experienced the transpersonal connection; she states, "The most significant thing in my healing is my connection with God. I've discovered the spirit within me."

The release of stored pain through art has given Jean a glimpse of her inner self. She says, "I'm an outrageous character." She has begun to experience self-actualization through her art. She says, "Since I'm creative, I'm much happier. The paintings just pop out of me."

Archetypal images have helped to release and heal her buried abuse pain. She has used colors and images of trunks, keys, and secrets. "I have this image running through my life of secrets and things locked up. I have a sense of wanting to find the key. I used a lot of red depicting a lot of rage, blood and pain."

Jean has moved into a heart opening through her art. She remarks, "I want to treat my images like honored guests. I am trying to be receptive to what I see. I want to listen to the gifts in this for me. I'm starting to dialogue with my art."

Her art has empowered her. She said: "My overwhelming feeling was: God, did that come out of me? I've finally got my voice and now I don't need to choke off the memories. This is what's so empowering about the painting. The other side of its empowerment is its scariness.

Jean has opened to the transpersonal healing power of transcendence through her art." She says: "I have a lot of healing to do from the memories. I am trying to reach and have the Holy Spirit help me. I realize I need to step back and let a greater truth lead the way. Purple is me: anger, light, humanness, a spiritual being becoming human."

By surrendering to her own higher essence (God), some of her painful memories have been released. She has consciously used art as her therapy. By actually painting imagery of her earlier sexual abuse, she finds it easier to assimilate these painful memories and move beyond them. She describes her painting, *The Penis From Behind:* "This is an image of a giant man, grabbing my arms and abusing me from behind. The perpetrator is my father. I was hiding behind a tree. He jumped out and got me. Now I don't feel afraid like that anymore, not about physical places. It's easier when I see it on canvas. This painting was so intense because I didn't want to let go of it. I felt like the blinders were coming off."

When "Everything was coming up violent," Jean realized she needed help. Out of primal darkness came a kaleidoscopic archetypal flow of healing energy. She said, "All of a sudden I realized I needed help. This was a breakthrough for me. I knew I was going to look at these things [paintings] and get better. I knew I could do it."

As she was in the depths of painting and one day was flowing into the next, Jean discovered her center through mandala art therapy. She remarked: "There came a sense of center in me, a mandala inside me. This is what I am like in my core. This core is steady, it goes all the way through me growing with health. This is what I have always been and what we are all from. We are pure and whole from antiquity."

As her healing progressed, Jean's wounded child began to transform into the divine child. She says: "I saw I was in a child space and didn't know how to get out of it. The second I saw I was an observer looking at the child in that space I knew I'd get well. I was starting to have to move on from childhood memories and old projections. A feeling of strength, solidness, and freedom came over me."

As painful memories about her parents surfaced, Jean externalized them onto canvas board. She used photographs of herself during earlier stages of her life, buttons, cards, and frames. First she glued any object she was moved to include onto the board. Then she smeared, brushed, and threw paint at the piece as she expelled anger, grief, and pain. In such a way, she transformed wounding memories into something she was proud of: a piece of art. Jean is an expressive, imaginative artist.

Lastly, Jean began to connect with her own masculine and feminine in her heart. She says: "I knew I was cutting away and getting at the real me. Most of my work was learning to own the masculine and feminine part of me. Not projecting it out, but giving it to myself. I felt like a growing edge was coming from my heart. I felt a spiritual self surge all through me, my own essence. I'm amazed how beautiful this is."

Defining Jean's Current Issues and Strengths

The *abuse theme* is the major theme and runs through her story until her adulthood. Secondly, she is always looking for fairness in the midst of chaos. She said: "Mom hit me with the wash stick, it was so unfair. My teacher made me carry water when she hit the wall with her fist instead of my face. That was also unfair. I even did the other kids' work at home so they wouldn't get hit."

Jean was always *creating things.* Even while her life was torn apart in childhood, she managed to create things. As a child, Jean employed her imagination. "I loved making pretend things like mud pies. My sister and I made rooms out of the bushes by tying rope to them. I was always making things." Later in life she made collages, paintings, sculptures, and masks. "When I made masks, I learned where subpersonalities came from."

Another theme is that of *cluster illnesses,* accidents, and other physical experiences. Was she having transpersonal encounters with "fate?" Jean remembers, "In 1966, I got pregnant, had the baby, gave him up for adoption, and a horse fell on me crushing five of my vertebra." Two years later, she was planning to be married. A month before the wedding she was knocked unconscious in a car accident and given a neck brace. Two months later, the father of her child committed suicide. A month later,

Jean broke her leg in a skiing accident and dislocated her shoulder. All of these misfortunes occurred within a two-year period.

In 1981, she was again hospitalized for back surgery—only months after she underwent surgery for the removal of a uterine fibrous tumor. In 1992, she developed complications after foot surgery on both feet and was in a wheelchair for two months. The next month she encountered an angel, perhaps a near death experience (NDE), when her car careened over a cliff. Four times in her life Jean experienced clusters of illnesses and accidents.

The experience of *things jumping out to get her or being surprised in an attack*—which originated in reaction to her father—has continued as a theme in Jean's life. "My father hit me behind the head. It was always a surprise. I dream my father is hiding behind a tree waiting to get me. My father was like a wolf, always stalking me. The memories still jump out and take over my psyche."

Another theme in Jean's life is that of *constant amazement* at how art has helped in her search for self and healing. It is her transpersonal vehicle for transformation from fear to self-empowerment, a sensual release of unconscious pain for her. She says, "Painting activates all my senses. I like the sounds of painting. I'd rather be throwing paint than anything else. I get satisfied and fulfilled. I'm always surprised." Also, "Painting and writing have changed my self-acceptance for the better. The other side of the scariness is its empowerment. This is what is so empowering about painting."

The final theme in Jean's story is her *connection to spirit.* She manages to find transpersonal meaning in the midst of chaos. She said: "The most significant thing in my healing is my connection to God. I've discovered the spirit within me. There is a higher power guiding my life. I am trying to reach and have the Holy Spirit help me. I realize I need to step back and let a greater truth lead my way. I'm looking forward to the truth coming in."

Jean's Reaction to Participation in This Book

I have healed considerably since the interview in the following ways: first and foremost, while I was reading both the transcript of our interview and the transcript of "dialogue" with this summer's paintings, I was so moved by the write-ups that I read and reread them—as well as worked with the material in several sessions with my therapist. It is significant to me that after your validation I did a lot of processing and have "shifted" into a very hopeful stage in my life.

Your validation of my work in processing the "healing-abuse-memory paintings" has been enormously important to me. By reading the words, and realizing that there was a witness to this process, I really validated myself and told myself, "Yes, Self, you do know how to do this work: heal by creating; and you know how to dialogue with images and figure out what they are trying to tell you! Bravo!"

Acknowledging and moving through these issues with excitement, good health, and gusto are important steps in my ongoing process of healing for me! I now find myself in an objective, witnessing place with this sensitive material I'm emerged in.

I've been afraid of most things—for most of my life; just recently I have been feeling a lot stronger and more hopeful that I really have integrated a lot of my childhood and adult history and that I really may be a good supporter of others whether I do work as a one-on-one psychologist or with individuals and their creative processes.

MARI'S STORY

Mari was born in St. Paul, Minnesota, in 1954. Her parents were both age 23 when they married. Her father was in the Navy and was on leave from fighting in the Korean war. Her mother was a housewife but she had finished college. Mari says: "I was conceived on my parents honeymoon; they were virgins." When her father came back from service she was nine days old. She noted: "He and my mother never had any time alone together and it turned out that I was the cause of a lot of stress in the relationship because I was already there." Mari feels that her mother was very jealous of her father's attention to her. She commented: "When I was two weeks old, my parents made an agreement that I would not be touched except for basic care, feeding, and changing. It bothered my mother when my father touched me." She went on to say: "I sensed that my mother came from a very emotionally deprived background and she didn't know how to give affection. It was very hard for her to understand that I was robbed of some things." Mari tells her story:

My earliest recollection of affection was when I was about three. My father's mother was really kind to me. I had a terrible flu, and she made me a cotton nightgown and made a matching one for my doll. That was my only recollection of someone doing something nice for me. I remember being overwhelmed by that gesture and I totally loved my grandmother. She was also an artist. My parents had my sister when I was three years old and, in rapid succession, four other children followed. My mother had a total of six children in 10 years. I was the oldest and had to help her with my sisters and brothers. Because I had to help my mother with my brothers and sisters, I didn't have any free time. As a result I hated my siblings.

When I was five we went on a picnic with my godmother who was a single older woman. She wasn't a demonstrative woman. I was in the back seat getting tired and she invited me to lay my head on her lap. She stroked my head as I fell asleep. I just felt like I was in heaven. It was incredible to be touched like that. It never occurred to me that I deserved to be touched like that. That woman was really awesome.

My father was really attached to his mother but she died when I was five and one-half. It was a sudden death from a blood clot after gall bladder surgery. The clot dislodged and went right to her heart. It was traumatic. Shortly after that my father started hitting me. I'd do something, and didn't even know what it was, but he'd be screaming at me. He'd just start flailing away at me and then he'd apologize. So I always felt sorry for my father. I'd think, "Poor man, he just can't help himself." If I'd just do things right then he wouldn't have to hit me. As the years went on, it continued. It was always out of the blue. I never knew when he was going to hit me. I tried to counterbalance it by being an "A" student, by being as good as I could possibly be, but it never helped.

I asked Mari if she had any dreams that had themes to them when she was a child.

She remembered some dreams with escape symbolism in them.

When I was a kid dinosaurs would chase me and if I could get past a cyclone fence they couldn't get me. I had flying dreams when my father first hit me, but they stopped. Dreams of falling, too.

My mother was also very critical. If I had an "A" why wasn't it an "A+"? My mother was very critical and verbal, and my father was unavailable because he was always mourning the loss of his mother. When he was home he was very volatile. I was the focus of his physical abuse. I remember him hitting my next younger sister and brother and then he'd say to me, "See what you make me do? If you would just behave I wouldn't have to do this." He didn't hit them as much as he hit me and the three youngest didn't get hit at all. It was terrible never knowing when something would come down on you and always living in fear. I didn't know what it was about me that caused him to react that way. There was also the sense of having to hide who I was.

I had to make really sure I was always the person who my father and mother wanted me to be. For instance, I had a habit of sighing as a form of tension release. My mother would get absolutely furious when I sighed and she would say, "Who do you think you are? Do you think you're better than us, better than me?" She would load little physical things with meaning. I was so self-conscious it was incredible. I don't know how I survived. My mother was always scrutinizing me.

My only escape was books and I would read a lot. Once my father barged into my room, pulled the book out of my hand and threw it across the room and said to me, "No daughter of mine is going to lay around reading books. I want you to go outside and be popular." He chased me out of the house. By the time I had finished grade school I'd read all the books for high school. I was a reading nut.

I read a book about fathers who love their daughters too much. It really helped me because I knew my father hadn't sexually abused me but I always felt that there was some weird sexual undercurrent in our relationship. That, I was very uncomfortable with. He looked to me for what he didn't get from my mother and then his mother when she died. I remember standing on the steps of the church after my grandmother's funeral and my father took my hand and in that instant I felt this awesome responsibility. Then he started hitting me shortly thereafter. I believe he wanted something from me that he couldn't have and he was really frustrated. But he didn't know that. I think that's why I always felt that he wanted something from me that wasn't right. I was so uncomfortable around my father. I didn't want to be alone with him; not just because I was afraid of him physically; I just was uncomfortable.

When I was in high school, we moved to California for a year. Mother hated California. She manipulated my father to move back to Minnesota. While we were in California in 1969, I experimented a little bit with drugs. It was important that I got good grades so I didn't do much. I experimented a little bit, I lost my virginity. That was the first time I felt physical contact. It was a discovery for me. Even though with teenage boys it was not much of an experience, it was a lot more than I was used to. My mother discovered it when she read my diary.

I came home from school and none of my brothers or sisters were home. My father was home at 3:00 in the afternoon and that was unusual. My mother and father were standing in the kitchen drinking wine. They drank wine from the time they got home 'till they went to bed. They didn't get drunk, they were just high. So anyway they were drinking at 3:30 in the afternoon.

They walked out and my father backhanded me across the face and I got pushed up against a divider. He kept hitting me. I remember he had a wine glass in his left hand and he was hitting me with his right hand. I remember my mother saying, "Robert, STOP! STOP!" and I thought, God, mom is going to protect me. I was blown away. Instead she said: "Give me your wine glass so you don't break it." He gave her the wine glass and continued to wail at me. It was such a betrayal, absolutely tremendous. When that happened, I said to myself, I don't care how hard he hits me I am not going to cry. I am never going to allow him to affect me again with this behavior. He's not going to hurt me inside ever again.

According to Jacqueline Small (1991): Sometimes their parents' feelings were so explosive and dangerous there was physical abuse, and the children were not allowed to feel at all. They simply had to shut down in order to survive and they then became completely out of touch with their feelings. They may have felt responsible early in life for their parents' feelings; in other words, it was all their fault.

Mari goes on with her story:

I have TMJ now because I clenched my jaw so hard. I know I put up some tremendous walls just from that one incident that didn't come down 'till this year. That was a real, critical experience. After that I was very cold. I just went through the motions. I felt like I was totally at my parents' mercy until I could get away from home.

When we lived in California, they made me go to modeling school. I won this beauty contest, but they wouldn't let me do the things you're supposed to do as the queen. They were always giving me things with one hand and taking them away with the other. I was always confused. I wondered, "Am I pretty or am I not pretty? Smart or not smart? Capable or not capable?" I lived in a sense of never knowing; never knowing if something bad was going to happen; never knowing inside of myself what I had to rely on. I didn't feel confident.

When we got back to Minnesota, my old friends didn't seem the same. I had changed in California. I had phenomenal stress and tension, no friends, and I hated Minnesota. We were staying in some people's house who were on vacation, and I took all the pills out of every bottle in their medicine cabinet and ate them all. Nobody knew, but they wouldn't have cared if they did. I went to sleep that night with my sister. I knew I was going to sleep and that I would never wake up. It was so weird when I woke up. I was shocked. I couldn't even kill myself. I was sick for two weeks. My dad had to carry me to the next house. I never told my parents.

I never had anyone saying you are so "whatever." So I could say, "Yes, I really am." An experience of validation. Never had any experiences I could use to validate myself. There was nobody in my life who validated me. But there was always the memory of my grandmother. I always said if I ever have children I am going to treat them like my grandmother treated me. I made her into a mythical figure. She was really neat. I always trust my gut feelings. It's a combination of gut feeling and a sense of what is a psychic sense. My grandmother was very psychic. I will frequently see things before they happen. I call it being tied in. I think we are all tied in but it depends on how much we pay attention to it. I trust my intuition.

She has always impacted me in terms of my interactions with children. I always want my interactions with children to be positive in case they don't have other experiences in their lives that are positive. At least the experiences they have with me will be validating for them. I don't do a lot with children but those I do are important. I graduated from high school in three years. I was 17 when I graduated. I always knew I wanted to be an artist from the time I was five or six. All I did was draw. I drew and drew. Even during grade school and junior high. I loved art in school. In high school I was the first in my school to graduate early, and I had to create a whole system to allow that to happen. I did a lot of independent studies in painting, history of art, and paintings of the Vietnam War. I did a slide show with collages of women, bodies with different positions in a solid color outlined by pictures of fashion magazines. Dealing with the subject of "What are our bodies?" Showing that they are different than what is represented by the media.

After I graduated from high school I was working at a hospital trying to earn money to start college in the spring. One day I came home, walked into kitchen, and took a Pyrex bowl with green beans in it from the refrigerator. My father walked in out of the blue and said, "If you're not going to be the kind of person I want you to be then you're not going to eat my food." It was the first time I stood up to him when he got that way, and I said, "Well, Dad, I don't know what more you can expect of me. I am a straight "A" student. I graduated from high school in three years. I do everything around here anybody asks me to. I've got my own job. I've saved money for college" and I went on and on. He got really angry and started hitting me, and I just wasn't going to take it. All I can remember what happened is that we made our way from the kitchen up the steps to the back hall. I was trying to get into my room and close the door. I could see I wasn't going to be able to make it to my room so I got my coat on. He picked me up and kicked open the door and threw me into the snow. I landed on the sidewalk. I realized he still had the sleeve of my coat in his hand. He had torn the sleeve off my coat in the process. (I thought about it symbolically later in therapy and realized he was throwing me out and holding on at the same time.) I said, "I'm out of here."

No pictures of Mari's work exist for the period of her life prior to leaving home because as she remembers:

I burned my paintings after I got thrown out of the house when my father ripped my coat sleeve. I told my boyfriend's mother about the abuse. We still have an ongoing relationship. She was a nice lady.

I got myself an apartment with some other women and, from that time on, I was on my own. I never got an apology from him or my mother. It was like it never happened. Nothing was ever discussed.

I started college the next spring and got married to my high school sweetheart a year later. The day I told him I thought I was pregnant he left and I didn't see him again. My oldest son went and found him last year. He's a heroin addict. He's real messed up.

I had my son in 1974 and went back to school in 1976. I got on a welfare program. They gave me food stamps, tuition, rent, everything. I was able to maintain a "3.5" average. I was so happy I could focus on my art. Our assignment upon arriving at class was to "draw it" [the room] which had been wrapped in a large four foot wide roll of tissue paper. Everyone set to work trying to draw everything: the whole room with all the people, easels and tissue paper. I just said to myself, "No way!" and proceeded to draw one *"Single Fold In The Tissue."*

I love this piece because it showed me how I have the ability to make a daunting task manageable and how I can take something mundane and make it marvelous. I guess it says something to me about our power to transform something, about the power of art to transform and transcend.

"The Hand" is another college piece from a photography class. I photographed the shadow of a plant, my hand, and a piece of cloth on the carpet. Although not as powerful for me as the above piece, it represents a continuation of my experimentation with the transformative power of art, taking shadows and light and giving them texture—something we don't associate with shadow or light.

I got married again in 1978. We moved to California in 1979, and I had my son James in 1980.

I maintained this relationship with my parents where everything that had happened was like a secret, and because it was never talked about, it was like it never really happened. It wasn't like I wanted to talk about something we weren't dealing with, it was just easier not to talk about it. We had what you'd consider on the surface to be a very nice relationship. So I moved out here because my father was here.

I never finished my degree so my plan was to finish it, but my husband and I realized we couldn't live without two full-time incomes. So I went to work in the semiconductor industry and ended up in management within a few months. In college, I ended up working on my masters degree in business. We had the house in Saratoga and all that stuff. I realized I was unhappy. My husband at the time was not treating my oldest son very well. Not abusive, but not well. I started therapy to see how I could help my son and the therapist said, "Well, you have a lot of stuff you have to deal with. Ever since then I have been in therapy. From 1982–1985, I went once a week. In 1985, what had happened was I got to the point of realizing I had married a man who was very much like my mother. I wasn't happy in the marriage. He was highly critical of me and totally unaffectionate. From the outside looking in, everyone thought he was great. Just like my mother. Everyone thinks she's Dinah Shore. Anyway, I got a divorce and was out in the world again. I met my current husband right after I got separated, but I told him I needed time alone. Two years later I called and asked him if he was still available and he said, "Yes." We got married a couple of years later and it's been great.

Mari had two near-death experiences. They both happened within a couple of years of each other. As she tells it:

My husband and I went to Tahoe skiing. We were on the outside with just a cliff next to us. I remember being dead calm, it surprised me. My husband said, "I have no control of the car." I put my hand on his leg and calmly said, "It's OK; I know you're going to do whatever you can do. Whatever you do, don't put your foot on the brake." I had grown up in Minnesota and know how to drive in icy conditions. So the first thing he did was hit the brakes. The car spun around in slow motion. We were going toward the ongoing traffic and the next thing I knew we had our rear end out back over the cliff. I remember I still had my hand on my husband's thigh and I started thinking about my children. I was so calm. My whole life was there and I knew the next sensation was going to be falling back over the cliff. I saw my whole life and it was good. I felt really sad that I wouldn't see my kids. I was totally calm. The next thing I knew the car had stopped and we had turned around again and we were facing out over the edge of the cliff. He asked me if I had any guardian angels. It was just incredible.

The second NDE happened a couple of years ago when I got real sick with a cold. I got medication for it that didn't work. I called another doctor and asked for something else. The new medication made me really nauseous. My temperature remained 103 degrees. I was on the couch in the family room day after day. It was just awful. I wasn't eating and was getting weaker and weaker. She prescribed these suppositories for the nausea. It worked for the nausea but I started getting cramps in my legs and then all over my body. I was so weak by then that my husband had to carry me up and down the stairs. One morning I started to feel the cramping go into my throat. I couldn't breathe or talk. I managed to get myself up. By the time I got to the top of the stairs to get my husband my tongue was starting to go down my throat. The muscles were doing it. He drove me fast to the emergency room and they gave me a shot of Benadril and all the cramping went away in 10 minutes. I was having an allergic reaction to the drugs. During that time there was a sense that I was going to die. I couldn't get over my sense of calmness. I didn't want to die that way because it was really uncomfortable. I had a real sense of acceptance about the whole thing.

I was really driven after that. I stopped going to medical doctors and started going to a homeopath. That changed a lot of things for me. That's when I started seeing a new therapist. No more fooling around. It wasn't like I was fooling around, I was trying to get issues resolved but I just wasn't getting anywhere. It wasn't acceptable anymore to not have issues resolved. It was time to get myself together. It was time to be me, not waste any more time being less than who I was. The near-death experiences speeded my process up. They made me realize how fragile life could be. My process would have happened anyway eventually but I think almost dying speeded it up.

From 1985–1986 I didn't do much therapy. From 1987 on I did intensive therapy. I wanted to be free but didn't even know what I wanted to be free of. It was a process of realizing I had been abused. I just always thought everybody was beaten up by their dads. I didn't realize that wasn't the way children were supposed to be raised. Realizing that was a big thing. Ultimately I got to the point where I confronted my parents. The reaction was really bad. As a result I didn't have any contact with my parents until this last year. Just yesterday I had to deal with them because of what has happened to my sister. She was recently in an automobile accident and she is paralyzed. I was the contact person who had to tell them about it. When I talk to them it's like there's nothing there. When I talk to my father about the abuse (I had my brother and sister confirm it because they witnessed it) he said it never happened. It was four years ago that I confronted him and he still says it never happened. My mother refused to even respond to me. It was like I wasn't even there.

I realized I had to mourn the loss of parents, that in fact, I didn't have any in the sense of people who can nurture me. What I had lost was a sense of nurturing. I got to that point and didn't know where to go with it. I wanted to draw. I was not working at the time and had the freedom to draw but couldn't do it. I would sit here and do the drawings but it was so hard to get them out. I felt there was so much more but it wouldn't flow out. It had to be dragged out.

I started with drawings after the earthquake; to get down on paper my feeling of being on shaky ground. I did those drawings but they were stiff and difficult to do. In art school ideas just sprung out of me, art was easy and I loved it. After the quake I tried to express emotion and feeling but I couldn't do it. I started to have weird dreams, fish dreams. There was a series of them.

The first one had a deep pool, an indoor pool. I went into this room. The water was black. I had a key and it fell into the water. I believe it was my mother's car key or something. I couldn't see the keys and I didn't want to put my hand in that water but I started to do it and then I realized the water was moving. You know how when there are lots of koi under the water it starts to boil almost? That's what it started doing and I realized there were lots of fish in the water. I thought well, "I'm surely not going to put my hand in that water now." Then the fish started coming out of the water and flying around. I just can't stand fish that leave the water. After the earthquake we had this huge fish tank that fell and the fish were all over the floor and I couldn't save them. I can't deal with those slimy writhing things. I had to get out. In the dream I had to get out and my mother and one of my sisters was outside of the building and the fish were following. My mother had a purse. The key came back. I don't know why but somehow I had to get the key in the purse. It was important. I knew I just had to get that key into that purse. My mother and sister were not being of any assistance at all so I had to pursue my mother to get into the purse. The fish were chasing me. I put my hand into the purse and said, "Yes, the key's in the purse." That was the end of the dream. The purse was deep, sort of velvety black inside. There was nothing else in the purse. There were also more and more keys that went on this key chain as the dream went on so it was a key chain with a lot of keys that went into the purse.

I had this dream after I confronted my mother. The confrontation was a part of my therapy. After that dream I painted *"Fish Out of Water."* I had this really overwhelming urge to get that dream outside my body. I had to put it on paper. I remember being really fascinated when I was done. It was iconographic. I was amazed at how important that image was to me. When I put those feelings out on paper their importance was so clear to me.

In the second dream, the fish were flying out at me and they were barking at me. They never got me. I sensed that they were angry fish. After that dream I painted *"Barking Fish."* To me the barking fish was my father coming at me. This man was screaming at me. It was the first time I'd ever put anything like that outside of me. It was the end. It was two years until I could do something I was comfortable with after that. I did a lot of drawings but nothing approached the level of emotion of that piece. I did it in 1990.

In the third dream, I was at a party where everybody was wearing black leather. I was also there wearing black leather. I went to the bedroom to get my coat and as I was passing back through the main part of the house I saw there was a bird cage full of fish. When I walked by they tried to get out. I turned around and said, "No." They all went back into the cage and that's the last fish dream I had. I felt like I had control over the fish. After this dream no image came to my mind so I didn't do a painting of it. When the fish in the cage dream came it was like a closure and I didn't feel the need to do anymore.

My understanding of the initial fish dream is that the dark water is stuff I didn't want to deal with or know about. The fish coming out of the water was threatening to me but I wanted it. By getting to the point when I could say no to the fish I was getting to the point that I could handle it. That's how I felt about it. After that, my therapy focused on what had happened with my parents. More than that, I went beyond that period in my life. I said to myself, "I'm tired of talking about my parents." I'm talking about what happened. I'm ready to move beyond them. I want to go past them. I want to know how it affected me. So I spent from 1990–92, looking at everything I could see, taking myself apart, asking why am I so insecure about this. I could always trace it back. I felt that over those 2 years I was trying to integrate the parts of myself, the parts that I didn't like. I wasn't successful in that process. My therapist was aging and retiring so I changed therapists. I found a younger woman in Santa Cruz, a peer. Going to someone my age was scary. The night before my first visit I had a dream.

During the period between 1990–1993, Mari was struggling. She was putting all sorts of barriers in front of herself regarding her art. She would say: "I can't paint because I don't want to get the room dirty. I don't want to get paint on the new house. I can't paint because my kids need me. I can't paint because my husband needs me."

The work that she did do was very detailed and methodical. She was using graphite rather than paint. Her drawings starting with depiction's of shields. She describes her painting of the *"Mandala"*:

I had not been using color for a year and a half. This was one of the first ones that had any color in it. It was my struggle to find images I was connected to. As I did it the same geometric forms that drew me were reflective of my own emotional restrictions. I wasn't able to just let go and draw the things I wanted to.

"Kestrel With Poppy Pods" reflects a stage in evolution from the mandala format to the pelican paintings. I still needed the structure of the mandala paintings. I was afraid to work outside it. I think I was afraid of what would happen if I really got loose so I kept myself controlled by the borders.

I did manage to bring in more movement in this piece which preceded breaking out of the bordered format into the less structured pelican pieces.

I think it is interesting that I went from drawing static forms to birds with folded wings to pelicans with wings that could be just opening or just closing. It is as if I was slowly beginning to open up my work emotionally and structurally through the subject matter.

Mari was trying to present something but didn't know what it was. Then the work evolved into birds, birds in abstract forms. One of the bird paintings, *"Pelicanamore,"* was done from an image she saw in a magazine. Mari notes:

I started to play around with it. I was still not liking my artwork but I was intrigued by the image. I did a bunch of pieces of it. At the time I was struggling with my work. I was trying to do something that was more meaningful to me. For years I did work that had no meaning. My therapist told me that it appeared as if I was doing a series of shield-like images. I was protecting myself. In that series I was using more color than I'd used in a long time. The use of color for me seems to reflect how emotionally connected I am to the work. The less color the less emotionally connected I am.

I was trying to integrate and was in a period between the old stuck Mari and the new integrated Mari. I painted *"Anger, Sorrow And Tears."* In it I played around with the tear images. I did this one before the word series. It was a blending over, an integration. It started out as a writing piece. If you look close you can see the words. I had the image of the sorrow and the words that explain the sorrow.

The dream she had the night before her first new therapy session was this:

I went into the future but the buildings were adobe and I went into a pueblo. I was a reporter there doing a story on a mystical order and their responsibility was to preserve art and I don't mean to preserve it like a museum but for what art is. There was a monk who was the head of the order. Being the head of the order was a self-sacrificing thing to do. There was no ego involved, you were simply a vessel for this thing to happen, for art to be preserved. He told me all about what they do there and I realize there is an altar in this room. It was made out of smooth stone, all one piece with a candelabra. There were three bronze hammered disks laying on this table. They were three and one-half or four inches in diameter. There was meaning for me but I didn't know what the meaning was. I was overwhelmed by the experience I was having with this man. It just oozed meaning. As I was getting ready to leave, he said: "There are two spaces available to be members of this order, hint," and I said, "Yes, I want to do this." That was the end of that dream.

It characterized, for me, going from a window to being on the threshold of something. And I felt that way for a whole year. I was on a threshold of actually integrating. I was going to be able to take each part of me that was pulled apart and put it back on my own terms and own it. On my own terms, instead of the terms that had been defined by the abuse when I was younger. It was a really uncomfortable year because I was always on the threshold, never taking that step. Finally I just accepted that I wouldn't take that step. It would happen when it was time. I started with a new therapist a month after I turned 40. I have always promised myself that I'd paint by the time I was 40. I was giving my children 20 years then that was it. This was my time. All the things that I've wanted are going to happen now.

When I went to this bioenergetic therapist I had a sense of a release I hadn't experienced before. When I tried to draw during this time I had increasing pain in my right shoulder, jaw, and head and radiating down my arm. It got to the point I couldn't draw because the pain was so intense. When I could just focus on my art I had time to focus on introspection. I remembered that when my father used to hit me I'd always put up my right arm to block his hits. It was my protection; it was so reflective that I was always protecting myself. That is why I had so much pain in my arm. It was stuck there.

All I wanted was to paint. I was telling my homeopathic doctor about this and she introduced me to a bioenergetic therapist. After the first session I thought I'd been hit by a truck. As I worked with her all of the painful physical body things disappeared. I talk about what happened and I did physical things that helped me express anger and sadness. As I dealt with things with her I felt like they were gone, that the integration process was happening fast. I went to the store and bought brushes. I didn't care what happened to the room. I'd scratch into the surface of the canvas or paper and scream, "I hate you Bob [last name omitted]." I didn't hold anything back. Then I started the writing paintings. I screamed, "You asshole" and wrote what I felt. I had never let myself feel the anger I felt toward him. In the process of letting it out and in the process of owning the anger, I said, "I hate him and I hate him for what he did to me." Compared to a lot of people, the physical abuse was minimal. It could have been so much worse. The net result was that I couldn't minimize what he had done to me. I had to fully accept that it had really stunted me as a person. It had really prevented me from being everything I could have been. I lost a lot of years and I was really angry. I was able to get that out in the paintings. It went from there to more of a sense of peacefulness. I have a series of methodical repetitive marks. The one entitled *"Warrior Marks"* was very healing to paint. It was very peaceful to do the same thing over and over again and to have permission to do it that way. I believe at that point I had integrated and for the first time in my life I accepted everything that happened. I wouldn't change anything about myself. My husband started calling me "wife with fist." I wouldn't tolerate anything that wasn't OK. He wasn't used to that because I was really quite submissive. All of a sudden I'd say, "It's not going to be like that; It's going to be like this." Regarding my relationships, my art sometimes gets in the way of my relationship with my husband because I'm less sexual when I'm creative. I find all my energy goes into my art. I'm more sexual when I'm not being creative. My children have more respect for me when I am creative, I know that. It's not that they disrespected me before but they are proud now. I have no pain now. It was during one of these periods that I painted *"Passion and Fear."*

I did this series before the repetitive series. It was a process I went through just getting out the emotions I was having. This one was interesting. It was like I was looking at those words as those emotions but they weren't charged for me anymore. I could just put them on the paper without being caught up in them. Before that I was in the emotion, the anger. I was just drawing the paint down; I was full of it. Those emotions don't hold me anymore like they used to.

I was this person that I didn't know was inside of me. It was like being reborn, a really neat experience. All those parts of me that were going out were coming back in. I was able to own all the parts of me as mine and not dictated by someone else. I painted *"Tears & The Emptiness Held So Long Inside"* when I was experiencing grief. It was pure sadness. For years I felt it as a big black ball. I was starting to feel the ball of sadness breaking open. That's why I used the tears. All my sadness started to open up and I started to get in touch with the grief instead of the anger. It was amazing.

Before that I had the desire to express what was inside of me, but I couldn't express it until I knew what was there. The integration was critical. I feel sorry for my father. I feel for his pain. I feel people don't hurt other people unless they are in a lot of pain. Both my parents had a lot of pain. I don't hate them. I can remember what they did to me and experience anger and hate but then I can let anger and hate be. I just accept it. That is just the way it was for me. It doesn't have power anymore.

When my sister had her accident I found myself crying. All my paintings began with black paint. I couldn't go past the black paint so I kept starting paintings. I was mourning her. I have eight paintings started. I started putting dark paint over the black. As I felt less, I could paint more. I don't have any ideas when I go out into my studio. I just trust in the process. *"Entombed"* was done when I had a lot of pain. I can see what

I've gone through as they become more professional, less tied to my experiences of healing and more of who I am. That's really important to me. How wonderful to have a medium you can scratch and rub and hurl, you can do anything with paint. I don't have to control it. I spent my life controlling myself. This is wonderful. My paintings are all titled "Spirit Songs" now. I began doing a series of repetitive mark paintings. I've gone through the anger and grief paintings. After the repetitive mark paintings, I was at a point that I felt peace. I'd gotten out a lot of tense emotion. I felt really empty in a good way. It was meditative. I was just being, without all that other stuff. My therapist said it was important that I used the color blue. She said the fact that I used another color than red meant that I'd had some sort of a breakthrough. When your heart starts to open you use reds, then you can go on to other colors. I'd gone through that explosion.

Around that time I was transitioning from angry paintings to the peaceful paintings, I remembered when I was a little girl, just before my dad started hitting me. I had a bike. I lived in a neighborhood where there were only boys my age, so I did boy things, like climbing up into tree houses and riding bikes. We lived in an area that went down to the Mississippi river and all of the streets were terraced. On each level there were houses that faced out to the river. There were alleyways between each block. We used to go up about six blocks to the top of this series of terraces and ride our bikes at breakneck speed all the way down to the Mississippi river and we never stopped for those streets that came across. I remember I just loved that. It was just incredible, going fast and being a maniac. I had never been like that. From the time my dad started hitting me I had to keep my head down. I was really under control. I controlled everything about myself. I just realized that little Mari who had been so wild was still inside of me. She never went anywhere. She's still inside. I've always been that way but I couldn't be because it wasn't safe.

I did the repetitive drawings and loved little Mari. Then it moved into joy and celebration. It moved to expressing a sense of movement and atmosphere. *"All The Little Spirits Flying Away"* was done in June of 1994. In it, I just wanted to show the sense of release. I went from the repetitive type to this type of painting. It shows something just going away. It was joyful, an exhilarating experience. I had a sense that I'd been released from something and I could fly. I did a whole series of paintings that were similar to that. Artistically, I wasn't pleased with them and I painted over most of them.

This is life as I know it, how I see the world. And I'm not ashamed to say I love it and this is what I do. You don't have to like it. I don't know where it will go from here.

I'm here on earth to experience all that I can be; the best wife, mother, artist. I want to experience all the things I can. Lately I've tried things I've never done before. I tried scuba diving. I want to find a way to contribute something by being the best that I can be. Emotionally, art is validating of my being on earth. I just do and be and when a painting is completed, or as I see it evolving I just experience great pleasure or frustration. When frustration happens, I have to trust. I'm always saying I trust because I just take the paint and I can't tell you what I am trusting in. I just trust and then I take the next color paint and do what I do with it. Its part of the process.

I turned 40 in January of 1994. I don't feel like I fit in with the rest of society. It's hard for me to do things that are outside my studio and my own home. I'm off in my own world. I'm not flighty. A lot of people don't understand my values, what I live for. I have lost all my past friends because they did not accept my choice to lead a very spartan social life. In that sense I feel like I'm in my own world. I am absolutely determined that my painting be the primary focus of my life. In order for me to do that and give adequate attention to my family, manage the household, the property and our finances, I have chosen to spend as little time away from my home and studio as possible. My need to be with others is (and has always been) very low. I am very satisfied with the spontaneous social contact I get as a result of my art activities, my monthly meeting with my therapist and occasionally getting together with other couples. This may change in the future, but for now I am content in this regard.

I know I am not finished with my transformative work. I know it takes a lifetime. I am glad I've done as much work as I have, and I am especially happy to have worked through the issues with my parents. To be able to go into the future without having to carry that baggage is a blessing for which I am very grateful.

After the interview was over and the story sharing had been done, Mari produced a series of paintings with triangles in the center she calls her *"She Series."* When I asked her about them she said:

My "She Series" of paintings arose from my experience of being in this study. As a result I felt a closer connection to women and a freedom to explore my femaleness which I did through reading.

Throughout this process I began introducing triangle forms into my paintings. These forms broke loose into their own series after I read that the triangle has stood for the Mother Goddess since Paleolithic times.

When I do these paintings I feel expansive and connected in a way I have never felt before. I also find that other people relate to these paintings more than my others.

This Author's Initial Reaction to Mari's Story

I left Mari's home and studio feeling wonderful. She has taken her natural artistic ability and used it as a tool and coping mechanism to work through some difficult times and memories. Her art has not only increased her own self-esteem but has given her more importance in her family. Mari's art has evolved from "coping" to "expressive" as she has worked through her personal issues. Her art now represents more "who she is" than "who she was." Mari's art experience with painful memories exemplifies how one can "dissolve" painful memories even in the face of knowing they will never be "resolved."

Mari's artwork, plus therapy, helped her move from feelings of "There was nobody in my life who validated me" to "I wouldn't change anything about myself." She has used her art to transmute anger into serenity and tranquillity. She says, "I didn't hold anything back. I had never let myself feel the anger toward him. I couldn't minimize what happened to me. A sense of peace came."

She is very expressive and has accomplished an enormous amount of personal transformation work. The release of anger happened through paintings that were actually words written on canvas, coupled with paint thrown and smeared and used in any way that expressed her emotion at the time. The art work is wonderful and clearly displays in a visual format her ongoing process of self-actualization. One of her last comments to me was: "I don't tolerate anything that isn't O.K." Obviously, she has claimed and maintained her boundaries. She is aware of the role pain has played in her body and experienced relief in her arms as she worked through issues with her father.

Her artistic ability may have originated from a desire to please the one person to whom she felt a deep connection: her grandmother, the artist.

Mari's years of personal therapy appear in her vocabulary, in which psychological terminology is interspersed. Clearly, she understands her life issues and how she is coping with them. For instance, she says, "I was able to get my anger out in the paintings." Self-actualization is a lifetime process, and Mari has learned how to turn angry energy into creativity. I was joyful hearing her last comments as I transcribed her tape, "My paintings have moved into joy and celebration; this is how I see the world. You don't have to like it." This means she is painting for her own pleasure. How many of us can say that?

These sentences convey the strong, dynamic person Mari is at age 40.

Her future in the art world seems assured. Her resume grows every week as her art consistently appears in galleries and shows, and her supportive husband has even put her story and artwork on the Internet. Meeting and getting to know Mari was like brushing up against a tornado. I felt charged with energy and ideas when I left her studio.

Even as a teenager, Mari felt driven to begin her "real life." She remembers, "I felt like I was totally at my parents' mercy until I could get away from home." A large part of her life felt like merely "biding time." She comments, "I always knew I wanted to be an artist from the time I was five or six." Interestingly, Mari was 5 years old when her grandmother died.

Mari always loved art in school and created a curriculum that allowed her to graduate early. When her father expelled her from the household, she cut the familial cord by burning all her prior artwork. It was as if she were saying, "My life begins today."

At age 40, Mari found a new therapist and felt it was time to reclaim her inner self. "It was time to be me, not waste any more time being less than who I was." She realizes that her NDEs may have accelerated her process. "They made me realize how fragile life could be."

She was searching for something but did not know what it was. She said: "I wanted to be free but didn't even know what I wanted to be free of." During this time of turmoil, she struggled to draw. "I wanted to draw. I was not working and had the freedom to draw but couldn't do it. I'd sit here and do the drawings but it was so hard to get them out."

Mari had an interesting dream that evolved into a painting called *Fish Out of Water.* She had "an overwhelming urge to get that dream outside my body" and had to put it on paper. This feeling came from deep within her as she struggled to find images within her. The experience of getting one's emotions out of the body is the key to healing. When we take rage or sadness for instance and paint it out of us it really feels as if it has left the body. There is a huge catharsis that accompanies such creativity. One can achieve the same experience punching a boxing bag, or banging a tennis racket on a pillow but there is nothing more powerful, in my opinion, than viewing repeatedly the anger that is now on canvas rather than in the body structure. When anger resurfaces in your life merely viewing the painting can be calming. The painting reflects back the anger and acts as an understanding witness for the viewer.

Mari has no trouble connecting the pain which manifested in her arm and right shoulder to when, as a child, she used that arm to block her father's physical attacks. She worked with a bioenergetic therapist, and the pain ceased. Bringing the memories to consciousness helped to remove the blockages in muscular tension. She had merely to talk about what happened and to do physical things that helped her express anger or sadness. As she did so, Mari felt as if old issues disappeared, as if she integrated them.

Once the physical and mental blocks were removed, her paintings again began to flow, and she expressed her anger on the paper and canvas. Once the anger was released, a sense of peacefulness emerged; anger transformed into peace. Mari comments, "I have no pain now." After expressing her emotions, certain words no longer held a charge for her. "I could just put them on the paper without being caught up in them. Before that, I was in the emotion, the anger. I was full of it. . . . Those emotions don't hold me anymore like they used to. It was like being reborn." This transformative aspect of art must be experienced to be believed. Artistic expression holds enormous power and was unimaginable to me before I actually tried it. Once the anger is released the underlying emotions begin to surface.

Mari noticed that she began to contact her grief once the anger had been released. One senses that her grief and anger have transmuted into compassion. She said: "I feel people don't hurt other people unless they are in a lot of pain. Both my parents had a lot of pain. I don't hate them. I can remember what they did to me and experience anger and hate, but then I can let anger and hate be. I just accept it. That is just the way it was for me. It doesn't have power anymore."

Painting has given Mari a feeling of "self." By that I mean she began to accept herself. She said, "I accepted everything that happened. I wouldn't change anything about myself." Her self-confidence and self-esteem have blossomed through her artwork and her therapy. Sometimes art needs a catalyst.

Mari surrenders when she enters her studio. "I just trust the process. If I'm creative and joyful, then that's what happens." She knows now that she does not have to control her art. She reflects that she spent her life controlling herself, but now revels in artistic spontaneity.

Mari went through a range of emotions in her artwork: from grief and anger, to peace and compassion, and eventually to joy and celebration. This last stage gave her a sense of movement and atmosphere. She felt released from something and as if she could fly.

Combined with psychotherapy, her art has freed her. "I'm here on earth to experience all that I can be: the best wife, mother, artist. I want to experience all the things I can. Lately, I've tried things I've never done before, like scuba diving. . . . I want to find a way to contribute something by being the best that I can be. Emotionally, art is validating of my being on earth."

From Mari's story I realized how a seemingly insignificant event in a person's life can impart a powerful impact. I am referring to the gesture by her grandmother of making Mari and her doll matching outfits. Mari said that this act of generosity was the only time she felt loved in childhood. I am now more cognizant than ever of the impact of my words and actions on others. Also, I have become aware of how wounding it is to be disbelieved. Being disbelieved by my mother has been almost as wounding as being spanked with a belt by my father.

The Transpersonal Dimensions of Mari's Story

Mari's early childhood abuse experience gave rise to a "false self" which served for protection and survival. "I had to hide who I was." Fear was a way of life. She said, "It was terrible never knowing when something would come down on you. I always lived in fear."

School was Mari's haven, where she could mitigate the abuse at home. "I became an "A" student to avoid blame. I was as good as I could possibly be. It never helped. Mother was also critical and verbal. Home was volatile."

From age five through high school, Mari experienced physical abuse from her father and verbal abuse from her mother. "Shortly after my grandmother died, my father started hitting me. He'd scream for no reason. Then he'd apologize. I felt sorry for him. He'd hit my sister and brother and blame me. He'd say, "See what you made me do!" It was always out of the blue."

Mari attempted to escape her pain through suicide and drugs. "I had phenomenal stress and tension. I took all the pills in the medicine cabinet and ate them all. I knew I was going to sleep and I wouldn't wake up. I also experimented with sex and drugs."

Pleasant memories of her grandmother, the artist, inspired Mari's art. Her grandmother was the only person who was nice to Mari during her childhood. Mari remembers, "I made my grandmother into a mythical figure. If I have interactions with children, I am going to make them positive."

Mari sought the transpersonal realm through meditation. "After my husband left I joined a meditation group. I felt like I needed something. The world I was experiencing wasn't enough, there had to be more.

"I married again and moved back to California. We had a son and I reconnected with my parents on a superficial level. I couldn't do art because we needed two incomes. I was unhappy and got into therapy." In therapy, her deeper self began to emerge. She began to realize that she was entitled to happiness.

"I wanted to be free but didn't know what of." Mari began to confront her past abuse issues. "My parents denied the abuse. I had to mourn the loss of parents, mourn that I was never nurtured."

Mari's grieving of her childhood neglect stifled her art. "I wanted to draw but it was hard to get the paintings out. I had to drag them out." Her creative energy was blocked. "I couldn't express emotion and feeling. Drawings were stiff and difficult. In art school they just sprung out of me, now they didn't."

Mari's has had a series of fish dreams. As she tells them:

> I had a dream right after I confronted my mother. In it there was a deep pool, and a key fell in it. I didn't want to put my hand in there. The water was moving. The fish came out of the water. I had to get out. The fish followed. My mother had a purse, the key came back, and I put it in the purse. I did it.
>
> The next dream had flying and barking fish. They never got me. They were angry fish.
>
> In the last dream I was wearing black leather at a party. The fish were in a bird cage and tried to get out at me. I said "No!"

Mari visited a bioenergetic therapist, who treated Mari for the pain in her right shoulder and arm. "It went away as I dealt with my issues." As her body armor dissipated, her art once again began to flow. "I was on the threshold of something for over a year. I was pulled apart and wanted to be put back together on my own terms. The barriers came down and my art began to flow."

The release of rage toward her parents opened the door to peace, self-empowerment, and life adventure. "I didn't hold anything back. I called him [her father] an asshole and told my father I hate him while I painted. I couldn't minimize what had happened to me. A sense of peace came." Finally, her wounded inner child began to heal, and as Mari's deep self matured, evolved into the divine child. Mari remembers: "When I was a little girl I went on wild bike rides. That little girl is still in me. She never went anywhere because it wasn't safe. Now I want to live life to the fullest and experience everything."

Mari's experience of healing through art resembles Jean's, the woman whose experience is described in the introduction to this book. Whereas Jean used paste and collage to form words, Mari used only paint to put the hurtful words on canvas; but, the effect was the same: to see what had happened and grasp how those emotions affected their lives. Externalizing the pain facilitated its cathartic release. Although the actual painting experience embodied the emotional experience of the child, the viewer was an adult who could observe the work as a witness.

Mari's art has evolved from the healing to the expressive stage as a result of her interaction with Saille, another artist in this study. In reading Saille's story, Mari realized she must claim her art as "female." Now she feels she has moved into another stage, one which expresses her essence rather than her pain. This exemplifies the beauty of the artistic process; once one's essence is expressed, art assumes a spiritual dimension.

Mari is both a special talent artist and a self-actualized expressive artist. Her healing has evolved to where the distinction in her style is blurred, encompassing both sensory and imaginative aspects.

Defining Mari's Current Issues and Strengths

Being perfect, one of the themes that ran through Mari's childhood, meant doing everything as good as she possibly could to please her parents, and, specifically, to avoid being hit by her father. "I became an 'A' student to avoid blame. I was as good as I could possibly be. It never helped."

She experienced the same anxiety that Jean did and for the same reason. She said, "I always lived in fear. I didn't know what it was about me that made him react that way." Mari, like Jean, could not go to her mother for help or sympathy. Mari said, "Mother was also critical and verbal. When I sighed, mother would get furious and say: Who do you think you are? Do you think you're better than us? Do you think you're better than me?"

Mari's boundaries were transgressed. Her mother read her diary and learned Mari was having sex and had smoked marijuana. Mari said, "I felt betrayed." Of course, the physical abuse by her father was also an invasion. Like Jean, Mari closed down her feelings saying, "I'm not going to cry. He's not going to hurt me inside ever again."

Another theme is that of having *no one to validate her.* At age five, Mari lost her grandmother. No one else validated Mari's experiences; Mari had only the memory of her grandmother and grew up with a lowered sense of self-esteem.

Mari is *industrious.* As a child, she was a vociferous reader. During her marriage she worked in the semiconductor industry while obtaining a masters degree in business. Now, in a good relationship with a successful man, Mari is creating painting upon painting.

Mari's Reaction to participate in This Book

It felt good to be part of something outside my usual world. It was validcating and very comforting to hear your empathetic comments and read about the similar struggles of other artists in the study. It was one of two recent experiences I've had recently that have catapulted me into a much fuller experience/acceptance of myself as a woman. . . . I believe your acceptance of me was probably another catalyst. I am most frequently used to being rejected by other women. If Saille and I correspond, I may even get a friend out of this experience. In summary, I would say that being in the study has helped me take a step into the larger world by validating my right to be there.

MARY'S STORY

I met Mary when I bought a house right next door to hers. We knew each other for six years before she mentioned that she was an artist. The first time she invited me in to see her art I was stunned. This quiet, private woman was reaching into the depths of her being and painting bright, wild, abstract, Mesoamerican godlike faces on 3′ × 4′ canvasses.

My former image of Mary was that of a shy, good-natured housewife. Boy, was I surprised! Mary is anything but timid in her artwork; it is bold, abstract, and colorful. It was Mary who peaked my interest in this subject in the first place.

Mary is a devout Catholic. She is 78 years old and lives with an adoring husband of 50 years. Mary's life was traumatized by the death of her only son which, in addition to its own horror, brought back to mind the unexpected death of her father earlier in her life. She has more recently suffered the loss of five siblings within a 12 month period around 1991.

Mary was born just prior to the depression, the fifth of Juan and Francisca Delgadillo's 13 children. She was born in Northern Arizona on the old Route 66 near the Grand Canyon. As Mary tells it:

> My father and grandfather had a restaurant, gas station and cabins. We all lived in a small town with cowboys and sheepherders near the Santa Fe Railroad. It was like a little Spanish mini-world. Route 66 was one of the main routes from the dust bowl to California, which meant that thousands of dust bowl immigrants came through our town. They were poor and having a hard time so they would trade us a blanket and other items for food. One family wanted to give us their dog but of course, we didn't accept it. If they were so poor that they had nothing to trade we gave them food anyway. That's the first time I ever saw biscuits and gravy. Mother said, "Look at what these people eat!" I was about 10 at that time.

Looking up at me with a twinkle in her eye, Mary added: "I like biscuits and gravy, now!" She went on to say:

> We had a lot of family gatherings with my cousins. My grandmother had most of them at her house. I remember on Christmas Eve we prayed until midnight, at which time we would be allowed to eat. So exactly at

midnight, all of us kids would run into the kitchen to eat tamales. I remember grandma passing a statue of baby Jesus around for us to kiss. That statue ended up with tamales all over it.

Mary claims: "Painting is in my blood." She may be right; she has a daughter and a granddaughter who both share her love of art and who are quite good artists themselves.

Mary refers back to that small town she called home as an Hispanic mini-world, because it was enriched by Mexican traditions and customs. In her large, extended family there was a tradition of story telling as was the case in many Mexican-American families. Through her relatives she learned about the Mayan and Aztec cultures and the history of her people. This nurturing and supportive atmosphere left her with an abundance of cultural memories and interests. When asked about her relationship with her mother she unhesitatingly said: "I don't think any girl could have had a better mother than I did. I praise her and think she was wonderful. She was about as good a mother as you could get. I look a lot like her."

Mary remembers drawing from earliest childhood. Like many young girls she cut out and colored paper dolls. But what distinguished her childhood from that of some of the other artists' was her family's encouragement to express herself creatively—whether it was mask and doll making, or painting. For example, she recalls an incident from childhood noting: "We had an aunt who lived in Colorado who came to visit us and who liked to embroider. She asked my mother if she had embroidering patterns for her to work on and my mother said: 'Well, Mary knows how to draw, I'm sure she can draw something for you to work on.'"

Mary explains how proud she was and how she drew a picture of flowers on fabric which her aunt then embroidered. Her aunt still has that piece.

Mary used cardboard and crayons to make doll clothes, and remembers acquiring her first crayons, saying: "They cost a nickel, but were they great!" In grammar school she began to use chalk and water colors. Her family taught her to make papier mache out of which she created a variety of holiday masks.

During the summers of her teen years, she went to California with her siblings to pick apricots and peaches. In 1937, after graduating from high school, she stayed in California. Her father died suddenly that year and her mother moved the entire family to San Jose.

Just after the end of the depression, she worked in both the fields and in canneries and liked neither. Her sister noticed an ad for a person who could draw diagrams and showed it to Mary. This led to a job at a title company and eventually to the County Assessor's office.

During this time she met and married Joe C. They proceeded to have two children. Mary didn't paint too often during her childrearing years but did do a few drawings.

Once her children were in school, Mary went to work and continued to work for the next 20 years. Over those 20 years, she painted nature pictures, mostly realistic landscapes and florals, but also a small number of seascapes. She intermittently took lessons from a local artist. To finance her instruction she sold these paintings to fellow employees, relatives, and neighbors. According to Mary: "I sold everything I painted. One man even bought two of my ocean scenes."

She painted a sweet, colorful picture entitled *"Flowers In A Basket"* at a time when she was contemplating her retirement. The major corpus of Mary's work is found in what might be called her mature San Jose period. This is characterized by two distinct approaches to art: realistic and abstract.

When her son Jim was killed in an automobile accident in 1968, it marked a turning point in both her life and her art. He had just graduated from high school and was waiting to begin college on a scholarship in the fall. Prior to her son's death, her artwork was representational reflecting subjects in nature. The death of her son materially affected her painting thereafter. For the first five years after his death, Mary could not talk about it. She noted: "I put his death out of my mind and didn't think about it for five years." She refused to think or talk about Jim for five years. She say's: "I wanted to be by myself, and that helped me. I didn't have any feelings." I couldn't mention his name or look at his picture. She turned his photo to the wall. She put his death out of her mind as best she could.

It is interesting to note that her focus changed from people and flowers to landscapes that were devoid of people during that five year period. While a few of her pieces included a small barn, for the most part, they lacked any human reminders.

After that five year period, the flood gates opened. Mary's mourning of Jim had realistically begun and painting became her self-administered therapy. Her creativity appeared to be an attempt to re-create unity (Haynal, 1985). She said:

When I painted I was lost to the world. Often I felt hot tears running down my face. I didn't realize I was crying until I felt the heat. I painted out my pain. When I'm painting I don't think about anything else. I don't know what I'm doing. I just paint what I feel."

Now, many years later, I can talk without getting the tears. I believe I'm all right now. All during those years I was looking for Jim in my dreams. He was lost. I dreamt of houses, strange homes. In one dream I lived on the second floor and the floor was all full of water. At the bottom and underneath me was a beautiful room that was not flooded and had a baby grand piano and beautiful rugs.

In another dream I'm in Tulare. There are trees and stuff and I walk in and it's not my house, it belongs to someone else. I'm getting married and I don't know who I'm expecting to get married to. It's never Joe. These are all weird dreams but I know they have something to do with my son.

During her earlier years she used oil paints, exclusively. But when she began to paint out her pain, Mary supplanted those oils, which took so long to dry, with quick-drying acrylics. It was as if she suddenly realized the brevity of life.

She entered San Jose State University's art program upon her retirement from the assessor's office, and subsequently earned her Bachelor's and Master's Degrees in Fine Art. Her art subjects changed from landscapes to abstract Mesoamerican gods. When this change occurred the art seemed to take on a life of its own and her work became more and more abstract. She noted: "During the time my art was changing, my daughter helped me a lot by encouraging me. My paintings are to be left to her and to my granddaughter to live with them after I'm gone."

Her lifelong interest in Mesoamerican history began to dominate her work. Her vibrant color combinations express enormous amounts of energy and movement.

Professor Garcia recognized in Mary's work some of the ancient symbolism of the Aztec culture. He commented: "Mary, do you realize the sea shell was the first thing the Aztecs painted?" He went on to point out the significance of the hummingbird, the skirt, and other features of her artwork. This all excited her so much that some nights she could not sleep because her mind was filled with brilliant swirling colors. On those occasions she got up and painted until dawn.

A numinous event happened to bring Mary out of her sadness, if only for a while. She recalls:

One of the priests from the Guadalupe Church came over and asked me if I wanted to paint the Blessed Virgin Mary. I said I would try. I painted it on satin and they really liked it. When I went into the church and saw my Virgin Mary being worshipped it was overwhelming to me. It's hard to explain how I felt. It was a shock, like electricity surging through me. It was a feeling of ecstasy; like something had transferred from the Virgin to me, and that thing was part of my son. We believe in praying to the dead. It was holy. I couldn't believe I'd painted it. I said to myself, "How could I paint that?" I had to pray to something that I'd actually painted. Inside of me I felt happy for the first time since I lost my son. It was an indescribable feeling. I felt very humble. God is so sacred; I don't know if I have any sacredness in me that big.

Greenwell (1994), describes this electric energy in the body as pranic energy activity. It is a physiological dimension of the Kundalini process. Other Mexican artists such as Diego Rivera, his wife Frieda Kahlo, Juan Soriano, and Pedro Coronel also have painted the symbols of ancient Mesoamerican cultures. The symbols keep coming through artists year after year.

"Quetzalcoatl," the first of her Mesoamerican god paintings, is also known as the plumed serpent, and associated with the god of priestly life and self-sacrifice. He is the aspect of Venus as Morning Star who lifts the sun out of the darkness as well as god of the winds and the breath of life. These wonderful metaphors, "self-sacrifice," and "lifts the sun out of darkness," and "breath of life," describe Mary's process of grief so well. It is interesting, and yet hardly surprising, that each of the Aztec, Mayan or Olmec gods she chose to paint was known for an aspect of her pain. She painted little parts of herself and her son's fate into each picture. For example, *"Huitzilopochtli"* was called the "omen of evil." He was also known as the Hummingbird and led his people in their painful journeys until they arrived in the promised land. *Itzpapaloti,"* known as the Deity of Darkness, is also known as the Twisted Obsidian One. The deity in this painting reflects the auto accident that took her son's life. *"Mictlanlecuhtli,"* Lord of the Land of the Dead. This deity cares for the souls of those who find their way to his restful silent kingdom.

Another current of Mary's creative energy is expressed through her papier mache mask collection, a series of skeletal faces celebrating *"El Dia de Los Muertos,"* the day when the dead come to life. In America, this day is called "The day of the Dead," and is celebrated in November. She sculpts these human-head-sized paper pulp masks, dries them in the sun, and then paints them—simultaneously revealing her preoccupation with death as well as her pain. It is as if she would bring her son back to life if only for a day through her art.

In summary, the paintings and masks Mary has created, since the death of her son, are more than priceless memories; they represent her search for transpersonal sources of inspiration and meaning. While Mary did not say it, I thought it was quite evident, based on her stories and how each painting came into being that she has worked through much of her pain through her art. Her last mythical painting took a year, whereas the first one took less than a month. It may be that the therapeutic work accomplished through these masks and paintings is complete, and that it is time for her to move into another stage of the healing and artistic process.

Indeed, after completing thirteen paintings, she switched her focus from individual mythological figures, to larger works that tell a story. One of her works illustrates the *"Confrontation Between Cortez And Montezuma."* The painting depicts a variety of subjects such as horses; Cortez and his soldiers; Montezuma; the jaguar; the eagle; and La Malinche, Cortez' wife, who was an Indian girl who helped the Spaniards in their victory over Montezuma.

It would be unrealistic to believe that she has already worked through all her pain; no doubt it will continue to motivate her search for meaning through creativity. Art has very much played a key role in her healing especially after her son died. I remember her saying: "After I lost my son the urge to paint was strong."

After the series of 13 abstract faces of Mesoamerican gods, and after *"The Confrontation Between Cortez And Montezuma"* painting, Mary went on to paint identifiable women into her work. She has painted two works with three women in each painting. The first represents the three bad women of Mexican mythology and the second reflects the three good women. I feel that the women in these two paintings reflect different aspects of herself; her own sub-personalities, if you will. The first painting reflects her own less than desirable aspects. Getting in touch with some of the "shadow" parts of herself has enabled Mary to identify her own guilt and pain and to integrate these aspects of herself into her healing process.

"Las Leyendas del Barrio" is an acrylic painting of Llorona, the wailing woman; La Malinche, the Indian princess who was given to Cortez as a gift; and La Bruja, the witch. These figures were known to Mary as the three bad women of Mexican mythology.

As Mary tells it:

> Llorona had two children by one of Cortez's soldiers, then he abandoned
> her. They were never married. After he left, she drowned his children in
> anger. She wails at night because she can't find her children, nor enter
> heaven without them. Mexican mothers tell this important story to their
> children. My mother told it to me. It warns daughters that they should
> remain pure until marriage, and when they do marry, they should take
> care of their children to ensure family happiness.
>
> La Malinche was a Mayan princess who was given, by the Aztecs, to
> Cortez as a wife. She was angry at her people for being given away. She
> knew the trails and the culture of the Aztecs, and helped Cortez defeat the
> Aztecs by giving him invaluable information. She spoke Mayan, Aztec,
> and Spanish. I always thought she was a traitor but some people think
> that she wasn't a traitor because a woman should be true to her husband,
> and Cortez was her husband.
>
> La Bruja casts spells on people and gives them the evil eye. She can put
> a spell on a pretty girl, and change her into a frog. She has the power to
> make people ill, even to the point of death. She makes dolls and sticks
> pins in them. However, she could also be employed in more creative ways.
> For instance, if a girl wanted to heighten the affection of a boyfriend, she
> would go to the witch who would cast a love spell on the boy.

Her next painting shows the counter balancing, positive side of this
triad; *"The Three Good Women of Mexican Mythology."* This painting
represents Mary's strengths. The story in the painting describes La
Comadre, the godmother; La Patera, the midwife; and La Curandera,
the one who counteracts La Bruja's spells. Mary has identified with all
six of these women, at one time or another, in her life. Mary tells the
story of this painting:

> La Comadre, the godmother, is a very important figure in Mexican life.
> As it is baptized, each child gets a La Comadre, who helps the mother
> with the baby. After one of my brothers was born, my mother had to get a
> gallstone operation. My brother was only two months old and his La
> Comadre, a woman named Celestina Rincon, with 10 children of her
> own, took little Johnny and nursed him along with her own baby. She
> kept him for five months. My La Comadre is my grandmother.
>
> La Patera is a midwife who comes to your house to deliver the babies.
> Hospitals were only for the rich. I had a La Patera but some of my
> brothers and sisters were born in hospitals.
>
> La Curandera is the woman who cures the spell of the witch. She has
> herbs hanging in her home. She removes a hex, or spell with the evil eye.

Once, I went with a friend to visit a woman and her new baby. In the Mexican tradition, complimenting a baby without touching it results in misfortune for the baby. A few days after our visit, the baby became ill. The La Curandera asked for one of my handkerchiefs because she thought we cast a spell on the baby. Luckily, the baby recovered. I knew I had nothing to do with causing that baby any harm; I'm sure we touched it.

Mary is now attempting to paint the more human aspects of women. Her use of symbolism is powerful. For the first time, since her childhood, Mary is again introducing people into her art. This is highly significant. Note the flesh tones in the faces. She has not tried to achieve realistic flesh color since childhood when she made paper dolls.

Her painting of *"Little Flora"* appears to be a breakthrough piece. It is the first painting in many years to be devoid of abstraction. With this work, I wonder if Mary has not come full circle. This work is a positive acknowledgment of that little girl that resides in each one of us, and especially in Mary. She drew in her own lovely high cheekbones, dark hair and eyes; and she has even surrounded herself with the artifacts of her childhood. There are flesh tones and a pretty dress. This little girl, though surrounded by flowers, has a daunting gaze. She appears to be looking into one's soul. The foreshortened arms, coupled with the absence of legs and feet reminds us how powerless we are as children. This work takes us all the way back to the child in Mary herself. Mary even sold flowers on Sepulveda Boulevard, in Los Angeles as a child.

"Tico," the companion piece completes Flora's story. These two mythical children preceded the painting of *"La Familia."* This couple are Tico and Flora's parents and are woven into a story about a young boy who becomes a hero with the help of a hummingbird. Mary plans to turn the story into a children's book someday. I found it fascinating to find the hummingbird theme repeated in this work and ponder the connection between the hummingbird and her son. Cooper (1992) notes: "In Mayan tradition the Hummingbird is associated with the Black Sun and the Fifth World and is said to know the solution to the riddle of duality."

"Route 66" is the story of the westward migration of the "Oakies" along that once famous highway. Remember Mary grew up along this road. Her house address was actually Route 66. Steinbeck wrote about this migration in his famous novel "The Grapes of Wrath." The families who passed her home were poor and desperate to reach the lush fields of California. Her family helped them when they could. She identifies with the migrants, because she too was a field worker, who migrated to

California after her father died. This work shows the forlorn faces of those who left their farms and traveled along that arduous trail. Each state flower reminds us from where they came. A cherub appears to be standing in the birth canal of a womb. Mary says: "All of a sudden I want to paint angels and cherubs." Mary is about to birth herself in this painting in much the same way as did Frieda Kahlo.

Is the birthing of a new series of art about to begin? Will this next series be the story of her life? I am continuously amazed at how this wonderful woman paints directly from the unconscious and through her heart. Recently Mary telephoned me and excitedly told me about her new painting. She said, "Linda, the people are going to be alive! I've never painted anyone who was alive before and these people are going to be alive. I am going to paint "Proposition 187." I want to tell people about the plight of the poor immigrants. Proposition 187 was a California ballot measure designed to deny public education to illegal immigrants.

This Author's Initial Reaction to Mary's Story

I've known this artist for so long that my initial reaction to her and her art preceded the interview by at least five years. When Mary first showed me her art, I was amazed that this quiet homebody of a woman could produce such outrageous paintings. After hearing her story, some of which was too personal to print, I felt a deep emotional connection to her.

The way Mary has been using her knowledge of Mesoamerican art is uncanny. Although she wasn't aware of it at the time, she delved into her psyche to evoke ancient archetypes that give fullness and depth to her art. She, as artist, intuitively displays the wealth of the Mesoamerican gods' legacy. By bringing them to life for us with all their drama and spectacle, Mary, through the color, energy and vitality of her work, has invoked them as both co-creators and therapists in her ongoing artistic process. Mary, unintentionally, used art as a coping mechanism. She knew she had to paint but was thinking about her son, not about her own healing. She painted to have the time alone to think about and mourn him. She says:

> For five years I couldn't talk about him. Now I can talk without getting the tears. He was lost. After I lost my son the urge to paint was strong. I'd get the brush and start painting and feel the tears come. I didn't need any

therapy because I was lost to the world when I painted. I didn't realize I was crying until I felt the heat on my face. I painted out my pain. When I'm in my room painting, I don't think about anything else. I don't know what I'm doing. I just paint what I feel. I wanted to be by myself and painting helped me do that.

Mary did not begin her artwork with the idea of healing but recognizes how healing it has been for her. She does naturally what many people "try" to achieve by reading books and doing hours of meditation. Artwork is very powerful, and at one point her art facilitated, for her, an access to the divine—perhaps a Kundalini experience. Mary recounts:

When I went into the church and saw my virgin there, I can never explain how I felt. It was like a shock of electricity surging through me. It was a feeling of ecstasy. It was holy. I said to myself: "How could I paint that?" I had to pray to something that I'd painted. Inside of me I felt happy for the first time since I lost my son. It was an indescribable feeling. I felt very humble. God is so sacred, I don't know if I have any sacredness in me that big.

During the experience in the church, Mary experienced a transference of energy. In eastern traditions this is often called a "direct transmission." When a person, rather than a statue, is involved, a guru for instance, this energy transference is called shaktipat.

Mary has had traumatic life events, and I think she has handled them so well because of her strong family of support. Since childhood, she has been nurtured by loving people. In adulthood, her husband has been her biggest fan. He makes picture frames for her, hauls her artwork to shows and exhibits, and never complains. He accompanies her to art openings and smiles as he looks on with pride as her adoring fans mull around her.

Mary has a sense of connection to family rather than a sense of disconnection or alienation which occurs when there has been abuse. She says: "My paintings are to be left to my daughter and to my granddaughter to live with them after I'm gone."

Mary faced the extremely difficult trauma of the death of a child and integrated it into her life. Just reading this story is a loving event. I, as reader, transcriber, and interviewer felt very respected and loved in this woman's presence. She extends the love that has been given her all her life. She is truly blessed. I recall her words: "I would like to help people; it reminds me of what my grandmother did. It makes me feel happy."

Mary has always had the support and blessings of her family, and it has had a positive affect on her life.

The Transpersonal Dimensions in Mary's Story

Mary's individuation process was accelerated with the death of her son. Her repressed grief was released through her art and became the nudge to the deeper journey into self. She remembers, "My son was killed in a car accident. Painting became my self-administered therapy." She moved through solitude into archetypal images where alternate states of consciousness flow through feelings. "When I'm painting I don't think about anything else. I just paint what I feel."

Her process deepened through dreams into contact with the deep feminine energy of God. She experienced a transpersonal journey through solitude into one of self-actualization—an archetypal soul space. "My paintings changed from scenery and flowers to Mesoamerican gods. I didn't know it. Professor Garcia named it for me. Some nights I couldn't sleep. My mind was filled with brilliant swirling color, and I'd get up and paint until dawn."

During her experience in the church, archetypal dream-space energy emerges into divine feminine archetypal imagery which opens the Kundalini life force experience in her body. Mary recounts, "Something had transferred from the virgin to me, and it was part of my son."

This was the beginning of integrating contact with "big sacredness" as her unconscious life purpose. She said, "I'm on earth for a purpose but I'm not sure what it is. All of a sudden I want to paint angels."

Mary's artwork has changed and evolved during her 78 years. It has always increased her pride and self-esteem. Her art defined her uniqueness among her 12 siblings; later, during the most painful time of her life, her art provided an access to her interior, her connection to God and her son. She used Mesoamerican symbolism—her own cultural gods!

Mary's paintings document her history. They tell the stories of her culture as well as the stories of her childhood. *Route 66* depicts the white man's pilgrimage; her work-in-progress describes the story of the Latino pilgrimage in America. Mary is an expressive, imaginative artist who uses self-actualizing creativeness.

Defining Mary's Current Issues and Strengths

Mary's religious life began in childhood. She recalls that when she was young, "On Christmas Eve my grandmother would pass around a statue of baby Jesus for all of us to kiss. We got tamales all over baby Jesus."

Mary is *family-oriented*. When asked about her relationship with her mother she said, "I don't think a girl could have had a better mother than I did. I praise her and think she was wonderful." Mary has a close connection to her nuclear family and invites her husband, daughter, and granddaughter to her art shows; and, they join her with genuine interest.

Mary's artistic ability was *nurtured* from earliest childhood. Her family taught her how to make holiday masks out of papier mâché and doll clothes out of cardboard. She remembers her mother telling her aunt, "Mary knows how to draw, maybe she could draw something for you."

While working for the county assessor's office she was encouraged by people who bought her paintings. After the death of her son, her daughter encouraged her. At that time, Mary's style changed dramatically from representational to abstract art. Professor Garcia also encouraged her when he identified that she had tapped into the Aztec culture.

Family issues show up in her artwork. The following personages tell family stories of loyalty, motherhood, nurturing, and romance: Llorona, the wailing woman; La Bruja, the witch; La Curander, the one who counteracts La Bruja's spells; La Comadre, the godmother; La Patera, the midwife; and, La Malinche, the Indian princess.

Traditions and customs are important facets of Mary's life. She remembers the tradition of storytelling. From earliest childhood, she heard tales about the Mayan and Aztec cultures, and the history of her people. This nurturing and supportive atmosphere left her with an abundance of cultural memories and interests.

Her painting of the story of *"Raices"* (Roots), gives a vibrant peek into her history. It depicts the story of the battle of Cortez and Montezuma. *"Las Leyendas del Barrio"* (the legends of my neighborhood) is a set of two paintings and appear to be Mary's transpersonal search for the archetypal origins of the good and bad elements in life. Together they tell the story of the different women of her tradition. *Las Hechicheras Malas* shows the shadow side of traditional family life; La Malinche, the betrayer; La Bruja, the witch who can also cast love spells; and Llorona, the one who killed her children are in this work. *Las Hechiceras Buenas* depicts the three good women of her culture: La Comadre, the godmother;

La Patera, the one who helps deliver the babies; and La Curandra, the person capable of dispelling the witches' spells.

The rich combination of history, tradition, and family life combines with Mary's artistic ability in her search for transpersonal sources of inspiration and meaning. She has combined the personal with the transpersonal and filtered both through her artwork.

Mary's Reaction to Participation in This Book

My art is one of the most important things in my life and I felt honored. I thought it was nice to be included. You mentioned one time about me changing my technique and adding flesh to my paintings. That was interesting because I hadn't realized that. I did *Highway 66* and that had some flesh in it. It's all about Anglos during the dust bowl migration to California, and now I'm doing *Proposition 187* and that's all about Latinos. This is the first one I've done with people that are alive. First came the flesh, and now they are going to be alive. I've gotten to the stage that I want to do cherubs. It's kind of difficult for me because I don't want to paint a cherub like a human being. I want them to look "cheruby."

I want to join some of those art groups. I want to meet more artists and get some help and feedback.

MYRTLE'S STORY

Myrtle was born in Merritt, British Columbia in 1923. She has been married to Ed H. for 44 years. They have two grown children and two grandchildren. She describes herself as an extraverted introvert and jokingly claims her goal is to get up in front of a crowd without going to pieces. She is the most extraordinary society painter I have ever met. Her portraits of adults, children and animals are unsurpassed.

Myrtle has had a lifetime of continuous trauma, one type after another, and yet she has endured unbelievable pain and suffering with a positive attitude and a great desire to give something back to this world. Her story is very interesting to read and I urge you to do so because you will come to love this woman. She is quite amazing and a role model for us all.

In Myrtle's humble words: "I had an unusual childhood. I'd say what happened to me is the reason I am the way I am today." She credits her place in the art world today as a direct result of her early life. She has won numerous awards and is a highly paid portrait painter. She credits her patience and understanding to the time she spent trying to get each muscle to move during the seven years she lived with a full body brace as a teenager.

She began to draw at a very young age; in fact, at nine years old she was drawing as well as most adults. She drew a picture of two young children entitled *"Boxing Gloves,"* when she was ten or eleven. She says: "It represents the squabbling that siblings go through growing up. I did it when I had tuberculosis and couldn't go to school. I had a great imagination and I'd conjure up ideas and settings." She painted a picture of a *"Child With A Dog."* I asked her if the child was someone she knew. She responded: "I got the child out of my mind, it was not someone I knew. My mind is photographic when it comes to faces and proportions." According to Myrtle: "I had no idea I had talent then. It was the farthest thing from my mind. I painted for my own pleasure.

At age 15, her paintings were beginning to resemble professional work. She grew up on a farm and painted her siblings and the farm animals that were all around her. There was a time during her teenage years when she considered being a designer of clothes and her rendering of models wearing hats is wonderful. According to Myrtle: "I had visions of being a clothing designer. I designed *Hats*. I was in the 4-H and did sewing as a project. I never made any hats though, just clothes. While I was raising my children I made clothes for the whole family, even my husbands shirts. I can't believe I ever had the time."

Myrtle never went to grammar school like other children because she had a myriad of diseases. She had tuberculosis which she may have gotten from her mother who also suffered from this disease. She also suffered from rickets and severe scoliosis of the spine. The tuberculosis and rickets led to hospitalization in a sanitarium when she was nine. She was released when she was twelve.

Her childhood experiences at the sanitarium were traumatic in themselves. Two events she readily recalls are: (1) "I had a real poor appetite so they put me in the basement and dangled a caterpillar in front of me to scare me into eating," and (2) "I knew there was no Santa Claus, so I told the other kids. I was the only one who didn't get a toy from Santa. I was devastated. Somebody donated a doll so I did get that. It was a Patsy doll, a real treasure; I still have it."

Myrtle had her first numinous experience the day she left the sanitarium. While riding in the car on the way home she was amazed to see how each blade of grass was so bright and each flower glistened. The landscape come alive for her. At that moment she marveled: "I wanted so much to express the beauty of the world around me. I'll never forget how beautiful everything seemed to me." In reflection she commented, "I believe that experience was the seed that was planted for me to become an artist."

By the time she entered high school she was wearing a steel and leather body brace which she wore until she was 22 years old. Until the very end of that period she wore it 24 hours a day to try to straighten her spine. The physical education teacher helped her off with the brace and helped her do her exercises. She recalls: "I felt like I was in this square box, and if anybody was to pat me on the back they'd be ringing their hands. It caused me to have pressure sores, and it was hard to heal them." Her mother and the teacher spent hours trying to help her get just one muscle at a time to move. Each muscle could take a month or more to regenerate because her back was partially paralyzed. She attributes her patience in painting animals and children to those years she spent trying to move each muscle. Her reflection on that time of her life was that she wanted to make up for what she lacked physically. She had to work harder to pass because she was always tired. According to Sandblom (1989), "artists have, above all, an urge to seek new and personal means of expression, paths of communication with fellow beings who can appreciate their deepest feelings."

Myrtle was extremely shy and grew up with a very deep inferiority complex. In high school she had no friends because she avoided people lest they knew she had an iron body. She would eat her lunch sitting on the john with her feet up rather than face the humiliation of sitting alone in the cafeteria. Once she went to the library to see if she could find a painless way to commit suicide. She did try but her mother saved her. She notes: "I am so thankful. It taught me a lot. Now if I hear of someone contemplating suicide I feel I can talk to them and understand them. When I look back on it, it was a cry for help." She recalls a young man she thought was cute also liking her. She says, "He thought I was a strange person because I'd never let him close to me." If she dropped her books she couldn't pick them up. She felt like a freak and considers it a blessing to have had her art. This brings to mind a poem by Byron (who had a deformed foot) that may capture Myrtle's feelings at that time.

Deformity is daring.
It is its essence to o'ertake mankind
By heart and soul and make itself the equal—
Ay the superior of the rest. There is
A spur in its halt movements to become
All that the others cannot, in such things
As still are free to both, to compensate
For stepdame Nature's avarice at first.

When asked what her experience of art has been, she commented: "There is a lot of excitement when I am able to express my feelings. I paint all as I see it and art is better than medication for pain because the intense focusing obliterates the pain." She also says: "I get excited about my accomplishments, being able to do it." She goes on to say: "The acknowledgment and the enjoyment are good for healing, and they help my self esteem." She has always thought of lavender as a healing color. Peaceful ocean scenes of the meditative type give her peace and calm. In reflection, Myrtle said:

I see the beauty of life; not the downers. I've had enough sickness and depression. I want to see the good. I'm not a person in agony. I'm a positive person. I helps me deal with life when I can see the good that comes out of it. When you go through something bad, you learn to cope. It makes you stronger. The challenge becomes a game. You say to yourself, "OK Lord, this is going to be worked out. I just have faith and start some brain storming. I take things calmly now. Being in the prayer ministry has helped me a lot. I chose to be of service to God.

Myrtle remembers: "In high school and before that I did have self-pity. I was worse off than anybody else, and I didn't count my blessings. As the years went by I dropped the self-pity and the blessings came my way."

She feels that you get distracted by self-pity, but when you start counting blessings, they come rolling in. She says: "Things work out for the good, you just have to be patient." Her comment was: "I had more nice things than negative things in my life; acknowledgments and accomplishments, God's compensations." She notes: "You can't do what everybody else can, but you work with what you've got."

Reflecting on the past she said: "Now people look so beautiful to me. This may have began way back when I felt so homely and everybody looked more beautiful than I thought I did."

Myrtle remembered: "Dorothy, my father, and I had a little band—a threesome. My mother sold angle worms and tomato plants to get Dorothy some violin lessons. Then Dorothy taught me to play. She was the genius in the family." But Myrtle learned to play the piano from a book. She says: "I'd cry and play the piano. It was real good therapy for me." She expressed some sadness at not having had much of a relationship with her siblings growing up when she says: "They had their own friends so I learned to entertain myself."

Once she overheard her mother recount to her father what her doctor had said. The doctor had said that he didn't expect Myrtle to live to be an adult. That Sunday she went to Sunday school and prayed: "If I live to be an adult I will do something with my life to make a better life for others in my situation." She has never lost sight of that prayer. Myrtle has done more work with the handicapped than one would think possible. There is more about this later in her story.

Her mother encouraged all the children with their artwork because she hoped one of them would grow up to be an artist. She would insist that the children painted from life, no copying. She brought butcher paper home by the roll. The children would draw on it on the floor. Myrtle fondly remembers: "I drew all the animals on our little farm. We had a cow and calf, rabbits, a raccoon, and even a rat. Little did I dream that in my adult life I'd become a professional artist of animals and people. This talent must have been in me all the time. Now I realize it more than ever that an artist is what I was destined to be."

It has been said that children sometimes live out the dreams of their parents. Myrtle is a good example of this statement. After high school she wanted to work as an artist but her parents told her she couldn't make a living at it and encouraged her to attend college. They felt it was a wonderful hobby but not a good career choice. She listened to them against her better judgment and got a degree as a science major.

She met and married Ed H. and moved to the campus at The California Polytechnical Institute until such time as he got his degree. She remembers: "When I married Ed there were 19 shut-ins I was writing to. I could relate to them because I had been a shut-in." During the few years previous to their marriage she didn't do much in the way of painting but did continue with her music. She says that after they were married Ed was so surprised to learn he'd married an artist.

The doctor told her it would be a big risk factor for her spine if she were to become pregnant but her desire for a child was so strong she was willing to risk the consequences. When she was pregnant with their first child, she and Ed went into an art store and bought a whole set of oil paints, $40 worth. She told Ed, "I'm going to be a portrait painter and this child I'm carrying is going to be my first model." Her next comment was: "I painted a picture entitled *"Our Child,"* and do you know, when she was born she looked exactly like that painting."

The doctor was right, her back got worse after each birth. She could never lift the children; when they were old enough they had to walk into their own cribs. She could hold them sitting but could not stand up while holding them.

It was during those childrearing years that she took art classes at college. She took every art class given by Hartnell College, San Jose State University, and Santa Clara University. Ed worked until midnight so, after the children were asleep, she did her homework.

They lived in a neighborhood with lots of children and each day she did a charcoal of a different child in an effort to keep up her art skills. At the end of the year she had an open house and invited all the neighbors in to see the drawings of their children. She says: "Most of them saw them for the first time, and although some wanted to buy them, I knew someday I'd be a professional portrait painter, and I didn't want my little beginning pictures hanging in somebody's house." She still has them, 40 years later. They didn't appear to be little beginning drawings to me. They were well-defined expressive children. Each was more distinctive as Myrtle's artistic life unfolded. Her portraits got better as time passed. A few years later Myrtle made the portrait of a young *"Spanish Boy."* He was a neighbor and she painted him for practice. She entered that piece in the Cherry Chase Festival of Art in Mountain View, California and won first place out of 200 exhibits. It was this painting that provided the privilege of studying with Thomas Layton, a portrait painter, in San Francisco. Myrtle says: "He could see I already had knowledge of color."

At one point she went to the State Department of Rehabilitation to ask for some assistance. She wanted a job so that she could pay some of her medical bills. They initially turned her down citing her inability to sit or stand for any length of time. It was only after someone from the state saw her artwork at a one person show that they made the exception and offered her a job tutoring other handicapped artists. This led to an ongoing affiliation with the State Department of Rehabilitation.

She wanted to be a lecturer even though, as she puts it, "I'm the shyest person I've ever met." Her chance to practice came about during a class she was taking at San Jose State University when she had to give a 20-minute presentation on what she would do with what she learned in the class and her goals for the future. She was too shy to talk in front of the class so she assembled slides from the pictures she took of her handicapped students and flashed the pictures in a dark room onto the projection screen. She was nervous but in the dark it did not show and she was able to do it. She proudly recalls: "I got an 'A' in that class."

Myrtle has since given 71 inspirational lectures on subjects such as "Beauty is all around us even in the bottom of a drainage ditch," "Age is just a matter of opinion," and "No matter how bad off you are there is something you can contribute to this world." A compilation of over 500 slides of people in their eighties and nineties who are still working are used to tell her stories.

She gives these lectures at places such as Asilomar (a convention center), art clubs, rest homes, and hospitals. She shows people who have successful careers even though they are handicapped. She notes: "One man has only the use of his foot and hand. He has severe cerebral palsy, and he paints portraits and landscapes with the brush in his left foot.

This man refuses welfare aid. I strongly believe what you give you get back."

She was at the peak of her career when a dog, running at a high rate of speed, ran into the back of her legs in a freak accident. As she puts it: "I flew up in the air and my upper back landed on the ground. I couldn't breathe and thought I would die. I couldn't move my hands or feet or anything. My breathing was hampered. The lung problem was eventually resolved, but my arm remained limp. Doctors said she would never use the arm again, or paint again."

After four and one-half years she finally met a doctor who was an artist. He was a physiatrist, and as she puts it, "That's a physical therapist with a medical degree." He took time to review her medical records and found that most of her problem was not from the diagnosed fractured spine but from a vertebra that had slipped out of place. He wanted to crack her neck in chiropractic fashion.

The day before she went to that doctor she was talking with a neighbor, a nurse, who was taking care of a 36-year-old woman who had her neck broken by a chiropractor resulting in paralysis from the neck down. When she heard that the doctor wanted to crack her neck she was terrified. He said he could not do it unless she relaxed. She remembers: "It took a lot of faith, but at that point I was ready to try anything. I let him crack my neck. As I was walking out of the office I could feel circulation coming back into my arms. This was the beginning of a month-long treatment that put me back in front of an easel. I do know I never gave up because I knew God wouldn't take away a gift he'd given me.

Disease can influence creativity in many ways. When it comes to the direct influence of disease on the work, even the technical execution may be affected. "Disease occasionally may influence the direction of the art's development, independently of the creator's own intentions" (Sandblom, 1989).

She painted a *"Nigerian Woman"* in her native dress. The model was a young woman who wanted to earn money for beauty college. She was learning how to straighten hair and used the money she earned modeling to finance her beauty school education. She has since returned to Nigeria. This painting has won many awards.

Myrtle says, "My paintings have made thousands of dollars for worthy causes over the years. The wonderful events that have occurred as a result of my art have been great esteem builders." She's gotten awards, honors, and is now in 52 publications. She says the accolades just come to her now without trying. She was invited to the White House by President Ford to attend a worldwide meeting for the handicapped. She proudly states:

> Fifteen organizations from the Bay Area sent money to pay my way. Santa Clara City Council gave me $200. While I was there I promoted art for the handicapped. I'm the author of "Art as Recreational Therapy and Rehabilitation for the Handicapped." Writing that fulfilled my dream to become a published author. Landford Publisher was so impressed by the content of my program they approached me to do an educational program for them. I made an educational package with slides and a 45-minute lecture tape. A lot of subjects in the course were the students I had when I was teaching art to the handicapped. I had a waiting list for students, but the handicapped were always number one with me. I was prepared because I had studied photography, writing, and had given lectures.

In 1983, Myrtle had a stroke that affected her brain and her memory. The doctor told her it would be a progressive thing but she refused to give power to his words. She remembers having to let her family know if she was going out, because she could not be sure she would remember how to get home.

She says: "I figured by that stroke I probably learned something; that I shouldn't push myself so hard. I was good for a while, then I got too confident and started doing too many portraits. I couldn't say no. So anyway, I got under stress and had another stroke. I had to learn to walk that time."

It took all her effort to learn to walk and her painting career was put on hold again. During her recuperation, a woman with two sons came for a portrait. She wanted them painted together because they were "buddies" and one had kidney failure. Myrtle knew she could not put the woman off too long and this was what pushed her recovery forward. She did the painting. I know this story sounds embellished but in fact it is toned down. I've left out the numerous exploratory surgeries performed to remove tumors.

It was just after the stroke recuperation that she was diagnosed with breast cancer. In her words: "My father's family died from almost 100% cancer, so I knew the odds were not in my favor." She researched her particular type of cancer and decided, against her doctor's wishes, to try radiation therapy. The day after her last treatment when she was at a low ebb she was bitten by a Lyme diseased tick. This seems like an extraordinary set of events but they are all true. She went to the hospital to have the tick cut out and was put on the strongest antibiotic available for 28 days. The antibiotic didn't agree with her. She says, "I could not stop the medication because they had to make sure it got to the brain. As a result of that I developed a yeast infection in my digestive tract."

"Many . . . have ascribed a therapeutic effect to creativity, a means of enduring the suffering of life. In *The Birth of Tragedy*, Nietzsche says that it is only Art that has the power of diverting our feelings of disgust for a dreadful and meaningless existence into conceptions that one can live with."

Myrtle has had more than her share of traumatic life events. For most of her life she has had to cope with either illness or handicap. Her story reads like a medical encyclopedia, and yet at 73, she has all the energy and creative spirit of a teenager. She is an example of what a positive mind can do to overcome challenging life events. Myrtle's life theme has been meeting and facing challenging situations and growing for having endured them. Her spiritual life is flourishing. Each conquered challenge resulted in better art.

Sandblom (1989), notes, "Illness has often deeply influenced not only the life but also the work of great authors, artists and composers. Hans Christian Anderson of fairy-tale fame is emphatic about the power of pain and its prominent place in the history of culture."

Many artists have been well aware of the important role that their disease has played. "Of course, this does not imply that suffering is a prerequisite for artistic creation, nor that a creator has to be ill in order to make suffering real to us" (Sandblom, 1989)."

A few months ago, Myrtle went back to work and is free of cancer. She feels better than she has in years. She recalls that she was not focusing on the cancer as much as on the healing. Now she meditates every day and still has time to accomplish more, but at a relaxed pace. She has less pain since she began doing meditation. When asked about a catalyst for her painting she notes:

> The catalyst for me in my painting was way back when I came out of the sanitarium into this beautiful world. It really struck me. I will never forget the feeling. I wanted to express the beauty of the world around me. When I paint people or animals, I paint them at their best. I painted an *"Older Woman"* and had quite a challenge. Her husband came to me and asked me to paint her portrait. The problem was that she had died. He looked so lost and lonely I couldn't refuse. I told him to bring me some

photographs of her and a nice dress. I chose from five pictures and created this portrait. He brought me old, dowdy clothes so I sent him back home to find something more cheerful. When he brought this dress I knew it would come out nice. When he came to pick it up I was very nervous. He was very rich and sort of particular. He took one look at it and the tears started to flow. I knew I'd done a good job.

You might say I'm like a psychologist when I'm painting people because to paint them at their best you have to first let them talk about their problems. Then we go on to happier times. Maybe we talk about a vacation that's coming up. It is amazing how their expressions change and that's the expression I want on the canvas. Painting people from life takes a lot of energy and I am "starved hungry" when my subjects leave. I work so hard at it. It isn't a relaxing job.

The biggest joy comes when the portraits are framed and hanging up. I think to myself: You did it again! When I'm starting out I wonder. That blank canvas can be intimidating but I don't let a negative thought enter. This is the challenge. I'm sort of intuitive and if I think they're going to be negative I won't paint them.

She wants her portraits to be positive images, ones that will provide good impressions of the subject. A comment Myrtle made that particularly fascinated me was: "I look down the line of relatives in their albums to see if one has a hooked nose, how many have hooked noses. What are the main features of the family." She can look at a picture now and tell if that person is a sister. She can identify relative traits that run in families. She made an interesting comment to me which was that painting one's own family members is the hardest thing to do because after you live with a person for a while you do not notice their distinctive features as readily as you do with strangers. For instance, she says, "If a man marries a hook-nosed woman, he won't notice it after thirty years." Therefore the *"Portrait of My Daughter"* was the hardest portrait to complete. She feels she has captured her features correctly but it was more difficult than the others. "I'm so close to her. It's harder to paint your own family." Myrtle's desire to be more than a portrait painter, a society painter, has been accomplished. She can paint anything. She told me: "You have to be able to paint anything if you want to be a society painter because you have all different types of backgrounds to put in. If it's a businessman, you need to be able to do an ocean or the books in his study. If it's a woman, the background may be a drapery and you have to make velvet look like velvet and satin look like satin."

When she was growing up, she was around more animals on their farm than people because as she puts it: "My family wasn't the social type." Myrtle says that when it comes to animals they are all different: "The poodles take more breaks than the basset hounds, and bassets don't cooperate unless they want to. I always send the parents away; animals and children are so much better when the parents are not around." She goes out to dog trial meets and watches the animals in action. The basset hound in one of her animal portraits has won over 500 obedience awards. The reason she loves the animals is that they are themselves and not trying to make an impression. It is important to her that people also be themselves. She even took a course in self-hypnosis to learn how to calm herself so that the animals would calm down and have relaxed expressions.

She notes that as a portrait painter you have to notice every little detail: "I must have been observing those details at a very young age as I look at these old paintings of mine."

Myrtle has done a series of encaustic paintings in additional to her portraiture. Once she was at an art show 25 years ago and saw a painting that excited her. She contacted the artist and learned the techniques from her. She comments: "I loved it so much that I researched it further and have since created recipes of my own." She feels that doing these keep her technique from being too stiff. Encaustic painters are few and far between, perhaps only 300 in all of the United States. The paintings themselves consist of beeswax, pure pigment and a blow torch. The heat brings the color out and melts the wax creating what she calls "happy accidents." A red one, entitled *"Fire,"* was created because she loves warm colors. I did both of these paintings after I had my stroke and before I had my cancer. I paint during bouts of health. A blue one is called *"Ocean"* and won a world wide award from East Washington University. Myrtle notes: "My closest friends are my subjects. I fall in love with them. I've got people who have been my friend for 30 years as a result of owning my paintings or taking art lessons. There's a bonding. I don't understand it but I think it's wonderful. When I'm painting a subject it's a very intimate affair because I am there for them to make them comfortable."

The experience of "falling in love with her subjects" may be one of release from ego values—into the divine connection, perhaps oceanic—healing in itself.

Myrtle feels as if she is following in her mother's footsteps. Her mother was still working with shut-ins well into her nineties and was doing volunteer work the week before she died. She says she had a lot in common with her mother who began her art career at age 70. Myrtle noticed too that her own daughter is a lot like herself. She had a good relationship with her mother and finds herself copying her. She says: "Even though my mother had rheumatoid arthritis she walked every day. She didn't take medication—only natural things. We always agreed on everything." She feels that she is healthier than she has been in years noting, "I haven't had a cold in eight years."

This Author's Initial Reaction to Myrtle's Story

I got an inner reaction on a body level as well as on emotion and physical levels from this artist. I find something quite disconcerting about Myrtle's life theme of getting sick, overcoming the illness, and becoming stronger through the process. My subpersonality, "the arrogant rescuer," ran forward saying "Oh, Myrtle, you don't need to be sick to be cared about and loved. We'll all love you anyway." Then the "preacher" part of me came forward and said, "Don't be ridiculous, it is the will of God that she endures this pain. She has something to gain from all her suffering."

Something about Myrtle's story continues to rattle around in my mind. My reaction isn't one of quiet understanding; rather, it is more like running my fingers over sandpaper or filing my nails. A shadow part of myself gets activated when I read it.

I wonder how one person could endure such a life of constant trauma and still have a sense of purpose and humor about it all—and Myrtle has. She was an ill child who felt alone and freakish. At the same time, she had a great talent for art and was encouraged by her mother who dreamed at least one of her children would become an artist. Although Myrtle was limited in what she could do, in art she could paint well and please her mother. This was a healthy bond. One might say her art was her gift to her mother.

Were Myrtle's illnesses the result of trying to keep that promise she made to God when she said, "If I live to be an adult, I will help people in my situation"? Was that too hard a promise to sustain? Did that promise require more energy than was available? Were her illnesses and handicaps an escape from the pressures of one's mind to fulfill such an enormous promise? After all, her commitment to the handicapped did not end with a few art lessons. This woman gave 71 inspirational lectures, taught, and compiled courses for University Publications—all while raising a family and suffering the daily pain of scoliosis. Was her unconscious crying out for rest by mandating that she be flat on her back in bed?

I got goose pimples from some of her comments such as, "After those four and one-half years of paralysis my paintings were better than they had ever been." Was that comment simply a fact? Or does some part of her believe we must overcome challenges to be better people?

Myrtle did not intend to use art as a coping mechanism or a healing modality, but it seems to have worked out that way for her. Although she does not dialogue with her paintings, or paint spontaneously, she relies on her quiet focused time painting as a way to make a spiritual connection with the divine.

Through Myrtle's story I learned how powerful a contract can be. Myrtle believes she is trading service to the community for her life. Her promise to God, "If you let me live to be an adult, I will help others in my situation" has, she believes, kept her alive.

The Transpersonal Dimensions of Myrtle's Story

The transpersonal aspects of Myrtle's story are her simplicity of heart; her wonder about nature; her gratitude for life; her patience in the face of trauma; and, her artistic purpose as a connection with God. It appears that her soul growth comes through trauma. She said, "God gives you patience and understanding when you've had a lot of traumatic things as a child."

Wonder became the source for her artistic expression. Myrtle remembers, "On the way home [from the sanitarium] the blades of grass looked so beautiful. I wanted to express the beauty of the world around me. That was the seed for me to become an artist."

Her connection with God resulted in a soul contract. "I prayed, if I'm allowed to live to be an adult, I'll make it better for others in my situation. This dream has come true."

The transpersonal faith and trust from a human source began the fulfillment of her dream. Myrtle recalls: "A couple in San Jose had faith in me. They had a one-woman show. Someone from the state saw it and they held a special meeting. They said, 'We'll help you go to college or take private lessons. We want you to teach other handicapped people about art.' I did both."

A transpersonal vision emerged from the severe life trauma and from the radical medical experience that followed. After four and one-half years without the use of her arm, she came to realize that God would not take away a gift he'd given her.

For Myrtle, journaling began her healing process. She learned that crying was O.K. She also learned that it was all right to refuse to listen when her body wanted to include her in a wounding process. Through trauma, she has developed a transpersonal purpose as part of her soul growth. She notes, "I'm healthier than I've been in years. I have a strong purpose."

Also, artistic expression has been healing medicine for pain. It has afforded Myrtle gratitude, wonder, patience, and life-affirmation. "I used to have self-pity, I didn't count my blessings. Now people look so beautiful to me. Things work out for the good. You have to be patient."

Myrtle has used her purpose as a foundation for self-realization. She says, "If you have a purpose, it's unbelievable what you can do. I get a lot of support and prayers. I haven't had a cold in eight years. I have a strong purpose, my mother had a strong purpose."

Myrtle's story is incredibly ripe and rich with transpersonal aspects. I felt the simplicity of her heart, which has gone deep with her life struggle. There is a simplicity about loving life amidst what she has endured. She is wondrous about nature and has a deep gratitude for being alive which comes out repeatedly. There is a deep transpersonal space in her heart: she believes in God, and her art delivered her to that faith. She is incredibly patient while ill and says, "I can make it through this breast cancer, and I have the patience to move through the pain over long periods of time." That to me comes from a deep place in her spirit and is a deep spiritual peace which generates her patience in the face of misfortune.

Finally, her artistic purpose is directly connected to God. "God gave me my art to mitigate the pain. . . . Sometimes it seems hazy like a contract. . . . I'll go through this pain if you'll give me my art and give me my life." It appears her art emerges from her connection with God; however, there is a bright side and a dark side. I sense a beautiful depth in her mind and spirit. In considering the transpersonal dimensions of Myrtle's story, I sensed depth that suggests a strong connection between creativity, spirituality, and the healing, or transcendental aspects of engaging in the act of art at this level.

Myrtle's art began as a means to relate to her mother on a level of health and has continued in the same way toward the wider community. The quality of her artwork surpasses that of most portrait painters. Her painting has given her a sense of self-worth and realization that she is "superior" to others in that aspect of her life; she has always felt inferior to other people.

Defining Myrtle's Current Issues and Strengths

The major theme in Myrtle's story is *recovery by strength of will* from illness or trauma and a feeling of betterment for having had the experience. "The challenge becomes a game. You say to yourself, "O.K. Lord, this is going to be worked out!" Myrtle experiences the transpersonal process of soul growth through physical suffering. "My paintings were better than they'd ever been after my accident. . . . When they told me I would never paint again, I didn't give those words any power." She is painting better than ever.

The other main theme that runs through Myrtle's story is that of *service* to the community—particularly to handicapped artists. Myrtle spent the better part of her life proving to herself and her mother that Myrtle could make a living as an artist. In high school her parents said, "You can't make a living at art, go to college and study science." Later, the Department of Rehabilitation denied her assistance, citing her inability to sit or stand for any length of time. She was always having to prove herself.

Myrtle's art has been the vehicle to high self-esteem. "My paintings have made thousands of dollars for worthy causes over the years and the wonderful events that have occurred as a result of my art have been great esteem builders."

Myrtle's Reaction to Participation in This Book

What this process was for me was a validation; realizing my life purpose was always to be an artist, a portrait artist of animals and people. I never realized I had the talent at such a young age until we pulled out all those really old artworks. You got me to realize that I am really good at portraits. I'm really one of the best. I never realized it until you came into my studio and we went through my paintings. I never realized it but I was destined to be a portrait artist since before high school. All the things that happened to me in the past contributed to the wisdom and the knowledge that I have now. It does make me feel complete.

DOROTHY'S STORY

Dorothy was born in 1924. She is the second of four children and is Myrtle's younger sister. She married Nick when she was 26 and they have four grown children and two grandchildren. Dorothy considers herself a spiritual person and has done a substantial amount of personal growth work. Some of this personal work began when Dorothy joined Al-Anon, a support group for people living with family members who are suffering with alcoholism. When asked if she felt God is within her she unhesitatingly answered, "Yes, absolutely!" Her artwork is representational and the focus is on landscapes. Dorothy is an expert in the use of shadow and placement. Her work is warm, friendly, and calming. She has a special talent for capturing people doing everyday things and rendering them in a way that captures the heart and mobilizes our own fond memories.

Dorothy says, as a child, she remembers loving "people." When very young this surfaced when working with paper dolls and painting. Her early painting of a *"Girl In Nature"* was done when she was about 12 years old. She recalls drawing lots of little girls and flowers of nature. She would become very involved in designing clothes for them, and found that her designs became more and more intricate and creative as she focused on her project. She says: "Creativity feeds upon itself, it grows." As a child she usually had to entertain herself, since her older sister Myrtle was quite ill, and her younger sister and brother were just babies. She was lonely. Her painting *"The Little Girl Reading a Book"* exemplifies her loneliness, and was done when she was about 14 years old. Dorothy loved to read, and she spent most of her time either reading or painting. She remembers:

> In my family nobody talked. When my mother and father were upset with each other, they'd clam up. My parents were very honest people, but they didn't know how to communicate. They paid all their bills, neither one drank, they'd get angry but there was no screaming or yelling. They'd hold it in, which was worse. If someone doesn't communicate, it's like emotional abandonment. It creates a fear. I was an afraid little child. I was cantankerous at home but I was so afraid in school. It frustrated me.

This idea of holding it in took its toll on Dorothy as she matured. It first manifested itself in grammar school. In Dorothy's words: "Once, when the teacher asked me to speak, I stood up but no words would come out. So I sat back down again without saying anything." This wasn't the case at home however and she remembers, "I got more spankings than anybody. I was the rebellious one in the family." According to Barron (1968): "A person who is neither shy nor rebellious in his youth is not likely to be worth a farthing to himself nor to anyone else in the years of his physical maturity. Rebellion, resistance to acculturation, refusal to adjust, adamant insistence on the importance of the self and of individuality—is very often the mark of a healthy character."

At age 15, she read a life transforming book but unfortunately she cannot remember the name of it. She remembers in amazement: "I didn't know a person could change their thinking. My thoughts could be a choice." After reading that book her life started to open like a flower. She says: "I learned that there was a way to live happily." She remembers:

> In school I got good grades and didn't miss a day until my senior year of high school when I got the flu. I was on the scholarship society. In junior college I was a whiz at getting the basketball into the hoop at Hartnell. I never had a date or a boyfriend in high school; never 'till after high school. No one asked me, it just never happened. I was totally opposite from my own children. I was skinny and busy with my own life.
>
> My mother went to a night school program. I was 20 and she asked me to go to a dance. A relative of my future husband thought he should get out too, so he was talked in to going to that same dance. Nick and I met doing the do-si-do. The first thing I noticed about him was when he reached out his hand, it was big and warm. He has wonderful hands. The first thing he liked about me was my legs. We do-si-doed for about a year. We always took my mother along. Then one evening he asked me to go to a dance alone with him. He gave me a little peck on the forehead. We courted for about a year, I guess. Then I decided that I wanted to see more of the world. So I went to San Jose and got a job at Goushe map company and worked there for about a year. I decided it wasn't that great in the city. I was raised on an acre with a garden. I decided to come home. I told a friend of Nick's that I'd like to see Nick again. He came to a Grange dance and we got back together again. But you know what is interesting? I must have had something in me at the time. I recall one night we went out to a football game and my back was hurting really bad. I was trying to get out of going to the game. I remember he got really mad, he thought I just didn't want to be with him. Before, I'd always seen

him when he was really nice. This showed me another part of him, and it's strange, but then I realized, he can show feelings like that. Something about that intrigued me. There may have been something unhealthy in me at the time, I don't know what that was, but I got more interested in him then. So we got married and had four kids.

We had three children one right after the other, and one ten years later. He was wonderful with the children. He has healing hands according to this psychic. One time we went to the psychic fair and my hand showed stress but his showed healing. His hands are comforting. He'd hold my hand when the children were being born, or if I was sick, which I rarely was. He has some kind of healing in his hands. I don't know if it is the earth or what. He'll give me a back massage and it feels so good. He has many good qualities and it's all worked itself through. He's always been real close to all the kids. We had all our struggles during their growing up years. For a while, during the teen years, the oldest three children became alcoholic, but they all have overcome and they are all living independent lives. The youngest one doesn't seem to have been touched by it. They are all very close. They love their father and they love me. They went through a lot. I guess we're all overcomers. It's very special. They all got help.

I started going to Al-Anon many years ago. I was in my thirties, in 1955. The kids were seven, eight and nine. They were all excellent students in grammar school. They were in the highest level and got the highest grades but when they got to high school, I guess it was the alcohol, but they started losing control. So, later, the two girls went to continuation school to get their degree. They both got it the same year. The oldest boy never finished high school but he's OK. Life went on and eventually they got help for their problems.

When Dorothy started painting children and adults she felt control over where she wanted to place the figures within her composition. She knew exactly where she wanted each person in each painting, and she would usually place them where they looked like they were having fun. She won first prize for a painting of two young boys who were fishing. The award came from the Society of Western Artists. That award left her feeling elated. Another painting of a *"Boy Fishing"* is of her grandson. She comments on this work:

He has such beautiful little legs. I wanted to paint his sturdy legs. A little girl came at a perfect time and I thought it would be nice to include her. I remember my grandson being rebellious that day and I had a hard time getting him to cooperate. My husband was there too. I got pretty much the painting that I wanted. I gave it to my daughter.

Completing this painting left her feeling powerful, ecstatic, and relaxed. She loves painting figures and gestures. When painting on site, Dorothy has the feeling that the right people will just come into the work. She says: "They just seem to arrive when I need them to, then I do the placing." A painting she calls *"Fun in the Sun"* is a typical example of how Dorothy places her subjects in just the right spot for aesthetic effect. She tells about her painting:

> The location is an inlet from the ocean. I was trying to entertain my grandson on his summer holiday. I took photos while he was off having a great time somewhere. Figures are so fleeting; so for that one I took photographs. But I changed the boy into a girl. I put a little girl in front of woman with a baby and she was a boy originally. You can do all kinds of things; that's the creativity. I moved all the figures around to where I wanted them.

She loves painting natural settings; loves the process of being within nature while creating. She has often has the experience of being outside of herself while painting in these beautiful settings. She acknowledges that the paintings just flow out of her freely and easily. It appears she is touching a dimension of spiritual connection; accessing her higher self, if you will, during her painting processes.

"Yellow Spring" is of a little blue house sitting in an orchard where mustard is growing. Dorothy says:

> I painted it along with an older friend of mine who was a wonderful buddy because she would never speak when we were doing our paintings. She was busy doing her own work. I like to have quiet so that my mind can stay completely focused on my work. I get outside myself when I paint, I become totally enmeshed in the process.
>
> I remember when I did that one, it was a beautiful spring day. The orchard was full of mustard and it was gorgeous. I'd gone by there a number of years and always wanted to paint it. One day I got permission. I sat on a little red weather beaten chair. It is metal and I carry it when I paint. My friend sat on the other side of the orchard so that we each had a different perspective. I just love the sun beating on my back on a spring day. I just sat and tried to make the focus come in the way I wanted. We went back the same time each day to capture the same light and feeling. I just grasp what I see. It took a couple of weeks. I did it live. Photos are a more recent thing I've tried since my mother is gone and my friend is getting older. I am a slow painter but I can be fast if I have to. Sometimes I get a little picky with the blossoms and all. I like the little details. I did

that one about eight years ago. I enjoy gazing upon blossoming trees and flowers. I become intimate with them. It is like meditation.

Her mother grew many beautiful flowers. Painting them brings Dorothy back into connection with these lovely memories. She has a special reverence for her paintings of natural settings which have been replaced by development. She usually takes a friend with her when she paints outdoors. "Things in nature as well as people call me to paint them," she notes. I painted *"Blue Mountain"* about three years ago:

A friend of mine wanted me to do a picture for her husband as a secret surprise Christmas gift. So she bundled up the kids and took me along in the car in the Aromas area which is near here. We went on a beautiful spring day. I was beside myself. It is so seldom that I have the luxury of a driver. I sat in the passenger seat and could just jump out when I'd see something. We looked for a scene that would please her husband. This is not the picture we chose for him. This one was for me. I'd always wanted to paint this hill. I did one for him of my husband's farm. From the top of the hill we could look down into a valley, and then across to another hill. This man is a farm advisor so we chose the rolling strawberry hills and Mt. Madonna. That's the one he ended up with.

I am reminded of a painting I did a long time ago. When I first started my membership with The Society of Western Artists it was my first entry. Mother was with me then. We were on the dunes and found a little isolated spot with a fence behind us. We were comfortable. The scene was *"Moss Landing,"* the old wharf. The painting should be a historical piece now because the pier has been taken down, and now we have a modern wharf. It's not the same. These people were all in different positions. I love doing characters and they were wonderful.

We heard little noises behind us, and then I looked around and there were holes in the fence. I looked closer and there were some eyes. We saw someone peeking at us. It was students from Santa Cruz University studying marine life. I became self-conscious. I painted anyhow. It was a pure fun painting.

I focus intently when I paint. My mind is only in this one place as I create. It is meditation, escape. It also brings the life force into my body and stimulates expression of color, form, and feelings. I feel buoyant and alive. It is my essence.

My mother was great for my art, all the way through. If I needed a tube of paint she'd see to it that I got it. If I needed a frame she'd buy it, then I'd pay her back right away. If I needed anything to do with art, she was always there. She was my great supporter. I painted a picture of *"My Mother"* just as she was, no frills. I really captured her likeness.

My daughter married a fisherman so I gave them the painting of Moss Landing as a wedding present. They've since gotten a divorce but he won't give the painting to her. He loved it so much. I haven't seen it since. I would love to get it back. That was pure joy.

Doing light happy paintings takes my mind off the heavy things in my life. There is relief in it. Artists draw because it is their life's purpose. True artists realize this creative side is part of their make-up. If we don't live this out, we are dead inside. I come alive when I paint. It has been a burning desire in me as long as I can remember. When other things get in the way of my creative work I feel like I am slowly starting to lose my life's purpose. In these times I feel frustrated and fed up and greatly dissatisfied. If I don't balance my life with my art I feel dead. I desire to stay healthy and alive.

In my painting of *"The Old Plum Orchard"* life and death are represented in the same painting. After I did it, I started thinking about the psychology of it. Each plum tree is in a different stage of life, just like people. People who come to see it say they themselves feel like this tree or that tree. An old nun, in her nineties, looked at this picture and pointed to the dead tree in front and said, "I feel like this one." She is now living in the Mother House in New York. Another younger nun who was with her pointed to one with more blossoms and said, "I like this one." She chose one with many blossoms and is working as a teacher. I feel that each blossom is part of the life force.

My husband was the one who pointed out the scene for me. It was a rainy day, and the sun was trying to come out. The place where we would have to park was precarious. I was hesitating; the weather was so lousy. He was so excited to show me the spot, that I went. I just fell in love with it myself. The big clouds, the sun going in and out, showers; it was all so beautiful.

Dorothy says: "I feel there is a big connection between emotional and physical health. Painting is my emotional healthiness. This healthiness is the wonderful effect of loving to paint."

When she gets inspired she turns out some real prize winners. For example, her painting of *"Hecker Pass"* won first prize in The Society of Western Artist's Competitive Show. This painting was done about 15 years ago. As Dorothy remembers:

I was up in the attic and it was cold. I had a hot water bottle on my lap, and was peering out the window. I was looking down on the lake and hills. It was a beautiful sight. I love those Mt. Madonna hills going down into Gilroy. Those were harder times for me. I'm speaking of the way I was feeling at the time. Of course, when I paint I'm outside of any problem or domestic stuff. There is no recollection of any mundane problems when I paint. I'm only interested in the moment.

From statements such as these one gets the feeling that through art, Dorothy is able to connect with her highest essence, a place of wholeness. She relates the story of having to deal with an alcoholic family. She had a pattern established with her husband, in which, he would drink at a bar, come home, she would chew him out, he'd go to sleep happy and then she'd be awake half the night.

All this changed when she joined Al-Anon. She talks about some of the things she has learned from Al-Anon, a support group for people whose lives have been touched by alcoholism in one way or another: "You learn to become an independent person. It freed me as a person. It gives a lot more energy in my life, when I'm freeing it for myself. It's a wonderful mental health program. We get into our own lives. We don't let their crisis' effect us. We allow them to experience their own crisis. We remove ourselves from the guilt of taking responsibility for them. We give them back their own responsibility. We don't have to suffer."

She says: "You become co-dependent when you don't want to face your own life so you get busy into someone else's." According to Lawlor (1992): "Co-dependency is the pattern of painful dependency on compulsive behaviors and approval seeking in an attempt to gain safety, identity, and self-worth. It should be properly viewed as an unconscious adaptation, an attempt to stay emotionally connected to people whose own capacity to remain related is severely compromised."

Dorothy says: "It's an excuse, a fear. It's easier. Instead of making a whole life for yourself, you help somebody else figure theirs out." Al-Anon teaches tough love. She says there is a fine line between interfering and helping. She says it may seem cruel but leaving the alcoholic to figure out their own problems sometimes acts as a catalyst to their seeking help on their own terms. Dorothy is really convincing when she tells me: "We don't need to know the answers for someone else. What they say, think and do is their business. We learn to mind our own business." She said that prior to Al-Anon she'd suffered from sore throats for quite some time. When she was able to exert herself and speak up about her problems, her sore throats went away.

She now thanks her husband for the opportunities she has had at

Al-Anon. It has given her tools for life. "I am trying to change my life so there is room for me to create every day. It is a great discipline for me to do this. To stop being "the helper" and "give time to myself. If I start falling back into co-dependency, helping others too much, I lose the time to paint. It's been nine years since the alcohol abuse stopped."

Dorothy says that her painting has gotten her through the alcoholic years. "Each year while I was attending Al-Anon I painted flowers to help them raise money." She remembers those 17 years when he "got a rise out of her" by going to bars. Once she quit giving him attention when he'd come home from the bars, he quit going to bars. She thought she could change him but now realizes: "You have to let them heal on their own."

When she first started to go to Al-Anon meetings she met a lot of resistance from Nick. He "fixed" the car so it wouldn't work. When she had a friend pick her up he was upset. She remembers: "I left anyway." An Al-Anon member said: "Don't show fear, it drives them crazy!" Dorothy says: "I became so understanding in Al-Anon. I'd come home full of compassion and put my arms around him in bed." Transpersonal Psychologists refer to this experience as a transmutation of anger into compassion—a very big step in personal growth.

Dorothy tells me: "When I'm loving and non-judgmental, he responds accordingly. It takes reawakening of our inner power. When I'm being me and painting, he's his happiest." She says that art is a beautiful escape but that she needed Al-Anon to understand alcoholism and herself. She says: "Creative expression combined with therapeutic knowledge is a powerful thing." She recalls: "Al-Anon took me away from co-dependence and got us on with our lives. It showed me I was an artist. It showed me how to get my eyes off my husband and back into my own life. It's a spiritual thing which has given me meaning for my spiritual side. It opened my eyes to the value of the church. It clarified my life purpose. It keeps evolving."

Perhaps art needs some non-art support to be optimally effective in its contribution to healing. Dorothy confidently exclaims: "I am at the point in my life where I often wonder what the next step should be. I wonder where to go from here with my painting." Like so many successful artists she wonders: "Could I make a living selling my art? I often feel I could use the pressure of selling my art to move and create more and more paintings. I could use an agent, I'm sure." She says: "I wonder if other female artists have to keep themselves down because of ramifications in their personal lives if they truly go big time." She says: "The feelings of I'm me, I'm an artist, I'm successful sometimes effects close relationships." Dorothy vacillates between believing in herself and fearing the loss of stability in her marriage when she says: "But I believe there is always a higher way to do things. There is a way to live and let the chips fall as they will; a letting go, a gentle, non-defensive way. Be calm, and decide what you need to do for yourself as well as others. Be intuitive about these needs and try not to run on fear. Be true to yourself first and then you know you walk on solid ground. As St. Augustine said, 'Love and do as you will.' "

As she says these words one gets the feeling she would love to really deeply believe them but isn't quite sure. She notes: "Painting has always been my first love, and I fall in love with what I paint and become one with it." When she is painting in nature she is focusing on transferring the colors to the paper. She notes:

Sometimes there are obstacles even in the painting. Just like real life. Sometimes it doesn't go smooth, then there is the overcoming of every-thing to make it work. You need to shift things to make it pleasing. It's pure creation when you're outside yourself. When you're too conscious of yourself it doesn't go freely. I fluctuate between who I am and where I am. I have a feeling of triumph when I finish a painting. I feel as if it has filled my creative well. I enter competitions to fine-tune my artistic ability. Each painting gets better and better, and I become more important to myself. It is a great self-esteem builder. I feel better while I am painting and it rubs off.

Her painting of *"Oranges"* was done about six years ago. Dorothy said: That tree is right outside my kitchen window, near the walkway and my clothesline. It's very private. I looked at it often, and wondered what particular area of the tree I'd paint that would make a nice composition. I looked each day and meditated and gazed at it. I sat and really looked at each orange. I paint what I see. Then I take the liberty of exaggerating color. For instance, in the shadow I'll see a hint of lilac. Then I'll add more. I enhance the shadow color and it works. I can exaggerate. I learned that way back. It doesn't have to be exactly as it is. I can make it more my own; add my own touch, I create. I play God. No, he guides me. It flows through me.

Again, with statements such as these it appears that Dorothy is accessing the higher parts of her nature; she is acting as a vehicle for the life force to flow through her.

Although her artistic ability has been nurtured since childhood she has not neglected the more formal aspects of training. She studied art for 13 years in night school and at Hartnell and San Jose State University to learn the basics. She was told that her ability to set up composition was excellent, as was her use of color and shadow. Personally, I feel that this comment was an understatement. Dorothy's work with shadow is, in my opinion, incredible. Her work with shadow is actually full of color. She seeks out color in shadows, knowing there is life in shadow. She never uses just basic gray in her paintings. Nor does she ever use black in pictures of nature. She "drags" one color over another to create a heavier effect, a deeper tone. She makes her colors approximate what her eyes really see. She does not go by any hard-set rules for painting. She uses the intuitive process, stating: "Real artists break the rules sometimes."

Dorothy was an art teacher at the third and fourth grade levels in the Catholic school system. She remembers that her students loved her art class. They were always very excited to be with her in class because there was a freedom involved with her whole process. There was no grading, and the children could create in a setting without judgment, without right and wrong ways of creating their own work. This is similar to the way Dorothy's mother treated her art experience, very supportively. In fact she feels that her mother was the catalyst for her art. It may have been her mother's death that spurred this prolific flow of recent paintings. Her mother was one of those people who was most often with her out in nature while she painted. Perhaps the death of her mother brought home to her the knowledge that anything can be taken away and that she'd better use her talent while she is able.

Dorothy painted *"Potted Flowers."* She recalls:

They were on a porch. I must have driven past that building many times, but this was the first time they caught my eye. I parked in a lot across from the building for a few hours each morning to do my painting. One day the lady who lived there came over and introduced herself. She asked me if I would like to come inside to see her place. She had all kinds of flowers and potted plants in her house. She lived alone and each year she adds to her flower collection. It was wonderful.

Dorothy is an introvert by nature but, during her time at the Camera Club, she became its reluctant president. She confided: "I was terrified." She imagined giving her first speech would be like going to her own guillotine. When she heard the applause, she relaxed and admitted to me, "I was really a great president."

At this point in her life she uses painting as a discipline. She paints every day regardless of her situation in life. She feels that art isn't art until it is out in the public. She feels that we all have a gift that was meant to share. At one point someone told her she should change her pallet. She did. The first is called *"Magic at Dusk."* Dorothy describes the day she took the photographs that would culminate in this painting:

> My grandson was visiting from Oregon and wanted to go surfing. It was a beautiful summer afternoon. I thought to myself that I'd sit on the sand and watch that he's safe. I always carry a camera since I joined the camera club. As it grew later the sky became the most beautiful, gorgeous thing. I took all kinds of pictures. It was a memorable afternoon; I'll never forget the feeling. I went home and composed this painting.
>
> The *"Wave"* was done from assembling photos taken at a camera club picnic. We were on the rocks overlooking the bay eating lunch. I had my camera. I tried to capture that wave on the break. Then this little white boat came rushing in from the right side. I tried to get the boat as the wave was breaking. I create my own compositions from various photos. I prefer doing artwork live from the spot, but if not, I still create my own design and my own colors. I can be very creative.
>
> There was a time I was very pure about "no" photos. I'd never stoop to that. Since I joined the camera club and learned to use a camera I use it for inclination, not for imitation, because that's not art. If we can move mountains, rivers, houses and color we can be very creative with photography. This wave is for me. I'm going to make some waves in my life too.

Dorothy has a purpose and is beginning to acknowledge her own importance. She is no longer willing to wait until all is fine to paint. She looks forward to the future and plans to paint until she's 100 years old. She prays for the courage to take risks, adapt to change, keep learning and producing her art. She wants to live life to the fullest—only more so. Dorothy would like her story to end with a poem she wrote about artists. During the last conversation we had, she told me that she had gotten an agent and was in the process of accumulating a body of work. She wanted this poem to end her story.

> *An artist's life is special,*
> *For hours they'll sit and paint.*
> *Their soul goes into orbit*
> *and reality is faint.*

The mind strains to catch the essence.
While willing hands obey.
And the final stroke of color
Signs the magic of the day.

This Author's Initial Reaction to Dorothy's Story

After my first interview with Dorothy, I felt as if something was missing. I felt as if I'd only gotten half of her story—the good half. I wrote her story in only four pages, a stark contrast to the 20 pages from other artists who had the same length interview. After a month, I called and explained the situation. Her comment back to me was, "Oh, you mean you want my shadow stuff?" She agreed to a second interview which rounded out her story. Her story became more complete when it included her struggles with an alcoholic family and her own personal growth process.

It appears to me that Dorothy's life theme is learning how to get her own voice. This challenge began in childhood when she got up to speak and nothing came out and continued into her adult life when she was reluctantly made president of the local camera club. She recalls the first time she got up to speak, "I was terrified." When her voice came out, it seemed as if "someone else was talking."

Even her physical health problems were voice-related. Prior to joining Al-Anon she chronically had a sore, scratchy throat and deep cough. Her colds went away when she joined Al-Anon.

As Dorothy acknowledges her own power and her own voice she is getting stronger. "I don't have to get so emotionally churned up. I can be happy regardless of what other people think, say, or do."

Dorothy has tried optimistically to live an upbeat life. During her interview I felt there was some lingering pain just below the surface—a lifetime of pain, that was reframed daily, to enable her to cope and stay upbeat. As she said in her interview, she doesn't have to "suffer someone else's pain."

Painting has been her pathway into the beauty of life, and she recognizes the benefits of art in her life. "It brings the life force into my body. . . . I feel buoyant and alive. . . . It is my essence. . . . It is meditation and escape for me."

Besides art, caretaking has been a route to her soul and personal growth. She realizes now that she is just as important as those for whom she cares and is allowing more time for her art than ever before: her art is her life. An accomplished artist, Dorothy has won many important awards. The world recognized Dorothy long before she recognized herself.

After reading and rereading the stories of both sisters, Myrtle and Dorothy, I think some aspects of the trauma Myrtle suffered played a large part in their family dynamic; this seems particularly evident in the way Dorothy's life unfolded. Although Myrtle was the one with the illness, Dorothy also must have suffered as a result of those illnesses. A sick child needs attention and cannot be ignored. Possibly, Dorothy, only one year younger than her sister, felt very "unseen" or in Myrtle's shadow. It would be unusual, if as a child, Dorothy did not harbor some resentment or jealousy toward such a sibling. Perhaps some of Dorothy's "rebellion" reflected this unrecognized resentment. I asked Dorothy if these feelings were reflected in her experience and she said: "I've never resented Myrtle."

In Myrtle's story when she explains that although the school put them both in the same class so that Dorothy could help her, "Dorothy didn't see where I needed any help." Dorothy says, "I need to stop being the helper and give time to myself." Although Dorothy was speaking of her husband, I felt she was alluding to a lifelong pattern.

After listening to both stories, I role-played each sister. As Myrtle, I felt lonely and frightened. As Dorothy, I felt resentment welling in me, a sort of feeling that I felt guilty having. After all, Myrtle was involuntarily handicapped. But, in Dorothy's position as a child, I remembered my sister getting all the attention from our parents and not having to go to school or get up early in the morning. Is it any wonder Dorothy would feel that Myrtle didn't need any more help? Dorothy may have felt that Myrtle was getting too much help already.

Dorothy's talent for painting shadows may have originated from a feeling of living in her sister's shadow. Could the ambiguity she must have felt between wanting her own needs met and knowing Myrtle was even needier been the catalyst for marrying a needy man? Did Dorothy feel a certain sense of comfort in subordinating herself to a needier person?

Through Dorothy's story I learned that nature is a powerful stimulant to transformative experience. Her story has given me cause to begin an exploration of nature.

The Transpersonal Dimensions of Dorothy's Story

Dorothy stays in touch with her deep self through her art and notes the synchronicity in her life. "When I paint on site, the right people just come into the work. They arrive when I need them."

Dorothy unites with nature within the artistic experience. "I get outside myself when I paint. I become enmeshed in the process—one with rocks, trees, and mountains. I become intimate with it. It's like meditation."

She has a meditative focus in her art. "Things call me to paint them. My mind is only in this one place. It's an escape." This meditative state allows her to access an altered state of consciousness.

She embodies her awareness of the life force in her art experience. Art "brings the life force into my body. It stimulates expression of color, form and feelings. I feel buoyant and alive. It is my essence."

Dorothy connects her art with meaning and vitality. "Light, happy paintings take my mind off the heavy things in my life. If I don't do this, I'm dead inside. I come alive when I paint." Art is a healing body-mind experience. "I desire to stay healthy and alive. I feel a big connection between emotional and physical health, and painting is my emotional healthiness." Dorothy describes painting as a way of accessing spiritual unity and connecting with some part of herself that is whole and alive, her higher essence.

She has used Al-Anon plus her art as a healing tool in a relationship dysfunction. She said, "My painting got me through those 17 years. When I'm non-judgmental, he's perfect. Al-Anon showed me I was an artist, it's a spiritual thing." Al-Anon plus art led her into her life purpose and to spiritual growth. Art "clarified my life purpose, it keeps evolving." "Painting has always been my first love. I fall in love with what I paint. Sometimes there are obstacles, even in painting, just like real life. Then, there is the overcoming of everything to make it work. You need to shift things to make it pleasing. It's pure creation when you are outside yourself. When you are too conscious of yourself, it doesn't go freely."

Dorothy has used her artwork as a coping mechanism during much of her married life. Thus, when domestic situations disturbed her, she escaped into a world of beauty and calm. She feels her art has increased her self-worth and kept her healthy as well. Now, she feels her art facilitates a sense of spiritual connectedness.

Defining Dorothy's Current Issues and Strengths

The main theme in Dorothy's story is her *mystical encounter with nature* and her surrender to the deep self principle of synchronicity. "I become one with the rocks, trees and mountains. I become intimate with nature." She is so in tune with her surroundings synchronistic events seem to just happen. "When I paint on site the right people just come into the work. She seems to be in touch with her deeper self through her art.

Dorothy also has a theme of *relating her health to her art.* She says, "I feel a big connection between emotional and physical health and painting is my emotional healthiness. I desire to stay healthy and alive. Art is my healthiness."

Although Dorothy has been frustrated with some of the relationships in her life, she is happy with her relationship with her artwork. The *spiritual connectivity* always present in Dorothy's became recognizable to her through Al-Anon. "Al-Anon gave me tools for life. It showed me I was an artist. It showed me the value of the church and it clarified my life purpose. It keeps evolving."

There is also an attitudinal theme, common to women in all walks of life, that if one shines in ones own right, the male relationships in one's life will change or end. "I wonder if other female artists keep themselves down because of ramifications in their personal lives? I don't want my art to affect my relationship. I feel damned if I do and damned if I don't." Dorothy's higher self shines through when she says, "Don't run on fear. Be true to yourself."

Dorothy's Reaction to Participation in This Book

At first I didn't see what the value of it would be. I didn't know what this could possibly have for me. But, it's like someone witnessed it all. Someone outside the family has witnessed my feelings and it's like a validation. Something comforting; like it's OK. I've said all my secrets and I don't feel any guilt about the things I've said to you. You're a wonderful observer, listener, very good too. I wouldn't talk like this to just anybody. You were like an accepting witness. You didn't want to fix me or criticize me. You just sat and listened. I had no feelings of animosity coming from you, and I appreciate that. I want to thank you for that.

SAILLE'S STORY

While vacationing in Ireland in June, 1994, I met Saille in the little town of Killarney. We were on the same bus tour and it was delayed. We were all getting anxious by the wait and her husband decided to use the time to hand out some of Saille's sculpture flyers. She was visibly embarrassed by this gesture of love. Her flyers, her art, and her demeanor were all so intriguing that I got up and went to speak with her. As it turned out, some of her artwork was being displayed at the convention I was attending.

We hit it off immediately and she agreed to be interviewed for this book. We did her interview in the sitting room of the bed and breakfast where they were staying. It was wonderful for both of us. She talked about her life as we sipped tea and marveled at the synchronicity of being in the same place at the same time. We knew we were destined to have an ongoing relationship.

When not vacationing, Saille lives in Arizona with her husband Ray who she married in 1992. She has two grown children. She does fabulous water colors, but is most well known and proud of her sculpture. Saille is a serious artist who gets in touch with archetypal imagery in her productions. She uses her art to connect with the transpersonal and to try to understand the images that come through her. She has a strong need to find traces of tradition in her ever changing world.

It was in Milwaukee, in 1943, that Saille was born, prematurely weighing three pounds 14 ounces. She is an only child. Her father was ill all the years she knew him and died at the age of 49 when she was only five years old. Saille, reflecting on her father, says: "He gave me love; dearly, I felt loved." She was raised in a single parent household with a mother who suffered from severe asthma, manic depression, and eventually Alzheimer's. Saille notes: "During mother's manic periods she might suddenly decide we should move and that might include clear across the country. The only way we were able to get there was in a battered up old Plymouth."

Her mother often made decisions based on what was convenient for her but not for her daughter. In so doing she severely complicated Saille's life. An example was when she took Saille out of a nearby school in Milwaukee and placed her in a downtown school. Saille remembers: "She took me out of the local school and put me into a school two miles away so she would not have to make my lunch. The other school had a hot lunch." There was no bus service so she had to walk the entire two miles each way. Her path took her across four major intersections and she remembers: "It was cold in Milwaukee. I was a sickly child and was required to walk on bitter cold days. I had trouble with my ears. I can't imagine sending my own children off like that—the whole thing was just too much. I just feel like I barely survived my childhood."

She says: "It makes me want to give up and be taken off the planet. I just get tired; the struggle has been going on for so long."

As a young child, she suffered from physical illness as well as sexual abuse by her grandfather and male caretakers. Saille was a fragile child with chronic ear and adenoid problems which required many radium treatments. The combination of having had these problems, without the help of a mother who was capable of caring for her, has left her with lasting emotional scars. She has done an enormous amount of self-reflection and discovery and is slowly coming to terms with her past.

There was only one person in her youth without whom she says she would not have survived, and this was an aunt. Saille refers to her as her "beacon of hope." It should be mentioned however, that as her father was dying he gave her loving support that has sustained her throughout her life. Saille says that her childhood continues to affect her self-confidence and contributes to a lot of despair that she feels now. In her words:

I feel I had an extremely difficult childhood, to the point where it continues to open up for me how difficult it really was. As I get older, it seems to not be as resolved as I would like, and I keep hoping that the process of experiencing this pain will eventually cease and there will be a point where acceptance takes place. Often, I feel I've done it, and then life events will conspire to shake me up again. Feelings of insecurity and fear of estrangement on this planet resurface and then I have to process it all in some way.

What's happened as I've gotten older is that the feelings have gotten more intense. But now I have a vocabulary and tools that I use to deal with the pain that is surfacing. It's like having a library and you just have a lot of ways to deal with the memory as it imparts itself.

I access my creativity through emotions of joy, sadness, and betrayal. I've been to therapists who have said that I should be a raving schizophrenic with the history that I've had—event piled on event. I call it the crucible of childhood, rather than the cradle, or even the fire of childhood. Especially after my mom went through her period of falling apart. This confusing situation with her intensified as she began her process of aging and going into Alzheimer's.

I learned through her doctors that there was more wrong with her than I knew. I always thought it was me. I grew up feeling that I was too much for her, and that life was too much for her. When she died, I mourned not for her as a person but for her presence on earth as a mother. Being without a mother was an abstract pain for me. We moved a lot. My mother thought that moving would solve her problems. Alcoholic's Anonymous has a thing called a "geographical" that helps people solve their problems, so mother and I made tons of "geographicals."

My mother had a lot of anger and resentment. I felt like I was her sounding board; actually; she made me her sounding board. She'd say, "Now, don't tell anybody what I'm telling you; now, don't tell anybody where we live." I was three or four years old, real young, when I became her confidant. As I mentioned, my father died at the age of 49 when I was only five years old. I remember him being sick most of the time he was married to my mother. Despite his illness, however, he gave me much love. I felt this love dearly and subconsciously carry his memory to the present day.

Although I was sexually abused by different male caretakers it did not keep me from liking men. However, as I grew up, I did feel mistrustful in male company. In my first marriage I lived with 17 years of verbal abuse, which I guess I accepted, probably because I did not fully recognize what was happening. When the verbal abuse turned to physical abuse and he first hit me, I drew the line. I immediately made plans to leave him and was out of the house within the year. Emotional abuse is harder for me to judge.

I only like men if they are nice to me. I like men because my father was good to me: kind and loving. I never dated until college. I was terrified of dating then. It's been a long process for me of the male-female thing. A lot of women would have become men haters and I'm really not. I think that's because my dad called me his sunshine, his gift to me at the end of his life.

I was an only child and lonely, extremely lonely, bleedingly lonely. I wanted to have a brother or sister. I was left alone from kindergarten on. In my sophomore year in high school we had no formal art classes, but I painted a picture of *"Mater: Our Lady as a Schoolgirl."* I was intrigued, at the time, with the staff and spindle, perhaps, it was an early attraction to spinning and fiber work that was so much a part of my life with my mother. Mother was an avid seamstress and used sewing to relieve the stress of her job. She made most of my clothes, which I had a good time designing, in the sixth, seventh, and eighth grades.

Mother's greatest career move was to Chicago where she was given the job of designing the operating room suites at Michael Reese Hospital. This move allowed me to attend boarding school in Lake Forest, which I loved, and where I felt safe for the first time in my life.

As an artist I have sustained myself financially so far, but because of the nature of the economy my career provides me with no real security base. I've chosen to live off my art rather than opt for the security of a nine-to-five job. I think I'm a little bit too damaged emotionally to process stresses that happen in the workplace. I don't handle stress that well. I have a need for life without conflict. Other people who are healthier can deal with stress but I can't. I've always had to create for myself an environment that supports me, not financially but emotionally.

Walnut Seed Pod and *Strata Compression Panel* were both created in 1978, and were the first forms I worked with in my sculpture. Eventually, the split widened to incorporate the whole shape, and dissolved the linear straight edges. The shapes of the wall sculptures I design now are the culmination and fruition of many years of work. Since 1978, I have created and sold over 250 sculptures. My focus continues to be wall relief's, punctuated by paintings and the three-dimensional pieces.

In 1981, I did a *"Self-Portrait"* in a strong linear style in front of a mirror. I had recently divorced, and was living down the street from the family house. I tried to keep custody of my teenage children and stay with them in the house, but in 1980, the first major recession hit, and sales of my sculpture decreased to where I was not able to financially maintain the children well. At that time I asked my ex-husband to come back to stay in the house with the children, and I moved into an apartment. It was with a sense of failure, fear, and frustration that I did this drawing.

Once finished with the portrait, I propped it up at the end of the hall and clearly saw two people staring back at me. The split was obvious; one side was receiving the pain and maturing and the other side was still young and ingenuous. I have always avoided portraits of myself because it is hard to give a pretty face any character.

I like my self-portrait as the *"Old Woman Crone"* behind the triple spiral, with the owl goddess hovering on the right, as well as any portrait I have done. I have always felt that age would give my face the character that I miss when drawing it.

"Giselle" is welded steel, copper, and woven fiber. It was done in 1989, for the Toyota Corporation in Los Angeles. I had several large commis-

sions going, but this was the most important one. There was quite a bit of weaving in it which I created on my loom. I started weaving years earlier, using yarn created on my great grandmother's spinning wheel. I trained as a sculptor using a pure approach to metal but as the pieces were completed, I felt they had nothing new to offer the world of art. The spinning was an offshoot that I had developed to use as demonstrations in the schools. As soon as I began to incorporate the weaving into my work it started to sell through a local gallery here in Scottsdale. I still continue to create the weaving myself because it has the richness and heaviness I need to hold the pleated forms. I also concentrate on adding a lot of textural yarns. The striations continue to symbolize for me the layered deposits of the earth.

After the sculpture was completed and shipped, the designer was not happy with the finish I used. I insisted she show it to the client. The art gallery supported me. I renamed the sculpture "*Giselle,*" after the village girl who was rejected by the prince. The piece also looked like a dancer somewhat. The client loved the piece and the finish, which was a new approach for me, but I kept the name the same in honor of those two weeks of anguished rejection.

Commission work is not as creative for me as my personal work because of the difficulties of making changes from the original designs, but it is the only way to go if ones goal is to create large public works, which is what I like to do. I have wanted, from the beginning, to create monumental statements.

One thing I learned as an artist is focus. Focus is so very important. It was a painful process, discovering my art form. In the beginning, all I knew was that I had to do artwork. There was a point 20 years ago, that I thought I would die if I didn't get into my studio. I didn't know what I was going to make, but I did know it was going to be just for me. I had to have a studio, and I had to have space, or I was going to die. It was that bad.

"Artists are often compelled to express themselves and the failure to do so can bring about a crisis" (Levy, 1994). Saille went on:

I cashed in all my social security from the school I worked at, and bought welding equipment and all my tools. We put a loan on the house and closed in the carport and made it into a studio. I had taken vocational welding classes. Everything I made sold quickly. I started pricing things low so I would first establish a security base. As my work progressed I raised my fee. When you start out it's very important to sell. It's your method of communication to the world. It's also wonderful to have your work support you financially.

In 1990, I completed *"The Tree of Life."* It consists of polished steel, woven fiber, copper, brass, and painted canvas. It was a commission piece for a large lobby here in Scottsdale. At the time, I was using in my paintings, the image of a tree sprouting with my token animals. One tree painting incorporated a birth-tear along the trunk which appears as a dolphin-like fish. The sculpture more or less finalized that series for me, and is one of my most successful installations.

I continue to be fascinated with the tree of life as the axis mundi of the world and the shaman's tree. The shaman climbs up the trunk into the branches to enter into other worlds to heal his/her people. This sculpture has a combination of hand woven fiber and painted canvas.

My main identity is my sculpture. I've raised my price steadily every year to the point where I'm about as high as I can get until I get famous. I really can't charge much more. My lesser identity is with painting and drawing which I started to explore during the divorce process. Although my drawings have been slow in coming, lately, I've been happy with them. I wanted to communicate what was inside some fascinating tombs that I discovered in Ireland. I wanted to do this through my paintings.

With sketch book and paints I went to the Brugh Na Boyne, or Newgrange as it is called, then to Knowth and to Tara to capture the feeling of these lands. These rolling green hills with tombs placed on energy spots of ancient holy places pulled me into their mystery.

I needed to find the origins of my own people. This need began when, as a wedding present, my aunt told me that I could choose anything in her house. I chose the spinning wheel that belonged to my grandmother, Sarah McKenna. It touched my life deeply. It was what inspired my life work and my soul quest back to Ireland. This wooden wheel has brought me full circle—ready to spiral, at age 53, into one more inner revolution.

Inside Newgrange *"Brugh Na BoAnn"* is a watercolor completed in 1993. This is one of a series of four paintings that I did of interiors of stone age tombs in Ireland. The tombs are all oriented toward the sun and nobody knows who built them. Newgrange is a structure which was engineered to capture the sun on the morning of the winter solstice.

The painting was done from sketches and visits to Newgrange on two successive summers. The second summer my husband and I visited there on our honeymoon trip. I always return there. To me it is a place of pilgrimage and majesty.

I think the major artistic shift for me was having the confidence to return from abstraction to figurative. I could draw geometric shapes, but could not draw the figure and I think that is because of my estrangement with the human race. I only did pieces, and parts of people; like hands.

Prior to Saille's trip to Ireland, she had some very transformational fire dreams. In fact, it was this series of dreams that led her to Ireland to study the old Crone of Grecian and Irish mythology. One dream was of an old woman, dressed in black, hunched next to a fire on a high windswept hill. Inside that huge fire was the old woman's face moving and grimacing in the flames.

She notes: "I felt that face in the fire was a portent of transformation."

On her third trip to Ireland she was on the top of Queen Maeve's Cairn in County Sligo when she received a transformative healing of sorts. She remembers coming away with a more positive inner voice. Memories of her time in Ireland continue to nurture her in a way she says her mother never did. She feels that Ireland is truly a mother to her. Saille tells of another fire dream she had around the same time:

I am visiting some relations on my mother's side of the family, in an isolated dark multi-storied house. A raging fire started. It came up through the floor but no one did anything about it. I could not remember the fire department's phone number, so I dialed 911, and asked to be connected with the fire department. The man on the other end said: "There really isn't a fire." He told me I was making it up. I said, "No, there is a fire." He hung up. I looked around; the fire got worse. It was everywhere, so I called the fire department again. Again, he said I was making it up. My relatives said, "Stop that, we want the house to burn. We want the insurance." I was horrified and realized everything would be gone. I had brought some nice things in my suitcase; the bracelet Ray gave me, and some other pieces. I could not find them in time, and imagined retrieving them blackened and with soot. We sat on the lawn watching the fire. The fire chief came by. He accused my relatives of burning the house down. I said: "That's ridiculous, I called your station twice and both times I wasn't believed." So I went up to him and started to punch him in the face with my fist. He laughed at me and said: "Your whole family is full of anger." I thought, "Too bad Chris [her son] isn't here, he'd fit right in." That is where the dream ended, and the feeling afterward was that the police chief was a supportive figure, and all knowing. I woke up thinking of him as a friend.

In addition to dreams, I have had some numinous experiences that were quite odd. Once, while swimming, I got the distinct smell of peonies, and knew somehow, that I was to visit my father's grave. An opportunity came up so I did.

Another time, during a rebirthing session, I reexperienced the trauma of the attack I had before the age of five. During the memory, my consciousness shifted to my spirit which was outraged, that herself as a light being, could be treated in such a way. Then I separated from my body and went up to heaven and stood on the brink looking over earth. My father was there and he was with a woman angel dressed in glistening pink, that looked like Glenda, the good witch in the Wizard of Oz. Because of my extreme agitation the rebirther stopped the process; so I really don't know the final outcome. I have had no other memories of the incident.

In retrospect, it explains somewhat my faith in angels, and my alienation from this planet. Also, I have spent a lot of time reintegrating my body into my consciousness. I have lived in my head for a long time. I have to do a lot of physical activity; swim, dance, tai chi, and yoga to stay together.

Each time I leave Ireland I do drawings. The process of doing figure drawings began my personal process. During this period in the early eighties, I fell in love for the first time. With my first husband it was more of a functional union, and I thought that was the way it was. I fell madly in love with this man who came into my life and it was like he opened up all the flood gates. That's when I started having dreams of my father. I'd forgotten him. I sought a therapist who said: "This is about your relationship with your father, it's not about loving this man."

Another dream Saille had at that time, that seemed so unusual to her, was:

I go into an indoor amphitheater. There are rows and rows of verandahs; viewing platforms. People are fishing. They bring up a huge fish with a big smile on his face, even though he is caught. It makes a big flip and goes back in the water. Everyone is in awe and they stop fishing. That dream seemed like a redemption dream to me; Christ consciousness.

Now I meld pagan and Christian elements. I want to learn how to make those St. Bridget crosses. They're wonderful. I do a lot of work with the pagan Bridget and St. Bridget.

There is a destructive element to my work. When I first made the piece I call *"Solstice Pillar"* it was designed to be burned at an art event. I didn't know how important it would become. Because of fire regulations we couldn't burn it. I'm glad it was saved because now I use it to evolve new ways of participation. It's my first piece to use vegetation and it's the winter solstice and summer solstice from the Greek and Celtic traditions. One side is summer, the other is winter. This year at Beltain we had a party for 80 people at the solstice in celebration of a Hopi prayer tree tradition. Hopi women tie intentions to favorite bushes or trees and ask the universe to provide for them. On my sculpture the guests attached their prayers to the bundled sticks of the interior of the sculpture.

I want my pieces to have an interactive quality. If a spontaneous change happens I feel successful. We all danced a serpentine pattern around these pieces. They continued the snake of people through the house to see my new couch. Then we came in a long line through the house and outside to eat. They were all told to bring flowers. During the snake dance they chose a flower from all that were brought. At the end of the parade they placed the flowers down the center of the table where the food was served. The party was wonderful and the table centerpiece became part of the spontaneity.

"Dolmen Tree Sculpture" was done in 1994, out of rusted steel and brass. I did it for a Beltane party. The curve at the top of the sculpture will eventually have a companion sculpture emanating from it to create the final form of the dolmen. It was situated on our property to catch the winter solstice sunrise in the curve. On December 21st, it was exciting to see the sun refracted into rays, as it was caught by the edge of the steel. One can imagine the power of Newgrange as the sun enters that small aperture and lights up that midnight black interior. The construction of the sculpture follows the shape of the standing stone but in this one the stone is also a tree. It is done in plant form because of the base and the explosive quality of the brass forms emanating from it which can also be seen as light rays.

I'm in the process now of planning a companion piece that will capture the summer solstice sunrise that will be placed perhaps on the new location in Colorado. The "Solstice Pillar" of the winter and summer goddesses would be placed at the Equinox point on the horizon. This was the ancient use of the standing stones to provide a viewing point to locate the seasonal cycle.

The *"Stone Circle At Creggancenial"* is an oil pastel, done in 1994. This painting was my Christmas greeting. I did the original sketch in Northern Ireland, in 1993. My husband and I plotted a honeymoon trip in the shape of a mandala around Ireland. We wanted to begin in Northern Ireland where my great-grandparents were from. The day after we located the cemetery we visited the place in this painting. It is called by the locals the Druid's altar because of the inscriptions on the large stone in the center. This form of burial was utilized after the mound builders of Newgrange, and has several ceremonial ritual circles incorporated into the design. It is called a court tomb because there is a gathering court enclosed by stones before the actual entrance to the burial dolmen of the tomb itself. The stones were placed atop a mound and open to the countryside. The day we visited, the golden furze bush was in bloom all around and friendly cows gathered as we sat on the stones. A little white dog, who seemed to assign himself as tourist guide, appeared as we stopped our car on the road. He led us back the sodden side road, through and under gates, to find our spot. We learned early in our trip to follow the local dogs back to these places. They liked our company and we liked theirs.

"Dolmen Dreaming" is a watercolor done in 1994, after my return from Ireland. In it I use the designs used in the ancient Irish tombs. I wanted to document as many of these ancient structures as possible while the energy from Ireland was still with me. I painted these abstract notations in the sky above the dolmen because they are, some believe, shamanic inscriptions used to travel to other worlds. The dolmen form is traditionally composed of three stones—two upright and one large crosspiece. Sometimes the sides have two or three stones narrowing to the back to form a triangle. Since the triangle has traditionally been associated with the feminine it seems obvious that the dead bones interred there were returned to the original source of life-the earth mother. Some of these dolmens have crosspiece stones as heavy as five tons. How they were raised remains a mystery.

Saille gets her art images from dreams, travel, poetry, literature, archaeology, and mythology. She is particularly interested in light and fire as it relates to mythology and ancient cultures. Her art breathes life into her existence and allows her to feel closer to the earth.

She states that her art has helped her deal, and rise above, the handicaps of her childhood, and feels that she could not function in this world without it. The same things that made her feel good in childhood, making beautiful things, makes her feel good about herself now. She says: "Making beautiful things pulls me out of my morass." She notes: "I go from optimism to exhaustion in my struggle with the demons of my past."

Her sculpture truly mirrors her history, philosophy, and personality. She says that for most of her life her art has been ahead of her. Sometimes she cannot even relate to it. In times of alienation it seems foreign and she rejects it. In times of spiritual connectedness she sees it as absolutely appropriate, even inspired. On very good days she says she sees it as a physical conjunction and an actual energy conductor needed by the planet for balance. I found the statement about loving her art one day and rejecting it the next fascinating because it was repeated by Mari, one of the other artists, and also by Bruce Moon in his book *Existential Art*

Therapy, when he said: "One day I would look upon it [his art] with pride, the next day I found it repulsive" (1990).

This Author's Initial Reaction to Saille's Story

Reviewing Saille's story put me in touch with my own pain. Her interest in fire symbology startled me because my fascination with fire and light has been part of an ongoing process that seemed very personal. I wondered what the connection may be between trauma and fire. As I mentioned earlier, Dora Kalff (1971), the originator of sandplay as therapy, says that when a child lights a fire in the sand, or plays with fire outside of the sand, they are ready to tell their secret. I think this is accurate, because during the course of this research I have come in contact with many correlations between fire and a traumatic event.

For example, Jean almost burned down her cottage a month after her son was given up for adoption. She hadn't told her family she was pregnant. Another instance was when a friend of mine, with twin grandsons, tried to learn the facts of what happened the night the children's house caught fire. She thought she would talk to them on tape because they had refused to speak with the police. She had expected these four-year-olds to tell her that they had done it but did not mean to. What came out, instead, was a shocking revelation of how they were being sexually molested. It was as if with each fire, the participant's own house, his or her body, was on fire.

Saille had two fire dreams. In one, "an old woman hunched over a fire, and her face grimaced in the flames. . . . I also had a dream years ago of my house burning, and no relatives wanting to tell. Only the fire chief seemed a supportive character in the dream." Perhaps Saille's interest in fire symbology with the welding process and fire transformation has something to do with acknowledging her past by "telling her secrets" and purifying her life.

Fire symbology also represents purification and transformation: the life-giving and generative power of the sun. J. C. Cooper (1978) refers to it as a renewal of life; impregnation; power; strength; energy; sexual power and protection. Fire manifested as flame symbolizes spiritual power and forces, transcendence and illumination, and is a manifestation of divinity or of the soul; it is also inspiration and enlightenment.

Saille uses her art, both sculpture and painting, to ground herself, to "keep me together." Art is a very sensate function. It has a tendency to keep an artist in the here-and-now while simultaneously allowing that same artist to get in touch with other dimensions of reality. It is as if one can be whole, if only for the moment. Saille also uses her art to explore the deeper, more transpersonal aspects of her nature.

Saille's story, as in Mari's, shows one that validation from one person can impact one for life. In Saille's case, it was her father who lived only until Saille's fifth birthday.

The Transpersonal Dimensions of Saille's Story

Saille's childhood trauma was both human and transpersonal. Her human trauma was incurred by the death of her father when she was five years old, her sexual attack, and constant moving from home to home with her mother.

The transpersonal aspects of her childhood trauma came with her NDE and dreaming. "I get satisfaction in attempting a dream. I had a near death experience when I was about five years old. I saw my father with an angel and then I wasn't afraid anymore."

Saille uses her art as therapy and as spiritual growth to heal dark, buried abuse from her childhood. She uses altered states of consciousness accessed through art and exercise as a means of releasing the pain. She recalls, "I was sexually attacked. I use exercise to enter an altered state of consciousness. If I don't exercise I go into compulsive behaviors."

Her pain from the abuse is strong, and she commented, "Sometimes I still feel touched by evil." She uses her art to transform these dark feelings. "Making something beautiful helps me feel good about myself and helps pull me out of this morass of self-hate."

Her feelings change as she uses art as therapy to heal her inner struggle. "Sometimes I am optimistic about recovering from my childhood, other times I'm very tired. I feel healed when I paint something that truly reflects my experience. Painting has developed me personally." She even connects with the earth through her art. "On good days I see my art as a physical conjunction and energy conductor needed by the planet for balance."

Saille sees her art as demanding, both a sacrifice in her life and a savior. "I have a hard time leaving my art for a secure teaching job. I need to be a full-time artist because my art suffers when I try to work at the same time."

Although she sees her art as demanding, she realizes her art may be the only way to heal from her childhood pain. She says, "I was a lonely, only child and I was sickly. I still talk to my guardian angel all the time." Saille's spiritual despair comes from buried abuse pain. She says: "It's hard for me to fathom the abuses of my childhood. I feel like I barely survived. I have a lot of resentment toward my mother. I feel like giving up and being taken off the planet. The struggle has been going on for so long."

Art as a self-chosen lifestyle creates a transpersonal nurturing atmosphere with little pressure for Saille. "Although my career provides me with no security base, I need to have things my own way. I need a supportive workplace and environment that supports my emotion." For Saille, art is a transpersonal healing, centering, life-affirming tool. "Doing art, I don't get sick. Doing my art I stay centered. I thought I'd die if I didn't get into my studio."

For Saille, art is a means of transpersonal communication with the world on her quest for self-actualization. "Art is my method of communicating to the world. It is wonderful to have your art support you financially. Inch by inch, I've learned to trust."

Saille's transpersonal search for healing has included her body. "When I decided not to have more children, I made a break with the church. I had to reclaim my body. I've been taking back my body ever since."

Saille uses her art as a transpersonal vision and an interaction with life. She says, "I want my work to have an interactive quality. If spontaneous change happens, I feel successful. There is often a destructive aspect to my work. My art sense is about how I look at the world."

Saille's art has both healing and spiritual aspects. Her paintings express her pain and process, and her sculpture assumes the role of a spiritual connector. She feels this parallel processing—a split, occurring. Although her art combines special talent and self-actualization, the distinction is blurred by her two modes of expression: painting and sculpture.

Defining Saille's Current Issues and Strengths

One of Saille's life themes seems to be the issue of *self-sufficiency.* This is a personal rather than a transpersonal theme. As a child, circumstances forced her to be self-sufficient; now, as an educated adult she chooses ("I've always opted for my art") to live "on the edge" and maintain that self-sufficiency. She recognizes what is essential in her life and says, "I've always had to create for myself an environment that supports me, not financially but emotionally." This self-sufficiency also shows up in her financial situation. "I've always worked, but for extras it's been the sculpture. I helped my children with insurance and emergency funds."

Another theme is that she, like Jean, has *always made things:* mud pies, snow forts, plaster objects, and even embroidery. Saille commented, "That's where my creativity went as a child."

While this theme has personal aspects such as the actual productivity she experiences, it also has transpersonal aspects. Her experience of creativity is that of nurturing and honoring her deepest self. The best way she could honor and heal herself was as an artist. When she draws on different forms like fire and earth, she is drawing on her inner self.

Another theme that runs through Saille's life is her life-long *love of spinning* and fiber. She remembers:

> In high school, I was intrigued by the staff and spindle which is in my painting of *Mater: Our Lady as a Schoolgirl.* Perhaps it was an early attraction to spinning and fiber work that was so much a part of my life with my mother. This fascination with fiber began when, as a wedding present, my aunt told me I could choose anything in the house. I chose my grandmother, Sarah McKenna's spinning wheel. It touched my life deeply. That was what inspired my life work and my soul quest back to Ireland. This wooden wheel has brought me full circle; ready to spiral into one more inner revolution.

This theme spans both personal and transpersonal realms. Perhaps spinning and weaving gives Saille the feeling of being close to her mother; perhaps it fills the role of mother for her to some small degree. I think it is noteworthy that she puts the results of her weaving out into the world for all to see. It is like a transpersonal connection to "motherhood."

In fact, weaving is a metaphor for the cosmic web of life; the Great Universal Mother continually weaves the web of life. Saille connects with her historical mother and grandmother and to tradition. At the same time, she is exploring the mother and future grandmother inside herself. When she goes deep enough, it is the universal mother who is directly related to the development of her personality and her style. She says, "I continue to create the weaving myself because it has the richness and heaviness I need to hold the pleated forms."

This *sense of continuity* and a desire for connection also runs through Saille's life. As a child she longed for the feeling of connection she never had.

Saille's artwork has given her the roots she did not get from her family and offers her a transpersonal connection to all mothers, grandmothers, and great-grandmothers. Her art not only helped to connect her to her mother in childhood; now, her art connects her to her ancestors and to tradition. Remembering her mother, Saille said, "Perhaps, I was able with my childhood creativity, to help her develop her own. She lived very much off my success, and I felt a great pressure to succeed." Art has been a stabilizing force in Saille's life, a form of balance and comfort.

Saille's Reaction to Participation in This Book

It felt good to be understood at that level. It gave me an opportunity to be heard about areas that I think are important.

I haven't done this much work for years in such a short period of time. [She refers to work motivated by the interview.] Most of it's been done since I got back from Ireland. Going into my studio makes life all worthwhile. It's been a difficult year but I feel really good about the artwork I've accomplished.

MIA'S STORY

I met Mia through the plastic surgeon who reconstructed her ear; she was born without one. She is single, living in Seattle, Washington, and is a very talented artist and musician. Mia was included in this study because she is a living example of how our attitudes shape our lives. As she was growing up she was taught to deal with what ever came her way, that nothing happened randomly, and that she should use the gifts God has given her toward her higher purpose. She has internalized this set of principles and lives them out in her story.

Mia was born in Arizona in 1965, the youngest of four children. She has had quite an eclectic childhood and lived in many cities across this United States before reaching adulthood. Her natural father is an ex-monk with musical talent, and her mother, also a talented artist, is a therapist. Mia works in watercolor, drawing, and with colored markers.

Mia had a dream the night before our interview. It struck me that her dream spoke to the experience many of the artists in this study are having as a result of doing their life review. It is presented here prior to her story. As Mia recalls: "I was speaking to an older woman who had a golden retriever. I painted it. Then it turned into a Polaroid. I was using some kind of technology that doesn't exist yet. I had to wear sunglasses to do it. With these sunglasses on, you could go walk around the work you did. I was fascinated with it because I painted one side of the dog that looked like the actual photo, but then you could walk around and see the other side of the dog too."

Why I included this dream is because many of the artists in this study have said they were able to get a fuller picture of their lives, a more global perspective, if you will, after reviewing their lives and their artwork. It touched me that in her dream, although she only painted one side of the dog, she was able to walk around and see all sides of it. This dream reminded me of our conscious minds. So many instances in our lives have greater meaning when we look at them from all sides.

As a child she drew a variety of animals including a *"Dragon"* and a *"Cow."* Close inspection of the dragon picture reveals a princess atop a tower to the left of the picture. Cooper (1978) notes: "if the dragon is a guardian, it symbolizes the winning of the treasure of inner or esoteric knowledge, or in rescuing the princess it releases pure forces kept in bondage by the powers of evil." Mia has developed into quite the intellect. Some of her interests lie in art, music, Vedic spiritualism, and mysticism. She tells her story:

I was born with birth defects of my ear and a partial facial paralysis. I also have 20 percent hearing in my right ear. It was due to my mother having Rubella. I'm the lucky one really. That is a serious disease to get when you are pregnant, and I could have been any number of things; dead, retarded or whatever. I actually feel lucky in an odd way. Of course, I'd rather be normal, but since I can't be; I notice that this handicap gives me some things other people don't have. One of them is the strength not to expect certain things of myself. I knew I couldn't hope to aspire to be certain things; so I didn't even try. In some weird way, I think I'm better off for that, because it's enabled me to just be myself.

School was hell for me, because my face is a little bit imbalanced. My jawline looks like it's not even. One of my eyes is a little weak, so it hangs open more than the other one. I sort of talk out of the side of my mouth. It is all immediately apparent. I do the exercises I was taught to do. I don't think the muscles are paralyzed, I just think they are incredibly weak.

I was the youngest of four kids. We are all artistically and musically inclined for no apparent reason. My parents are both talented, but haven't made a career of art or music. Dad played the guitar and mother is an artist. She always dabbled but never took it serious. She is especially good at line drawings and has a very distinctive style. I see a similarity between our work.

I've always believed that artistic ability was somehow inherited. I started drawing at age two. I was always encouraged to be myself and to follow my path. Both my parents were very spiritual and trusted in the universe. They believe that whatever happened it was meant to be that way, and you just had to integrate it into your life.

At age four we moved from our little nuclear family into a radical life-style in this commune type place in the hills of Rancho Santa Fe. We lived in a big old Spanish adobe place. There were peacocks running around. The rooms had waterfalls in them. It was crazy, interesting but crazy. This is the place where my parents found themselves, and decided to get divorced. My mother fell in love with somebody who ended up being my stepfather and raising me. My parents were divorced when I was five.

Earlier my father had been a Jesuit monk who went soul searching, and found himself wanting to be married. He was a very spiritual philosophical person. He has a Ph.D. in English. He's an expert in Chaucer and Spencer, and he speaks Latin. He's one of those intense academics. He had his own reading room at the Huntington library. The divorce hit him very hard. Subsequently, it hit me very hard. That really rocked my world and I didn't understand anything at that point. My whole world was turning into something that was chaotic. I kept drawing. My sister and I went with my mother and my older brother and sister went with my father. That was difficult for me. My family split in half.

In the midst of all of this confusion Mia was drawing *"Angels."* She feels she had and still has a guardian angel watching over her. This little childhood drawing is particularly interesting to me because in it she has drawn her angels in both sexes. The center angel has a beard and the two angels on the sides appear to be female.

My childhood was hard. There was a lot of unhappiness. It was horrible. We moved on an average of every three years, into radically different environments. I look back now, and see how I've benefited from things. I learned how to adapt. I remember a time I only identified with animals. I was very interested in animals and thought I'd be a veterinarian or a biologist or something.

I asked Mia: "When you say you identified with animals what do you mean?" She answered:

I really think I felt like an animal. I really did. When I was six or seven, I was really a disturbed child. I don't remember a lot about that age, but I do remember being unable to talk to people. I was angry at my mother and didn't talk to her for a year after we moved to Berkeley. I was impressionistic. I could have almost been autistic, but I don't think it was that extreme. I started to come out and be a kid when I was nearly eight. We moved to Northern California and continued to move every two or three years thereafter. My life was constantly changing—new schools and different people from a young age. I always felt like an outsider. I didn't think there was any hope of me feeling like I fit in anywhere.

I remember, I had trouble relating to my sisters' friends. I also recall that I had a pet dog who ended up being brutally run over by an A. C. transit bus, right in front of me. That threw me into a turmoil for a long time. It was my first experience with death. It was as gruesome as can be. I still remember all the songs that were playing on the radio at that time. It was really a trauma for me.

School made me feel strange. I was always made fun of. The kids in school were horrible; they were the most cruel people. I'm sure that had something to do with why I never wanted to draw people. Since I didn't look normal, I ended up feeling bad about myself and neglecting myself. I didn't want to look good or to deal with who I was, so I didn't brush my hair or pay attention to what I wore. I really made it worse.

Even though Mia says she didn't draw many people, at age nine, she did draw a *"Profile Of A Young Woman."* I found it extremely impressive for a nine-year-old's drawing. In fact, it reminds me of some of the famous Native American artists who work in Arizona and New Mexico. It seems that her mother greatly influenced her artwork.

> My mother had the experience that school art education was the worst thing possible for a child who was artistically inclined. I was lucky enough to have her protection. When I started going to school, she'd go to the art teachers and say, "You are not to tell my daughter what to do, just give her paper and pencils and let her do what she does." I'm very lucky. I'm grateful. I witnessed the horrible stuff art departments put on kids.

At a young age, I was unusually talented at drawing things. I felt strange and apart but I was comfortable with it. I drew incessantly. I drew animals, never people at that time. In first grade I had a teacher who gave us a project to draw a family. I drew dinosaur heads on everybody. The teacher was very disturbed by this and went to my mother. She said: "Mia should see a psychiatrist." My mother may still have that picture, she's collected a lot of my work. Obviously, my mother didn't take it seriously. The grace and elegance with which Mia draws horses is wonderful. I asked her about her drawing of *"A Group Of Horses,"* and wondered why she is so fascinated by horses. She said: "I've been wondering why I do horses all my life; I wish I knew why I am so intrigued by them. There is something about their size; it seems as if they shouldn't be that graceful. That interests me. I like the way they move. They have a sort of grace about them. I did that one when I was about 20."

Her painting of *"A Green Horse With A Pink Mane"* was a quick sketch, done on a card for her mother. When I asked her to comment on it, she said:

> I've done hundreds of those. I like to work with Renaissance colors of green and red. I love water colors. I like the way you can mix the colors and you can let them dry. They have a flowing kind of strength to them. I like them because they're watery. I painted a lot of them in high school. The *"Tigers"* were done a long time ago, when I was about 19. I loved

doing tigers and zebras; any animal that has strange markings on them. They interest me a lot.

It wasn't until I went to high school, that I had any stability in my life. I went away to boarding school. It got me away from the difficulties my parents were in. I ended up finding a place that encouraged my art. I did portraits and landscapes. It was easy to do portraits because I could draw. It felt like cheating because I wasn't painting; in my mind I was drawing with paint. Some came out OK.

At that time my step father was a substance abuser of every type. There were a lot of things that went awry. He's since quit everything, and we have a good relationship even though he lives on the other side of the country. For all intents and purposes he is really my father. He still takes care of me. He sends money when I need it. We did endure a lot of hellish tribulations. I was lucky they understood I needed to get away from home.

I really enjoy color but paint frustrates me. I ended up using design markers. Architects use them. They are expensive but beautiful. What I like about them is that they saturate the paper so if you put them in a window they look like stained glass. I did one art show that was entirely mine in high school.

I've done pictures with color markers that are all from high school. They are directly out of my head. I love the colors of those markers. When I drew one I call *"Doodle,"* I was trying to use as many different colors as I could. I'd just start drawing and adding ideas as they came to me. I don't study things and then try to draw them. I'd be on the phone; half of my mind would be thinking about something else, and I'd just start doodling. The markers were expensive, so when I left high school I didn't have them and didn't use them anymore. My *"Swordfish"* is a spray paint thing. I did it when I was 20 or 21. Or it could have been in high school because in my last year of high school I got really into this spray paint thing.

What you do is draw something on a poster board then cut it out with an exacta knife, then you put it on a paper and spray paint over it with a few different colors. I did a bunch of those; in fact I did a bunch of post cards and sold them in front of the Met when I lived in New York. I sold a lot of those. My sister used to know a graffiti artist, who's pretty well known. Actually his name is "Futura 2000." He was an amazing guy who used to live with us down in the village. He taught me the technique. It was the way you hold the nozzle to get the drips that made it come out like that.

The school I went to was a place where unconventionality was OK. I guess by private school standards it was a hippie boarding school—a very cool place. I was able to do art two or three times a week, for three hour stretches at time. In my spare time I was able to go to a shed in the woods where they had a piano. I got really into that and would spend seven or eight hours up there. I just lost track of the time and did music. That is where I started to paint. I used oils and acrylic. It was pretty frustrating to paint. I was a drawing person. Painting is three-dimensional and I had to deal with light and shapes in ways I never really thought of. It frustrated me a lot. I gave all my paintings away. I do have slides though.

I never painted after high school. In college I was determined not to be called an artist. I wanted to break away from that identity. I wanted to know I could do something else. Maybe fit in. Now, looking back on it, I see how futile that was. Ultimately, I spent two years searching for subjects that interested me. My grades were good and it felt like I had some control over the intellectual side of myself. That experience culminated in Oxford for a year. I did that to prove I could do it, that I wasn't missing out on anything. I had a really difficult time. I spent a year in solitary confinement, isolated and strange, but it was rewarding at the end, because they reacted well to me. I was surprised to see how well they liked my ideas. They actually ended up asking me back. I'd done what I set out to do so I didn't go back.

I had my ear operated on when I was 22, in the middle of college. I'd get an operation, then a year would pass and I'd get the next in the series. With regard to my art, I've been obsessed with a variety of animals all my life. At age two, I was bitten by a dog and had stitches in my head. I drew dogs for a long time. I've loved to draw horses all my life for a reason I can't express. For a while it was wolves. I like the way they run in packs. Dolphins interest me a lot. At one time I studied oceanography. I love water—being in it. I could swim all day long. I became interested in cetaceans, [whales and dolphins] and how they communicate, and I am impressed by their intelligence.

Once a psychic told me I slowed my heart down so I could talk to the dolphins. What is so weird about that is she's probably right. I went to swim with the dolphins out on Cape Cod. There was a dolphin there who was rescued as a baby and couldn't be reintroduced to the wild. I got into the water and they said: "When you first go in he'll wait at the end of the tank until you stop being so excited. They can literally hear the blood coursing through your veins." It was really fascinating to me.

I went to a little private college in Bronxville, New York, called the Sarah Lawrence College. It's funny that I went there and studied philosophy and art history, because it's an arty and unconventional school. There were lots of openly gay people there. It was well known for its writing program. Interesting people, who taught there, were Alice Walker, Grace Pay, and Joseph Campbell.

What I learned was how to articulate, write, and argue. Some of my teachers were great. In fact, throughout my life, there has always been someone who has encouraged and protected me. I have been lucky in a lot of ways. All the time I was a young kid, I saw other girls trying to be pretty. I couldn't even compete. My handicap has been my advantage. I felt like a dog in school. It enabled me to hold onto my uniqueness in other ways.

I've known nothing but struggle and poverty since becoming an artist. It's unfortunate the way society has chosen to look at art, as an oddity. The fact is, everyone is an artist in some respect. If they don't pay attention to that it is a poverty of the soul that they have to endure. It's a horrible thing. I think we all pay for that in a lot of ways.

I came to the point, at about age 25, where I drove myself crazy trying to be acceptable, trying to fit in, and get a career together. I just couldn't do it. I finally gave in to myself and said if I have to live in a corrugated shack by the highway, I'm gonna do it. The moment I could say that to myself, this peace came over me. I realized how I'd been pushed into a corner.

Mia's words remind me of Bachold's and Werner's (1973) list of characteristics found in creative people: temperamentally independent, accustomed to going their own way, and independently making and implementing decisions. Mia continues:

I never thought I could do music because I felt I'd have to become a rock star if I wanted to make any money. That thinking kept me from a side of myself that's very strong. There was an issue about music for me, because when I was born the doctor told my mother the one thing I could probably never do was to have a career in music because of my ear. The operations I've had fixed the look of the ear, but not the hearing. I don't know what it's like to hear in stereo, for instance. I have an unusual way of hearing. I think it helps me sing. I can hear my voice clearly. I can stay in pitch easily.

The biggest problem with getting a music career going isn't about hearing or producing. It is dealing with the music industry. It is, without a doubt, second only to the illegal drug industry in the sleaze factor. It's basically run by the mob. That has been true since the 1950s. It's not like I have had to deal with the mob or anything like that, but I've had to deal with a lot of dishonesty, deceit, and greed.

I've had a lot of jobs because I've tried to live unconventionally and have some time that was my own. Most of my jobs have been situations where people have power over me. Unusual amounts of power, because they know I'm in a hard spot. This is what the music industry really capitalizes on. It has been interesting for me. I go back and forth as to whether I want to get too involved with it or not.

I've studied art history, lived in California and New York City, and saw the art market and the art world very clearly. That world has nothing whatsoever to do with art. The way it creates a market out of certain things is that it creates a certain standard by which you're supposed to judge your own creativity. I'm really repulsed by that. I think it had a lot to do with why I didn't pursue art. I was trying to think how I could turn something I like into a career. I always thought if I could make money doing something I like, then I could get my art across in my own time and in my own way. I also had faith. Trying to do it in a desperate way would never work for me. So I gave it up.

Now I'm in a lot of transition. I've been struggling with the music industry recently. Being in clubs, making records, fighting with men. Recently, I was in a band that was very promising. In our band we put together a group of people from different cultures and sexes. It didn't work out. The guys couldn't handle it. They just had to have control. We women weren't about to let that happen so it fell apart. I know they idealistically really wanted it to happen, but they just couldn't live that out in everyday life.

A lot of people thought we would hit it big. We had internal struggles. One of our members left with our master copies of recordings we've made. So, I've been mulling over why that happened. It was incredible. The person who took the tapes is a person who had nothing to do with writing the music. He's off in New York with our master copies, and I'm saying to myself, "That's amazing, what does he think he's going to do?" Just thinking about what just fell apart, and realizing that as a creative person you're at the mercy of other people, is frustrating.

I see now that the band never could have worked. It fell apart literally weeks before we hit the radio. If we had hit the radio the person who left would be famous right now. So, in a way, I'm glad it happened the way it did. I know I'll never have that problem again. Learning the hard way is a privilege if you can handle it. I did a *"Self-Portrait"* that reminds me of the work of Egon Schiele, an Austrian artist. He is very interesting to me as a drawer. His work reminded me a lot of my mother's drawings. He draws these intense portraits of people. The hand on my picture is very "Schiele."

I asked Mia if she had a life purpose. She said:

This sounds weird, but I saw a psychic who told me that I was in fact a healer. She said that I was born with some kind of difficulty, and there is a reason for that. She went on to say that I would help people in a way that I don't understand right now. I knew what she was talking about. And I knew, "Yes, it's been hard, but I've always been making some sort of progress that has not always been immediately clear." I know I am going in an unusual path, but I don't know where it is taking me.

I've always wanted to do music and feel I can give something to people. I was told once by a psychic that people aren't going to understand the music I do right away. I don't know what that means but I know that music is a healing thing for me. I hope that one day I can use it to heal other people.

I asked Mia if she had heard of vibrational healing. She said:

I know dolphins do that. I know we're on the cusp of understanding something very integral to the earth in a way we haven't understood before, and I think it has to do with sound and magnetic fields. Dolphins and whales need the magnetic anomalies in the earth to go places. They hear through the bones in their lower jaw. It conducts sound waves. Their whole lower jaw is like an ear for them. Some can hear a distance of 500 miles. It can't be an accident that my struggle has to do with sound and I've been so musically inclined.

I never really felt like I fit in, and I never really thought people would find me attractive. I'm over that. I've had many boyfriends, but they haven't been the focus of my life. On some level, I'm used to being lonely, and can derive something from that. There is a kind of freedom in it. I'm only now starting to feel that I could settle down with somebody. In the past, I've been head strong and independent. I'm not easy to get along with. I know what I want to do.

I asked Mia if she was more creative when she is well or ill. Her answer was:

I'm creative in response to pain. When I'm going through pain I can't do a damn thing. But it's right after it that my mind starts to process what just happened. I get creative. There is an aspect of sexual energy in creative energy. Music is sex in a way. It's exploring a kind of sexual aspect. It is another world four-dimensional. Sexual energy is communicative energy—trading energy. You are interacting. Like voodoo; you are using the body as a conduit for the spiritual aspect that is universal. This is what music and art is to me. I never felt my talent was mine; it's something that comes through me. Ultimately, there is an aspect of Vedum Religion that points to that. I don't think it's evil—it's spiritual.

Over the years, I think all the events in my life have been purposeful. I don't look at good and bad anymore. I suffer in relation to things, but I don't work them out in a historical, linear way. I've had some low times. When I was 13, my mother went away from my stepfather. We lived on Roosevelt Island and I had a hard time fitting in with other kids. I was an excellent student of science, and had a hard time because I became the teachers pet. I, once again, alienated myself from my peers. I had a lot of difficulty that year and thought about killing myself. Things looked so bad, for so long. I went through childhood making friends, then losing them. We were always moving around and I was constantly being put in challenging situations. I never tried to commit suicide, but I remember standing at my window looking out, and thinking about jumping out of that window.

I get depressed. I don't want to do anything. Recently, I've been very depressed because of what just happened with the band. It was very emotional. A lot of different people were involved. I got pretty close to where I was at 13. I never thought I'd get back there again, but I did. This time I had the ability to look at it in an objective way. I said "Wow," look at this.

I have my dark side. I think once you know that kind of sadness it will never go away. My music is incredibly depressing. Joannie Mitchell tapped into it in her music and I think it's the same for me. I don't want to make sad music. It's part of me that's there, and I only see that part when I do music.

I feel like I know myself better as a result of my paintings. I feel that when I paint, and look at the work, I see a part of myself that I'm not aware of otherwise. There is a certain style. I'm always surprised to see how distinctive it can be. Art is automatic for me. I try to use my intuition in every aspect of my life. Sometimes it is difficult to do that. By the nature of the society, I feel encouraged to intellectualize everything, and that is when intuition doesn't work. As soon as it gets into my head, it becomes an afterthought. Learning how to play music has been a way of getting back to that. I use my mind merely as a conduit to articulate what I feel. Language can't do that but music and art can.

When I get together with a musician who has a similar musical background as I do, it's like getting together with someone who has studied all the same things as you in college, or had the same kind of childhood. You can fly into deeper aspects of topics and things.

I asked Mia if she has had any UFO experiences. Her comment was:

Odd you should ask that. I went to a psychic when the band fell apart because I wanted to hear whether I should stick it out or move on. The first thing she said was, "You are not from this world. I do not know if you believe in it, but you're the only person I've ever seen who is from the Pleiadies." It was really odd for me to hear. She said she sees angels around me. I didn't take it too seriously, but I did go to the occult book shop because I'd never heard of the Pleiadies and I was curious about angels. Sometimes I feel like I have a guardian angel. I'd say I am spiritual.

I picked up a book and opened the page and saw a quote from a man I used to work for. He'd written a book about UFO's. It was a quote about somebody who had contacted someone from the Pleiadies. I thought that was also very odd. The timing was weird, and I knew the man. It's funny you asked me that. When I knew this man he had told me that he had just written the book and told me to pick up a copy. I never did. Gary Kinder was his name.

Next I asked Mia about near death experiences. She said:

Yes, I had one. It was related to one of my ear operations. I was operated on to have the cartilage taken out of my rib cage. The bone is used to sculpt part of the ear. It was very painful. I had a hard time breathing. I left the hospital and was sitting in front of the fire. I stood up and got half way to bed, when I fainted. I fell flat on my face. When I came to, I had the distinct feeling that I didn't know who or where I was. I didn't even know what planet I was on. I opened my eyes and they fell upon a piece of lead piping that was in a wall. I was trying to figure out what the hell it was and where I was. I remember a feeling of calm. Everything was OK. I had an unusual feeling of calm. As I started to come to, I said to myself, "I have to hold onto this feeling and remember it." Something just said, "It's OK, everything is fine." That experience never left my life. I never tried to attribute anything to it, but I will never forget the feeling.

As I evolve consciously, my art evolves. It doesn't always manifest itself in a big change because sometimes life only changes circumstantially. The content of my art changes with traumatic changes. For instance, when I was bitten by the dog, I drew dogs for a long time. It was an emotional release. My paintings are intuitive, they come out of my head. I have to turn off my eyes and just use outgoing tools rather than incoming tools. When I carry it off in a good piece of work it feels good, if not, I get frustrated. Then I work more on it as if it's an obsession. It's a need to get out what's in your head. Get it out, and do it right. I know I've cultivated this. It's the compulsion and the need to cultivate it. When I think about it I have a "Whoa" reaction.

Art set me apart and made me who I am. Anything you have in common with other people draws you together. I think artists are like that. If I see another artist whose work I really like it's a deep heavy thing. Art shapes my relationships.

I asked Mia about dream material showing up in her art. She said:

Rather than dreams showing up in my art, my art shows up in my dreams. I dream about doing art. I think dreams are the first expression of the way you are steering your life and if you listen to them they can teach you about the direction you are heading. One dream that stands out for me, is the one I had while staying with my mother and a friend for a short time in New York. It took place while I was in college.

In the dream there was a party going on in my mothers apartment. I could look out the window and see the city lights. In the dream the apartment window was much higher than in real life. I went into my closet to try on shoes. There were all these different types of shoes. None of them fit. My sister came in and told me that there was a party in New Jersey. I said, "Yea!" We get into a car with friends and went to New Jersey. We're in a little suburb somewhere and it is daytime. The sun had come out. There is a little house with an oak tree in front of it. We walk in and as soon as you open the door there is this massive place. It's a huge building with elevators and stuff. It's a crazy place. Drinks are being served, there are masses of people, jugglers, etc. It was dark. I immediately stood off. I was walking around and someone was following me when I looked behind me. It was a man with crazy hair and an eye in the middle of his forehead. He had three eyes. He looked crazy like a freak. He followed me. I was freaking out so I go to the elevator thinking maybe I can lose him in there. I get in with all the people. Everybody gets off, and I end up alone, and he's there. He disappears into the corner and comes back again. He dips into the fourth dimension and comes out again. That's odd. I get off and go into a room. There's a peaceful low hum. Against the wall is a rice paper shrine with three soap stone figures at the bottom of it. I have no idea what it is. I just feel like getting down on my knees and praying, so I do. All the while the third eye man is in the corner disappearing and reappearing. I get down and pray about my life. I don't understand it. I start to levitate and I hear a voice saying, "You can do whatever you want to do." It was a voice that wasn't mine. It was heavy. I was frightened and awed at the same time.

This dream sounds like it has a spiritual message for Mia. I asked her what she thought it meant but she didn't know. I asked her if she lived with either emotional or physical pain. She said:

I live with emotional pain. It's a sadness. Seeing pain in others and seeing how the world could be and the way that it is disappoints me. I'm very idealistic and I know the price for that is constant disappointment and pain. I never felt like being any different; I don't think I could. Through all that, I feel like I'm an optimist. Just seeing how my own suffering has brought about revelations for me, I can't help thinking it's true for everyone else. Life is a process in the path of the soul. I believe in reincarnation and life isn't just a useless struggle. My life has been full of change. When it all ends up people are looking at me for some kind of an answer. I don't think I have it yet.

This Author's Initial Reaction to Mia's Story

My first impression was that she was certainly articulate. This young woman has had such a variety of lifestyle changes in such a short time that I wonder what her life purpose is.

It appears to me that she is being led forward with each change. Mia's life impressed me as having a clear direction. Certain doors open at just the right time, and others close when they would have been too much of a distraction for her.

Mia is aware of the role that art plays in her life. "All the time I was a young kid, I saw other girls trying to be pretty. I couldn't even compete. It [handicap] enabled me to hold onto my uniqueness in other ways." With regard to the role art has played in her health she says, "I am creative in response to pain. Not during, but afterward, I get creative."

She is intuitive about her art.

> Art is automatic for me. . . . As I evolve consciously, my art evolves. . . . The content of it changes with traumatic changes in my life. For instance, when I was bitten by the dog, I painted dogs. It was an emotional release. My paintings are intuitive, they come out of my head. I have to turn off my eyes and just use outgoing tools rather than incoming tools. When I carry off a good piece of work it feels good. If not, I get frustrated. Then I work more on it as if it's an obsession. It's a need to get out what's in your head. Get it out and do it right.

Art is both an old friend to Mia and something she devalues. She has wanted to try something new, something else to expand her horizons. "I wanted to break away from that identity. I wanted to know I could do something else." However, when she surrendered to her artistic life, she felt at peace. She has sent little notes with wonderful drawings on them to me. The self-portrait included in this study is one of them. Art has given her part of her identity, as has her musical ability. She admits: "I feel that when I paint, and look at the work, I see a part of myself that I'm not aware of otherwise. I'm always surprised to see how distinctive it can be. . . . Art set me apart and made me who I am. My suffering has brought about revelations for me. Life is a process in the path of the soul. I believe in reincarnation, and life isn't just a useless struggle."

In Mia's story I observed how much she resembled her mother: this observation led me to see how much I resemble my mother.

The Transpersonal Dimensions in Mia's Story

Mia has reached transpersonal authenticity in the face of birth trauma. She says, "I'd rather be normal, but since I can't be, I've noticed that this handicap gives me some things other people don't have." Mia maintains inner balance through her art in the midst of outer chaos. "My world turned chaotic. I kept drawing. My family split in half. I drew angels."

She has a dark body image—a shadow fascination with animal bodies—a strange and apart self-feeling. "I identified with animals; I felt like one. I felt bad about myself. I didn't brush my hair or care what I wore." Her contradictory feelings about her physical handicap and wanting acceptance versus being oneself transform into inner peace.

She has a transpersonal vision of creative energy as sexual, life force healing energy. "There's an aspect of sexual energy in creative energy. Music is sex, in a way. Sexual energy is trading energy—you interact. Like voodoo, you use your body as a conduit for the spiritual aspect." She accesses alternate states of consciousness through both her art and her music. Both allow her to know different parts of herself.

For Mia, the darkness and light in creative tension move into art and music as she contacts the transpersonal with deep self-feeling. "I have my dark side. My music is terribly depressing. It's a part of me that I only see when I do music. Art and music are conduits to how I feel."

Mia has experienced soul growth which begins in suffering and evolves into insight but still has an element of continued uncertainty. She says, "Just seeing how my own suffering has brought about revelations. I can't help thinking it's true for everyone else."

Mia does not appear to use her art as either a coping mechanism or healing tool. For her, art is a natural part of who she is. Through her art, she experiences the connection she feels with animals. Her painful childhood experiences of "feeling like a dog" have evolved in her work; also, her animal symbolism has evolved as she has matured. I am interested that her body-as-animal theme continues to find expression through her work and has evolved into "beautiful animals with strange markings," which reflect Mia, the beautiful, young woman with strange facial markings.

Defining Mia's Current Issues and Strengths

Faith is a constant theme. Mia learned from her parents' transpersonal attitudes that everything has a reason: there are no accidents, and everything will unfold in its own time. Throughout her story one senses that in the face of severe trauma, Mia has found an inner sense of self. "Whatever happens is meant to be."

The main theme in Mia's story is her wonderful ability to *reframe her life events.* Mia was born with facial defects and no external right ear; her hearing in that ear is 20 percent. "I'm the lucky one really. I could have been any number of things—dead, retarded, or whatever." She notices that her handicap gives her things that many other people do not have such as "the strength not to expect certain things of myself." She has an incredibly positive outlook. "I don't think my muscles are paralyzed; I just think they are incredibly weak." She seems to tune into the higher aspects of her sufferings.

Mia is deeply *connected to her spiritual side.* Her reverence for all life comes to the fore in her relationship to animals, another of Mia's story's themes. Mia is most fascinated by horses. "There is something about their size. It seems they shouldn't be that graceful." Her fascination with horses, their grace, and rhythm reminded me of Mia herself and of Cooper's (1992) words: "In general the horse represents dynamic power, fleetness, wisdom and the intellect as well as the instinctive animal powers. It is also a prophetic animal, with psychic and magic abilities. The horse signifies the higher aspects of humanness."

Those words describe Mia. She is intelligent, wise, independent, powerful, and magical with her music and her art. It is as if as Mia's self-authenticity and self-esteem grew, the animals she related to changed into those which symbolize her own higher aspects.

Mia's life has a theme of *"not fitting in."* Between her facial disfigurement and the continual feeling of being an outsider, she never felt like she belonged anywhere. Once she even alienated the other kids by "being the teacher's pet." Mia feels that this issue of "fitting in" was never resolved. Even her art set her apart. "In college I was determined not to be called an artist. I wanted to know I could do something else. Maybe fit in. Now, looking back on it, I see how futile that was."

Another theme that runs through Mia's life is that of the *pioneer.* She lives an eclectic lifestyle and is willing to sacrifice the comforts of life for her dreams. "If I have to live in a corrugated shack by the highway, I'm gonna do it."

Her independence extends toward relationships as well. "I've had a lot of boyfriends but they haven't been the focus of my life. I'm used to being lonely. I derive something from that. There's a freedom in it. I know what I want. I'm headstrong and independent."

Mia's Reaction to Participation in This Book

I thought when you called me it was very funny because I always thought somehow that people would be interviewing me. But I didn't know how. I always thought it would be about music or something. When you called I thought, "Well this is one I never thought of." I thought it was interesting you found my story worthwhile and interesting. I always felt like people wouldn't understand it, wouldn't really get it. Not in a superior way, just in a way that I've gone through experiences people can't understand. Part of that may be a reflection of me being discounted because I'm not part of the status quo. I discount myself. I just felt real out of place in a way. It's amazing, it's a great thing you did. I know it gave me something to look at in how I relate to other people and how they look upon me.

HELEN'S STORY

Helen's story illustrates that even when the artist is severely depressed, artistic expression may facilitate the mobilization of healing influences from the deepest parts of a person's essence. The art has a way of touching that part of a person that remains "whole" in the face of life experiences that seem to fragment the personality.

Helen does beautiful collage work and has worked out some of her personal processing through her art. She was born in 1950, in Portland, Oregon, to parents who both had successful careers. She is an only child and grew up being raised mostly by different housekeepers. Her father was Jewish and her mother Christian. She was raised in the Jewish faith, and it was assumed she would take on that faith, but in adulthood she married a very religious man and became a Presbyterian.

She was not ill as a child but often feigned illness to get attention. She remembers being fat as a child and being screamed at and put on diets. She said: "My parents were not around a lot." When she was old enough they dropped her at preschool and went on to work.

In Helen's words:

My mother was a model and owned a modeling agency. My father was the advertising director for "White Stag" and was very conscious of the fashion world. I grew up wearing everything my mother wore. I remember them going to parties and I always felt like I was left behind. My parents were very protective of me and I went to private elementary school.

My mother was beautiful and when we went downtown everybody knew her. In preadolescence I was kind of chubby. My mother immediately thought I was going to be fat and when I was 10 or 11 she gave me diet pills. That is how it all began. My father was always putting me on diets. I remember one time in junior high he said: "You have to lose three pounds this week or you can't go to the dance." I wanted to please him. I was constantly trying to lose weight but some inner part of me was circumventing my efforts and I would steal food. Once I took the car out and went and bought cookies. They punished me, not for taking the car out, but for buying the cookies. It's interesting to reflect on this now. I never even knew what an eating disorder was until I was in my thirties.

When I was young I started to purge. It was an automatic response. I was in boarding school and I knew that I had to go home on the weekends so I'd eat all week, and then Thursday night, I'd purge and take laxatives. I had no idea what I was doing to myself. Somehow I figured out that this was how to do it. By the time I was 15, I was in the routine of taking pills and purging. I didn't measure up to my mother.

Dad bought his own company. He was building it up so he was never at home. Years later, I found out that he had affairs during that time. I really don't know about my mother. Whenever he was home I'd be sitting somewhere and he'd say: "Go get me that paper." He was really hard on me. I never ran away. My rebellion came out in food. I was scared of him. I wasn't as gorgeous as my mother. When I went off to college I was 20 pounds overweight. I wasn't really fat because I am tall. When I came home for Christmas, I'd starve myself so I'd look better when I got home. That cycle repeated itself until five years ago.

Helen is not fat, but she has a difficult time seeing herself the way most people see her: a lean, tall, beautiful woman. All her life she has had recurrent dreams of not being able to find her way out. This drama plays itself out in many settings such as houses, boats and mazes. She recalls her mother overstepping Helen's boundaries:

In college my mother opened a letter I left in the trash. In it I talked about marijuana and she reported it to my father. They thought I was really on drugs. He flew down to Whittier college and took me out to dinner. He confronted me. He said: "We're really worried about you." They found a psychiatrist for me in Los Angeles. I drove there once a week and I think it was a joke for him. During the time I saw him other issues came up. I was naive. I had been in this eating disorder cycle.

I got out of college and worked in the legislature in Oregon for 6 years. In college I majored in art. When I graduated I did this reverse. I moved back home and was in politics all of a sudden. I worked for Governor McCall until he went out of office. They were great jobs but nothing creative. A new psychiatrist realized I was depressed. That is when I realized there were problems. He gave me medications that were totally inappropriate. It got me on the track that something was not right.

The more I reflected on those years I realized what my parents had done to me. In college I remember I called home and my father didn't want to talk to me because he was watching a television show. That seemed wrong to me. I started doing therapy but also at the same time I was in my twenties and I started to starve myself. I became anorexic but not to the extent that I needed hospitalization. And I suddenly realized men were attracted to me because I was thin. I looked different. It was easy to equate being thin with being liked. I got caught up in that. My parents said: "You look so gorgeous," and all of a sudden I was wonderful because I was thin.

Helen notes that anger has been a catalyst for her painting in the past, and it has evolved lately into a need to find serenity and tranquillity. Her mind would be flooded with information and she'd get angry and need time to process the information. Helen reflects on her depression:

Now, after being in therapy, I think my depression is inherited from my father. Someone in his family even committed suicide. I tried suicide many, many times. I had a real thing about razor blades. When I get depressed nothing seems to matter.

I spent my twenties partying, being thin, not eating during the day and purging at night. When I worked in the legislature I had a relationship with a man 20 years older than me for about four years. I remember realizing I was replacing my father but I kept doing it. The man had children in high school that he was devoted to. I wanted to marry him. I was seeing John, too, and when he showed interest I had good enough sense to back off from the older man. That would have been miserable for me.

I couldn't purge anymore after I got married, because it was a secret, but I did sneak food. I didn't want him to see me eating. For years and years, I wouldn't eat anything major when he was there. I was getting heavier. Finally I got depressed. I was working at a job I didn't like. I'd be up all night worrying about the job. I thought of suicide a lot. I wrote poems about death and thought of suicide. I took a lot of aspirin but it just made me sick. I'd be on the floor crying; I'd be curled up; the whole thing. I was becoming more and more depressed.

John contacted a county program. He went and found a therapist. We went there together for awhile. He was a Jungian, probably not the best choice. I went to him for years. When we were about to move to California, he said: "I think you needed medication and I should have caught it." My present doctor caught it. I always knew I had a problem with depression. I just talked and talked with the Jungian. He was into confronting. I confronted my mother. I told her I thought she'd been married before. She said no. I always felt like this cousin of mine could be her daughter. She and my mother had a really interesting relationship. I wanted her to tell me the truth. Finally, she said her first husband went crazy in the war and that was why she had to divorce him. I didn't accept her answer. A lot was stirred up by the therapist.

I found letters my father had written to me in college by dictating them to his secretary on his Dictaphone. She typed them and he signed them. Which meant that she knew what they were all about. It felt like a violation of my privacy because they were about being thin and how much he would pay me to get thin and how I needed to manage my checkbook better. I found copies of all these letters and they hurt a lot. I became angry at him but couldn't confront him. I could talk to my mother so I did. She said he didn't mean to do it. It all came back to me in these letters. All the feelings of not being good enough, of having strings attached to everything I did. I burned them. I was burning things until three years ago.

I go to a great therapist now. I can't remember how it came up but I have a piano. I went to the piano bench and found the piece of music called *Yellow Butterflies* that I played when I was eight. I played that piece at a recital and I screwed up when I had my fingers in the wrong place on the keyboard. The whole song was off key. My mother and father were embarrassed. I'll never forget what they said. They told me, "You were fine, but so and so was the best." I came home from therapy and found the sheet music to *Yellow Butterflies* and burned it up. My husband was supportive when I burned the letters.

My parents were interested in the arts. They took me to museums at a young age. I had art history in school. They always encouraged me. They set me up to do my paintings. There were always strings attached, though, and I couldn't mess the floor, and I had to wear five aprons, but they always encouraged me. I think they encouraged me because I couldn't do anything else. They always wanted me to do something, anything, well. They wanted me to play the piano well; swim well; ride horseback well; I did them all mediocre. I really didn't have any passion for any of it. They saw I had more enthusiasm for the art. My mother is creative. She does water colors but believes she's really not very good at it. What creativity I have is from her. Even now when I finish a painting I feel exhilarated and then exhausted.

I'd take classes at the art museum in town. There was no question when I got to college that I would take art classes. Earlier in my life I had an interest in drama, too, but by the time I got to college I couldn't dream of doing that. I took journalism, too, and almost majored in journalism. I took art because there was a teacher who became my mentor. I have a degree in art but never did anything with it. I did Christmas cards and little projects but never much. I did a few things in Portland but nothing to speak of. I don't want to shine because that's what my parents always wanted.

When John and I got married I did not get pregnant because I thought I would get fat. That wasn't the real reason. I know my mother really wanted grandchildren. My godmother would say, "Your mother's really waiting for grandchildren." I remember having these fantasies. I'd picture myself seeing my father and being fat. We tried for a couple of years to have kids. I couldn't get pregnant and I was taking my temperature. I was 35. We had friends who adopted a Korean child. Suddenly it was the right thing for us. John was all for it. Usually men have trouble with adoption. I snapped onto that. It was my way out, a relief. I think deep inside I wanted to try the mother thing out. I latched right onto it. It was a wonderful experience. We have a wonderful little Korean girl.

My father didn't want to see her. He wouldn't come. My mom came to see her and left with pictures and stories. She got my father to come. It was difficult for him to look at that Korean face and to see her as one of his descendants.

I feel like I've been through so much therapy. John and I are going to therapy together now because he hasn't worked in two years. He has always wanted to go to seminary and the church we belong to said they would pay his tuition. He has a few options now and soon we may know which direction he will be going in. We've been focusing on ourselves as a couple.

I came down here to California. I did the house, got a part time job at a cooking school. When we adopted Amelia, I quit. I got progressively more depressed until I was scraping the bottom. I was suicidal. I tried to slit .my wrists, calling for help all over the place. They put me on anti-depressants. I was a mess. I think a catalyst for my artwork was when I got so depressed in 1990, that I went to Turner hospital. I was an inpatient for two weeks and an outpatient for two weeks. That is where my art got started. The art therapy was a kind of release. I could do it and no one cared what it looked like. I said, "I can do this." I didn't give a shit what it looked like. It was a turning point. As my paintings got larger I felt my confidence growing. I remember I was going to go back and look at it but I haven't had time. I talked to this person who had her doctorate and she said I need to get my anger out. She said you can't really heal until you can really feel your emotions. I kept going over and over that in my mind. The very first thing I did was some word pieces that said, *"You Have To Feel Before You Can Heal."* I did these collage pieces, I stamped out letters and pressed them on. I did about a dozen of them with words. One of them is called *"Survivor;"* they are very telling. Another is called, *"Out Of Control."* One I call *"Fish,"* it's symbolic. One of the pieces talks about *"Serenity."* One entitled *"Don't Stuff It"* is on a shopping bag.

For me it was important that I was going to do my artwork. It was my therapy and what I was going to give myself. For me it was building the self-confidence to do it. I didn't know I could do it. A month later I applied to the Festival of Arts and the Sawdust Festival. I made the first cut and had to take in my stuff. I was so nervous, it was incredible. I laugh now, but it was serious then. I got accepted in the festival. All along I had a mentor, a woman who also suffered from depression. She owned a picture framing business. She became the one who helped me all along. I was so glad to have her. She recently said to me, "Helen, you don't need me anymore." Maybe I can give something back to her now.

I have to tell you for so many years John helped me. We kept my depression a secret. When I was depressed he'd say I had the flu. Finally, I was strong enough to say I had depression and it wasn't a secret anymore. I feel that in this last two years I'm helping him. I'm doing it; it's an opportunity. It's kind of nice. I will be fine when I get over this depression thing. I feel like my hesitation in talking to you was that I was calm and I was very hesitant to trigger things. I'm glad I did because now I feel like I'm getting the big picture, a more expansive view of my life.

My art studio is my place of safety. When I'm away too long I have to go there. During one episode of releasing anger, I put lots of red paper down, one on top of the other, and let my anger out at my dad. I didn't go back to the studio for quite some time. That was hard to do.

I am trying to get more in touch with compassion. When you get that compassion, it's a whole incredible thing. I remember when I first got a feeling of it. It was wonderful. I hungered for more of that. When I first was going through that anger stuff, I got really involved in the church. I was a church Deacon. I visited people in the hospital and talked to them. I liked to be with them and talk to them. That is how I got a touch of compassion. It felt great to give something back. I started taking Prozac five years ago. I had a terrible sleep problem. I would wake at 3:00 in the morning and couldn't get back to sleep until 5:00 a.m. The depression was dragging me down, getting me more depressed. I got to the point I was so tired I was feeling numb. I remember liking Prozac. I was addicted to it. I thought to myself, "I like this." The thought of being addicted unnerved me. I saw my psychiatrist. He gave me Xanax to make me sleep. Then I switched to Lithium with a different psychiatrist. I had a lot of anger that came up in huge bursts. I took lithium with other drugs for two years. It really helped me. I got leveled out. About a year ago I was really depressed and decided I wanted to get off the Lithium because I gained 20 pounds. I weaned myself off of the Lithium but I kept taking antidepressants. I kept the 20 pounds on. I know the weight is there but it's not affecting my life. My parents were here at Christmas but they didn't say anything. I confronted them with my eating disorder, diet pills and all that. They were very upset. They didn't realize what they were doing giving me those pills at such a young age. They didn't remember giving me diet pills at age 11. I confronted them with all that. My father wanted to talk about it a bit. He said, "We think you're great and you've done all these wonderful things," but I have trouble believing it. Whether he believes it or not, that I am great, I believe I really excel in my art.

Last summer during the festival my mother came down to see the show. My father refused to come. It was a really big deal to me. He gave me excuses. I was really hurt. When mom went home she said to him, "You should have come." He called and said, "Your mother said you have a real flair, I should have come. I think I should come down for the day and see what you've been doing." I said, "No." I set my boundaries. I was hedging at first. I said, "You can see it next summer." I just didn't want him.

I have to tell you there are times I still want his approval. If I am in an art show, I think, "Maybe they're going to fly down and see me at the show." I have this little bit of excitement thinking they may do that. I'm not there yet. I still want their approval. I know it.

It goes back to when I was little and they never came to anything at school. Even on father/daughter night he would send some other father, one of the other kid's dad took me. I really felt emotionally deprived. I remember my mother slapping me in the face. That memory came back in the last five years doing therapy. I don't remember any physical or sexual abuse at all. I remember my psychiatrist telling me that giving me diet pills at age 11 was a form of abuse. It never occurred to me it was abuse. I got addicted to diet pills as a result of that.

One childhood incident that always comes back to me is a memory of being dropped off at day care because my mother went to work. The biggest thing that stands out in my mind was, when they had the parent-teacher meeting, the group decided to order little name tags for each child. My parents weren't at that meeting so a name tag was never ordered for me. When they handed them out I didn't get one. I was devastated. The kids wore them around their neck. I was the only one who didn't have one. I still think of that and feel awful. It was a big, big thing. That still gets me.

When I was seven, I remember my parents were fighting. They said they would get a divorce. I remember thinking to myself, "Thank goodness." Mother told me that there was a possibility we may be moving. I wondered who I would go with if they got divorced.

I know my father always wished he had a boy. I always did the projects with him. It was great when I married John; he got his boy. John has been out of work for two years and my father is upset and embarrassed by it. Our parents live near each other in Portland and have lunch together sometimes. Dad doesn't know things are so bad for us financially. Even so, I know he's really worried about us. Mom talks to me.

I've begun selling my art. I feel like I need to do it for money. It's put a little pressure on me but not to the point where it's affecting my art. I started out making note cards and sold them around town in different stores. It was an "up" for me. While John was working I could go out and buy all the expensive materials; now I have to research for lower prices. I'm thinking of a way to wholesale my art.

This is the first time I've been needed. For the last nine months every turn is a positive turn. It's just been click, click, click. I'm getting a really big picture: perspective. Right now I'm taking Prozac and Wellbutrin. I also take Klonopin at night. A year ago I was taking so much stuff: Lithium and two different antidepressants. My psychiatrist is very conservative. My problem was, nothing helped me. I've tried everything. Doctors are not supposed to give Wellbutrin to people with eating disorders because they can have seizures. Finally he gave me Prozac with Wellbutrin. He made me sign a letter of consent. I don't know whether I could sleep if I didn't take medication. I'm afraid to try sleeping without drugs. Once in a while when I don't sleep it's the worst experience for me.

Lately I've been thinking about wanting to experience my feelings, and I have to tell you, I called and made an appointment for next Tuesday with my psychiatrist. I am going to talk to him about reducing my medications. I read that Lithium suppresses creativity but it doesn't seem to suppress mine.

According to Reich (1961), "It is solely our sensation of the natural process inside and outside ourselves, which holds the keys to the deep riddles of nature. . . . Sensation is the sieve through which all inner and outer stimuli are perceived; sensation is the connecting link between ego and outer world." Helen goes on to say:

I'm concerned about reducing the medications because my father and grandfather were depressed too and this may be a genetic thing. A year ago I was drugged and didn't even know it. For 17 years I was taking so much stuff. I was always tired. I didn't realize it.

I want to believe my depression is genetic because the idea of going off all this medication is very scary. It hasn't been a year since I've been taking a couple of Prozac and three Wellbutrin. I've only felt normal since last March or April when I got on this combination.

I keep going back to the idea of helping someone else. It's a lot to think about. Until I really got sick and was in the hospital I was a child. I was 40 years old but I was a child. Now I think I am growing up.

What I hope is in my future would be for John to get settled so I could continue on with my art. I don't have huge goals for my art at this point. I do not need my art to be in museums. I'll enter shows and see if I can get into them. I just filled out a form for an art consultant.

I have this nice family. I just want to be able to afford to stay in this house. There is a possibility our life can get turned upside down and I don't know if I'm up to that. I just want a status quo. I feel like I'm getting healthier but I just want to live without a crisis. I don't want to worry about it anymore. I know we bring crisis on ourselves. It would be great if I could continue to do my art and be successful.

There is something about selling your art. It is a turning point. I did a whole series of art pieces about my anger. When I can't paint I scream, cry, kick, and hit. I get out of control. I'd go to bed for days at a time. I did one in red about my father. I remember going back and finding that piece on the shelf. For years, he was trying to get his business going. There was a financial crunch at home. I'm not at the point where I believe it even when I reframe his inattention like that.

I went to a group for eating disorders. It was a 12-step program. The leader of the group said: "Oh, my God; you are the first person I met who took diet pills." She was the first one I'd met, also, who took pills at such a young age. It was such comfort. It was a big "Aha."

Lately, I am beginning to want to give something back. When I finished the piece, *"What Will I Give Today?"* I had answered the question. I found a gift that was necessary for my life. I've become closer to a few friends and have more sincere interest, caring, and love for them. I'm becoming able to put everything out—show my naked self and feel more sure of myself. I feel as if I am fine-tuning my intuition.

This Author's Initial Reaction to Helen's Story

I was surprised by my first reaction, that of immediate recognition of her problem. A woman I know suffers from the same thing—wealthy parents, beautiful mother, weight gain, and a longing to be noticed and appreciated by her mother.

Even knowing the origin of the problem, I was not insulated from feelings of agitation. Although one may read this story as "poor little rich girl" and fail to appreciate the inner anguish the child endures, this is a very real problem of self-identity. What appears to me to have happened is that growing up Helen felt unnoticed and unappreciated. She felt "without an identity." She could claim nothing as her own. Even "victim" was more of an identity than she had otherwise.

Possibly, if Helen worked through her anger at her parents, she would lose the little identity she can call her own. I can understand her resistance to embark on this journey.

This story illustrates the depth of frustration a young girl can withstand in a family of well-meaning parents. I doubt that her parents would have voluntarily turned her into a drug-dependent adult if they had known they were crushing her self-esteem by badgering her about her weight. Perhaps, if her parents would have consulted a family therapist and explained the symptoms when Helen was 10 years-old, the underlying cause of the problem might have been treated rather than the symptoms. Instead, they chose the medical route, thereby pathologizing Helen. Her parents gave her an identity: the sick child. By cooperating, Helen was only being a good girl.

Helen has gained, through her experience in the hospital, an appreciation of her art as self-therapy. "Art therapy was a kind of release. It was my turning point. As my paintings got larger I felt my confidence growing." I think the real turning point in Helen's life is that her eyes have opened to the possibility of creating a positive identity: the artist. Helen feels, "My art studio is a place of safety." In her studio, she "is" somebody.

Helen processed much of her anger toward her parents through the use of words on paper. Helen externalized her feelings of anger, sadness, and grief in the form of paint and collage on paper. I think Helen is at the turning point of replacing "Helen, the victim" with "Helen, the artist." With her new identity, one that gives her positive reinforcement, she will be more able to release the old identity.

Helen referred to her art during her stay at Turner Hospital as a "kind of release." She felt comfortable doing her art because it wasn't being judged. She had felt judged all of her life. At this point she felt a turning point. She was able to freely express herself without being judged. "No one cared what it looked like. . . . I didn't give a shit what it looked like." As she surrendered, she began to get more in touch with her own essence. "As my paintings got larger I felt my confidence growing."

A therapist told her that healing could not occur until Helen could feel her emotions. Those words stayed in Helen's mind and acted as a catalyst in beginning her expressive art collages that used healing words. For instance, *"You Have To Feel Before You Can Heal,"* appeared on about a dozen pieces. She kept repeating these words in her mind; then, a change occurred. One of the art pieces came out with *"Serenity"* on it. And as her healing progressed, the last piece in her series was entitled, *"What Will I Give Today?"* I think that this transmutation of energy, even in its formative stages, is the beginning of Helen's real search for Self.

Instead of focusing on herself, Helen is now thinking of directing her focus outwardly. This feeling of wanting to give rather than receive is one of the transpersonal aspects to her art and has enabled her to form lasting connections with other people.

She is also able now, through the sale of her art, to give something back to her family in the form of financial support. This feeling of "giving back" has deepened her relationship with her husband by raising her own self-esteem. "This is the first time I've been needed. For the last nine months, every turn is a positive turn."

Working through her anger led Helen toward religion. At the time she was working on anger, "I got really involved in the church. I was a church deacon. I visited people in the hospital and talked to them. That is how I got a touch of compassion." She realized then that she could relate to another person on a deep level and share his or her painful experiences. "I keep going back to the idea of helping someone else. It's a lot to think about."

Helen's art, though used as a coping tool in some instances such as releasing anger toward her father, has also helped her to access the wholeness within her. Art has steadied her and put her in touch with the higher aspects of her creativity.

Helen's story taught me the value of communication. Helen's parents were very upset to learn from Helen that her depression was the result of their inconsiderate treatment of her weight problem as a child. Helen's parents encouraged her to do well in art as well as on her diet. Even though success in some walk of life was just what Helen needed to begin the formation of an identity, her anger about the weight issue blocked her ability to accept their encouragement.

The Transpersonal Dimensions of Helen's Story

Helen's feelings of a deeply negative body self-image created a serious bulimic disorder. Her anger at her parents became so great due to her buried emotions that it became painful to the point of suicide. "Anger has been the catalyst for my art in the past. I have a real thing about razor blades." Helen's art acts as a life preserver in a sea of unresolved abuse pain.

When Helen found old letters from her father which nagged her about her weight and about bad management of her checkbook, she burned them. Thus, she began to bring her parental abuse pain into healing consciousness. Once these feelings were conscious she was able to release them through her artwork.

Her art, as therapy, combined with spiritual growth for her healing. It was at this point that her self-image began to heal through her art. She got a mentor who encouraged her to enter an art show. When she applied and survived the first cut she was ecstatic. When she got accepted, she was overwhelmed. Helen has had some deep and profound changes in how she handles emotions. She said, "I can release anger there (my studio). I'm trying to get in touch with compassion. I remember my first feeling of it. I hunger for more of it." Recently, she senses the beginning of a deep heart opening. "Lately, I'm beginning to give something back. I've become closer to a few friends and have a more sincere interest, caring and love for them. She also comments, "I'm fine-tuning my intuition"—perhaps a spiritual opening is near.

Helen, an expressive and self-actualizing artist, uses words in her art, words which reflect the pain of her abuse. Like Jean, Helen likes collage and uses paint to place the words on paper. Because stencils filter the paint, I am interested that Helen uses a stencil when she applies the paint. A stencil prevents the paint from exceeding the design's border. Applying this to Helen's life, the stencil reminds me of the medications she takes to keep feeling balanced. They both inhibit her total self-expression, filter, and establish a boundary simultaneously. In my opinion, Helen's relationship to her art is still in the healing stage.

Defining Helen's Current Issues and Strengths

The theme that stands out in Helen's story is parental *expectations breeding rebellion.* "They wanted me to do something well. I didn't want to shine because that's what they wanted for me." In adulthood, Helen, an only child, achieved the ultimate rebellion by denying her parents grandchildren. She wanted to be a mother but was conflicted about not wanting to shine. She adopted a Korean child. "My father didn't want to see Amelia. It was difficult for him to look at that little Korean face and to see it as one of his descendants."

Another theme that piggybacks is that Helen views herself as a *victim*. Through her loss of identity she has claimed that of victim rather than have no identity at all. Her identity of being an artist has been slow in coming, but lately, as she gives it energy, she is slowly transforming her victim identity to that of the artist. She said, "It would be great if I could continue my art and be successful. There is something about selling your art. It's a turning point."

A new theme that seems to be emerging in Helen is the thought of *giving back* to the community. "Lately I'm beginning to give something back. I did a painting called *What will I give today?*

Helen's Reaction to Participation in This Book

I've always viewed my life as good and bad, black or white—fragmented. My immediate reaction after the interview was—the line was straighter— more connected—I have a place in the world. The line is angled upward. It was a positive reaffirming feeling. A quick high. I felt as if I was seeing the big picture I had never seen before from a new perspective. Then I felt not as sure about things as I thought I did and I felt numb and drained— quiet for the rest of the afternoon.

About a week after the interview for this study, Helen forgot to take her medication when she traveled to Los Angeles; she was without medication for three nights. She visited her physician, told him that she was feeling "pretty good," and that she did not care to continue the medication. She had taken medication for a long time and wanted it out of her body. He cautioned her that "it takes about 10 days, even 14 days to come down," but "there was really nothing he could say because I had made up my mind. I was in there on a Tuesday and by Saturday I was a mess. I was feeling suicidal and I talked to him on the phone." Helen was depressed and unclear as to what to do when he asked if she felt she needed to resume the medication. He said, "I think you really need to go back on medication, but if you want to wait another week, keep calling me, that's fine."

Helen chose to abstain, but by Monday she was really depressed; she had been without medication for longer than a week. Given her family history, the doctor believed Helen's illness might be hereditary and that she would need to resume and continue medication.

> It's taken me a good week to 10 days to get back on track again. I'm taking a new medication called Effexor. I don't feel depressed but I don't feel my old self again. I haven't really created anything in my studio. I've felt really depressed. I feel paralyzed. I'm not capable of doing anything. I go to bed, curl up in a fetal position and wait it out somehow. The waiting period is shorter and shorter. When I do get depressed, I come out of it more quickly. Just now I'm feeling better. I have a show in a month. I really need to start working. I got a few of my pieces into a big gallery downtown so I'm really thrilled. I feel, after talking to my doctor, I'm just one of these people who needs medication.

As Helen's identity as an "artist" fully supplants that old identity as "victim" she may be able to better release herself from her medication. She has hinted that her problem may be more psychological than hereditary when she says, "The waiting period is shorter and shorter. When I do get depressed I come out of it more quickly."

Chapter 5

RESEARCHER'S OVERALL IMPRESSIONS

All any man can hope to do is to add his fragment to the whole. No man can be final, but he can record his progress, and whatever he records is so much done in the thrashing out of the whole thing. What he leaves is so much for others to use as stones to step on or stones to avoid. (Henri, 1923)

During the interviews I was struck by the similarity between parts of their stories and mine, and as the process continued, by the resemblance between parts of their stories. As I read and transcribed each interview, I realized I was experiencing a deep healing. Details of a participant's story would match what I had previously thought of as insignificant details of my own life. The number of my "aha's!" increased as each story unfolded.

For example, I noticed that fire was mentioned in the stories of the artists who had been abused. Remembering the autumn when, as a young child, I set the back meadow on fire, I got goose pimples. I thought of sandplay therapist Dora Kalff's (1971) observation that when a child was ready to tell his or her secret, the child used fire in the sand or in other areas of life. I wondered what secret I may have that has yet to unfold.

Personal insights crystallized, ones that I had been moving toward for the past four years. With the movement, I realized I was moving into an experience where the sacred is accessed. Storytelling is a teaching tool which bypasses the analyzing part of the brain and affects the whole person. The researcher, those who are interviewed, and the readers of the resulting book are changed because to truly listen to another's story involves the willingness to be altered by it. This happened. Transcript readers commented, "You may think I'm crazy, but I feel like the cells in my body shifted when I read your stories." Another said, "I think your stories had an effect on me."

My curiosity has evolved into involvement in the lives of these eight artists. Our friendships will survive the end of this research because there is a feeling of connection, established through community and shared compassion. Because of this support, I decided to include my own story, something I had not initially planned. And, I experienced a sense of release in writing my own story.

Remarks such as "this was very validating for me" helped me to realize that this was not just abstract research. The artists and myself all feel changed in some way by having been part of this newly-formed community of artists who have had traumatic lives. There is a sense of connection. We are experiencing consciousness-raising and compassion as a transpersonal healing process.

By honoring the organic nature of this work, I have felt more comfortable including unusual data such as dream material, symbol interpretation, and information gained from psychics. As a result, I believe the end result to be an earthy and intelligible document.

I believe that the responses support my assumption that art has a healing component, fosters an intimacy with oneself, and is a method of dissolving, if not resolving, painful childhood memories.

RESEARCH QUESTIONS

After the interviews with these women I asked them all the same set of questions. Although these women range in age from 30–78 and come from vastly different life-styles, their answers to a few of the questions were so similar that I have included them here. The questions were:

1. What happened to you when you were about five years old?
2. Would you consider yourself an introvert or extrovert?
3. How far did you go in your education?
4. Was your childhood stressful?
5. What was the worst thing that ever happened to you?
6. Have you ever considered suicide?
7. What is your blood pressure?
8. Do you have recurrent dreams or nightmares?
9. What would it be like for you if you could not paint?
10. What was the best thing that ever happened to you?
11. Are you a spiritual person?
12. Is painting ever automatic for you?

13. Have you ever had any experience with either UFO's or Near Death Experiences?
14. How is painting for you emotionally?
15. What is your feeling upon completion of a painting?
16. Has your painting experience effected your personal relationships? If so how?
17. Do you know yourself better as a result of your art?
18. How do you work with pain other than with your art?

Trauma at Specific Ages

In Ken Ring's (1992) research regarding NDE's he found that those persons who were most effected by trauma in their lives were five years old when the trauma occurred. This I found very curious since five was a pivotal age in my life. I asked each artist, "What happened when you were about five years old?" I fully expected most artists would not remember that age. However, I was repeatedly amazed by their responses:

Mari: My grandmother died and my father started hitting me.

Jean: We moved to a rickety old farm in the country.

Mia: My parents got divorced and my family split in half.

Saille: My father died.

Myrtle: We moved here from Canada. The fissures in the earth frightened me.

Mary: I had to sell flowers to support the family.

Dorothy: Because Myrtle needed help I was put in the same grade as her, it was very embarrassing.

Helen: I was the only one who didn't get a name tag because my parents were too busy to come to the PTA meeting. I was devastated.

Extroversion Or Introversion

Jean described herself as an extrovert; the remaining seven artists described themselves as introverts. (This finding corroborates other studies which note that most artists are introverted.)

Education

All participants held a college degree, ranging from an associate degree to a master of fine arts degree. I found this fact particularly interesting since art is one of the least education dependent activities there is. Anyone can paint. The requirement for inclusion in this book was not that the artwork be of any particular quality, only that the women self-identified as artists. These women are interested in life-long learning. Most got their degrees later in life.

Stressful Childhood

Seven of the artists had stressful childhoods; I found Mary's "No" answer to whether she had a stressful childhood amazing since she grew up during the Depression. She was one of 13 children, had no privacy, and at a very young age sold flowers to help support the family. Her father died suddenly when she was 17, and she said she was humiliated having to be a field worker each summer. I am reminded of the adage that it is not what happens in one's life that is important, but how one reacts to such events.

The Worst Thing That Ever Happened

Many of the answers to "What was the worst thing that ever happened to you?" centered around death.

Mary: My son was killed.

Saille: My father died.

Mari: My grandmother died.

Helen: I got so ill I thought I was going to die.

These answers suggest that these artists thought about death. This life/death reflection is an existential contemplation of important life values and indicates a certain unity of psyche and a high degree of individuation. Other answers were very personal.

Mia: My mother got divorced, and I didn't fit in with the other kids [because of my physical differences].

Dorothy: I couldn't get my voice to speak up in class.

Jean: A horse fell on me and crushed my vertebra.

Myrtle: I had an accident and couldn't lift my arms for four-and-one-half years.

Suicidal Tendencies

A question which especially concerned me was: "Have you ever considered suicide?" Six of eight artists answered affirmatively. I was shocked. I had thought that because depression could be relieved through artwork, artists would be the least likely to contemplate suicide.

I was also surprised by how many of the participants actually attempted suicide.

Mia: I just stood at that window and thought about jumping out.

Myrtle: I even went to the library to learn how to kill myself painlessly.

Helen: I really had a thing about razor blades. I ended up in Turner Hospital.

Mari: I took a whole bottle of pills and just knew when I went to bed I'd never wake up again. When I did, I was in shock and very sick.

Saille: Sometimes I just want to be taken off the planet.

Jean: I didn't kill myself because of the kids.

Only Dorothy and Mary said they had never thought about attempting suicide.

Blood Pressure

Because I was curious to learn whether art might tend to lower one's blood pressure through the emotional catharsis that occurs during the painting process, I asked the participants about their blood pressure. Seven stated their blood pressure as low or low–normal. Myrtle responded that hers was 120/80 but she was taking a mild medication. Thus, 7 of the 8 artists have low or normal blood pressure. Only Mary had slightly elevated blood pressure and she is slightly overweight.

One might deduce that creatively releasing energy is good for one's health; however, these findings may not be generalizable. The artists in this study seem healthier than the average population with regard to blood pressure.

Creative expression facilitates health for a majority of people. In an interview with Olga Luchakova (1995) she said: "Positive emotional states, those states which are associated with states of freedom, foster a positive influence on the state of health. The biochemical correlate of this experience is the production of neuromediators, such as serotonin and endogenous endorphins, which are the carriers of positive emotional states. The higher the endogenous endorphin level, the higher the immune resistency toward infection."

Recurrent Dreams or Nightmares

Most of the participants either had or continue to have recurrent dreams or nightmares. The themes include: running, being chased, falling, being lost, and houses. One person described driving on a disappearing road. Their answers indicate to me that the artists' imagination is not limited to wakefulness. Some have painted their dreams or have had paintings influenced by their dreams.

If Painting Was Not Possible

Participants were asked, What would it be like for you if you couldn't paint?

Jean: I'd get irritable, [have] nothing to look forward to.

Dorothy: My life force would be gone.

Mari: My life wouldn't have meaning, it wouldn't have enough.

Helen: It would be like I had no hands.

Saille: I'd die.

Mia and Myrtle looked me in the eye and said respectively, "I have [been unable to paint]," and "I've experienced that, it's awful." These responses suggest that the artists find happiness in creating their work; their artwork gives meaning to their lives. Without their art, they fear that they would die or cease to experience the life force. These artists connect with the transpersonal through the experience of painting. They experience a sense of unity when they connect with their essence through their art.

Mary's response was less dramatic, she said: "I'd go into music or writing."

The Best Thing that Ever Happened

When asked "What was the best thing that ever happened to you?" the following artists answered with relationship-centered responses.

Mary: Having my children and family.

Helen: Adopting our daughter.

Jean: Marrying Tom.

Mari: Meeting David and having a loving relationship.

As well as being dedicated artists, they have broad interests which indicate an active social life. Personal achievements figured with others. A sense of achievement is conveyed in their responses.

Saille: Building an art studio.

Myrtle: Realizing she could paint anything she saw.

Dorothy: Winning prizes for her art.

Mia, the philosopher in the group, responded, "I don't look at things as good or bad."

Spiritual Self-Image

All of the artists think of themselves as spiritual. When asked if God is within them, they all responded affirmatively. Furthermore, most of the artists felt that the core of all religious experience is the same.

Altered State

All the artists feel that part of the process of painting is "automatic" for them. These answers suggest an altered state of conscious in which the artist reaches the depths of a unity experience.

Paranormal Experience

None of the artists had any Unidentified Flying Object (UFO) experiences, but 4 artists had a near death experience (NDE). This figure represents 50 percent of those questioned. (These experiences are detailed in the stories of Mari, Mia, Jean, and Saille and represent a type of altered state of consciousness.) Since all of these artists have experienced some type of abuse or abandonment pain, a dissociative factor may have activated the NDEs.

The Emotional Experience of Painting

Answers to "How is painting for you emotionally?" pointed to an emotional release that occurs during the painting process.

Myrtle: Exhilarating as it unfolds.

Mary: Pleasurable, it's in my blood.

Mari: I always trust the process, it validates my being.

Helen: Usually it is a high, I have to be alone.

Jean: Wonderful, I'd rather be throwing paint than anything. I like the sounds of painting; I throw it, make noise; and I have music going.

Mia: It's intuitive, the subjects come out of my head.

Dorothy: Good. I think to myself, did I do that?" It fills my creative well.

Saille: It is intense, sometimes draining.

Seven of the artists commented that they feel off in their own world when they paint. Their response suggests a state of expanded consciousness wherein the hidden realms of their psyches become available. This state is similar to meditation.

Feeling Upon Completion of Artwork

I observed an expression of relief and pride on most artists' faces when I asked how they felt after finishing a painting. This feeling of accomplishment is expansive.

Myrtle: Exhilaration and accomplishment and extremely hungry.

Mari: Pleasure.

Jean: Excited, because I'm satisfied and fulfilled. I forget time and food. I'm completely satisfied. There is no judgment, I'm always surprised.

Mary: I look and look and sometimes change them. Then I forget about them and start something else.

Helen: The majority of the time—exhilarated, then exhausted.

Saille: Elated.

Mia: Good or frustrated. It depends on how it came out. The need to do it right is great in me.

Effect of Painting on Intimate Relationships

When asked if the experience of painting affected the artist's relationships with the people closest to them, Mary did not see any difference. The others said:

Dorothy: Yes, for the better. I feel better and it rubs off.

Saille: Yes, I get in touch with my feelings, and I'm more open.

Mari: Yes, sometimes it gets in the way. I'm less sexual when I'm creative. . . . My children have more respect for me.

Myrtle: Yes, they are proud of me. My mother was so joyful because this was her dream.

Mia: Yes, it shapes them.

Helen: I've become closer to a few friends. I have more sincere interest in caring and love for them.

Most answers suggest heightened self-esteem, validation from others, and a sense of a job done well. Each artist agreed that painting did indeed affect their self-acceptance positively.

Art as Enhancing Self-Knowledge

"Do you know yourself better as a result of your art?" Two artists (Mia, and Mary) responded negatively, and six artists responded affirmatively. Helen commented that as her art got larger, her confidence grew. Their art works for them in different ways. Jean's art allows her to contact an outrageous, spontaneous character. Saille learns from her art and said that she knows her sculptures precede her.

Working with Pain Other than Through Art

I asked, "How do you work with pain other than through your art?" Jean and Mary use journaling. Other artists turn to music, sleep, talking with other people, a chiropractor, and antiques. Helen vented physically. She said: "I'd kick, scream and get out of control."

These artists are well aware of their own responses to both physical and emotional pain and recognize that they do indeed have pain. This recognition may be the beginning of healing. Unlike many people, who do not acknowledge their emotional pain, these artists seem to be coping well with their emotional and physical pain. They contain it rather than suppress or deny it. They have learned how to hold the pain and this is healthy.

Chapter 6

THE ESSENCE OF EACH STORY
AND THE COMMON THEMES

*Through Art mysterious bonds of understanding and of
knowledge are established among men. They are the bonds of
great Brotherhood. Those who are of the Brotherhood know
each other, and time and space cannot separate them. (Henri,
1923)*

A synopsis of each artist's life opens this chapter to refresh the
reader's memory. The statements which capture the essence of
each artist's life are words spoken by the artist. They represent the major
contents, themes, and patterns in each life story. These themes and
patterns emerged from my rereading each story. I listed the words that
struck me as condensations of themes and then reduced duplicate themes
to sentences that exemplified each situation.

Because these summaries read like poetry to me, I chose to use the
format of a poem. Each artist found the one-page summary of his or her
life quite powerful and emotionally moving.

Those artists who have consciously used art to heal psychic and
physical wounding (Jean, Mari, Saille, and Helen) are listed first, then
presented are those artists who use art as a coping modality (Myrtle,
Dorothy, and Mary), and these poems end with Mia, who sees little
connection between her artwork and her health. During some of the
interviews, I wondered if the health of all people would improve if they
were exposed to a technique for using their art in a conscious manner. I
leave you, the reader, to ponder this question.

THE ESSENCE OF JEAN'S STORY

Mine was not a happy childhood, too many beatings going on.
I used to hide under the dining room buffet. He'd kick me with his
boot.
Mom hit me with the wash stick. It was so unfair. I thought it was
normal.
Age 22, I started grad school, got pregnant, had a child.
I gave it up for adoption. It was heartbreaking.
Until the sex abuse memories surfaced, my career never took off.
Nobody was there for me.
The most significant thing in my healing is my connection with God.
I've discovered the spirit within me.
I'm starting to dialogue with my art.
I have a lot of healing to do, a bunch of healing to do from the memories.
I'm looking forward to the truth coming in.
My abuse perpetrator was my father.
He was hiding behind a tree and would jump out and get me.
Now I don't feel afraid like that anymore, not about physical places.
The memories still jump out and take over my psyche.
I needed to be in a "NOT" stepped-on position any more.
So I paint; it's easier when I see the memories on canvas.
A feeling of strength, solidness, and freedom came over me.
For the first time I was seeing the real me.
Most of my work was learning to own the mother and father parts of
me.
Not projecting it out but giving it to myself.
I'm enormously proud I was able to do this.
It feels freeing and I'm delighted.

THE ESSENCE OF MARI'S STORY

My father was attached to his mother. She died suddenly.
Shortly after that my father started hitting me.
It was always out of the blue
I always lived in fear.
I had phenomenal stress and tension.
I took out the pills from the medicine cabinet and ate them all.
When I woke up I was shocked;
I couldn't even kill myself.
I married my high school sweetheart. A year later I got pregnant. He
left.
I was unhappy. Got into therapy; did intensive therapy.
I wanted to be free but didn't know what of.
I had to mourn the loss of parents; mourn that I was never nurtured.
I wanted to draw.
I began to have fish dreams. The barriers came down and the art flowed.
I had pain in my right arm and shoulder.
It went away as I dealt with my anger.
I couldn't minimize what had happened to me.
A sense of peace came.
My paintings have moved into joy and celebration.
This is how I see the world.
You don't have to like it.

THE ESSENCE OF SAILLE'S STORY

My loving father was always sick and he died when I was five.
I grew up feeling I was a burden to my mother.
I was her sounding board.
I was bleedingly lonely.
I feel like I barely survived the crucible of childhood.
I have a lot of resentment toward my mother.
My childhood abuse is an ever unfolding crippling influence in my life.
I'm too damaged to process the stresses of the workplace.
My art suffers when I try to work at the same time.
I thought I'd die if I didn't get into my studio.
Sometimes I feel like giving up and being taken off the planet.
I could not function without my art.
Making something beautiful helps pull me out of my morass.
My main identity is my sculpture.
It truly mirrors my history, philosophy, and personality.
I am fascinated with the role of the sun.
Light draws me in.
I look for fire symbols in early mythology.
I see my art as a physical conjunction and energy conductor
needed by the planet for balance.
There is often a destructive aspect to my work.
I want my work to have an interactive quality.
If spontaneous change happens, I feel successful.

THE ESSENCE OF HELEN'S STORY

I was raised by housekeepers.
My mother was beautiful, a model. Everybody knew my mother.
When I was 11, she put me on diet pills.
That's how it all began.
Father put me on diets. I would steal food anyway.
When I was young I started to purge.
It was automatic; I took laxatives.
I didn't know what I was doing to myself.
By 15, I was in a routine of taking pills and purging.
I realized I was depressed. I knew I had problems.
Anger has been the catalyst for my art in the past.
Now I need to find serenity and tranquillity.
I've tried suicide many times. I have a real thing about razor blades.
I went to the hospital. This is where my art got started.
It was a turning point.
As my paintings got larger I felt my confidence growing.
I needed to get out my anger. I put red on the paper. You can't heal
until you can feel.
My studio is a place of safety. I have to go there.
I'm trying to get in touch with compassion.
I took Lithium with other drugs for two years.
I'm just one of those people who needs to be on drugs.
Now when I do get depressed I come out of it more quickly.
I'm becoming able to show my naked self and feel more sure of myself.
There's something about selling your art. It's a turning point.

THE ESSENCE OF MYRTLE'S STORY

I was very sickly as a child. I couldn't attend school until high school.
I had rickets and tuberculosis. I was put into a sanitarium.
I had scoliosis of the spine. I went to high school with a brace.
I cried my eyes out. I had a deep inferiority complex. I got depressed.
I went to the library to learn how to commit suicide.
I had a steel body. I felt like I was a freak.
The doctor said I wouldn't live to be an adult.
I was devastated. I realized I was a burden.
I was determined to live to be an adult and promised, that if I lived,
I'd make life better for others in a similar situation.
Now I realize I was destined to be an artist.
I learned to paint everything. I was a society painter. I gave lectures.
No matter how bad off you are there is something you can contribute.
Thousands of dollars were made for worthy causes from my art.
I've had two strokes. After the strokes came the breast cancer.
Painting is better than drugs for escaping pain.
My art is God's compensation for my pain.
I paint people and animals at their best. I fall in love with my subjects.
Every animal is different. I adore them. Poodles take more breaks.
To be a portrait painter you have to notice every little detail.
I want to express the beauty of the world around me.
I have a strong purpose. My mother had a strong purpose.

THE ESSENCE OF DOROTHY'S STORY

In my family nobody talked, they'd clam up.
The silence was so thick it was ominous. I was lonely sometimes as a child.
When I paint on site the right people just come into the work.
They arrive when I need them.
I get outside myself when I paint, I become enmeshed in the process.
I become one with the rocks, trees, and mountains.
I become intimate with nature. It is like meditation.
Things call me to paint them. Painting brings the life force into my body.
It stimulates expression of color, form and feelings.
I feel buoyant and alive. It is my essence.
Light, happy paintings take my mind off the heavy things in my life.
If I don't do this, I'm dead inside.
I feel a big connection between emotional and physical health.
Painting is my emotional healthiness.
I had to deal with an alcoholic family.
All this changed when I went to Al-Anon. It clarified my life purpose.
It is a spiritual thing. It showed me the value of the church.
Painting has always been my first love. I fall in love with what I paint.
Sometimes there are obstacles in painting, just like real life.
Then there is the overcoming of everything to make it work.
It's pure creation when you are outside yourself.
If my art was taken away, my life force would be taken away.
I pray for the courage to take risks.

THE ESSENCE OF MARY'S STORY

I grew up in a nurturing family in a little Spanish mini-world.
I learned about the Mayans and the Aztecs.
On Christmas Eve we ate tamales and kissed the statue of baby Jesus.
I drew paper dolls and made papier mâché masks.
My family has always been proud of me.
I worked and sold my paintings to fellow employees and friends.
My life changed when my son died in an automobile accident.
I cried and cried and then couldn't talk about his death for five years.
My art changed too.
I paint abstract Mesoamerican gods and paintings that tell stories of our people and our
culture.
I didn't need a therapist because I was healing through my paintings.
I painted the Virgin Mary for the church.
Then I had to pray to something I'd painted. It was overwhelming.
When I saw my Virgin in the church it was a shock,
like electricity surging in me.
Something had transferred from the Virgin to me and it was part of my
son.
God is so sacred.
I don't know if I have any sacredness in me that big.

THE ESSENCE OF MIA'S STORY

I was born with birth defects of my ear and partial facial paralysis.
School was hell because I look different.
I felt strange.
I was made fun of.
I felt like an outsider.
I didn't fit in anywhere.
I drew animals; horses, mainly.
My handicap has been my advantage.
It enabled me to hold onto my uniqueness in other ways.
I surrendered.
Peace came over me.
Music is a strong part of me.
I have an unusual way of hearing.
I am on an unusual path but I don't know where it's taking me.
It can't be an accident that my struggle has to do with sound and I've
been so musically
inclined.
Music is sex in a way. Sexual energy is trading energy. You interact.
Like voodoo, you use the body as a conduit for the spiritual aspect.
All of the events in my life have been purposeful.
Art and music are conduits to how I feel.
As I evolve my art evolves.
Art set me apart and made me who I am.
Art shapes my relationships.
Life is a process in the path of the soul.

COMMON THEMES

These Artists Have a Sence of Spiritual Connection

Most of these artists have experienced what Koestler (1964) refers to as a feeling of touching and being part of a universal experience. While in the experience of painting, an artist touches an aspect of oneself that is whole and complete and facilitates spiritual connection and personal growth. Myrtle and Dorothy both spoke of being summoned to paint by certain subjects, and of how nature comes alive for them. Dorothy talked of feeling "at one with the trees, rocks and mountains." It is as if these artists access an altered state of consciousness or a meditative state while painting. This may account for their sense of unity and connectedness while in that expansive state. They experience the transpersonal dimension of reality, the place where a connection to spirit exists.

Most of these artists have touched the numinous either through an NDE, in nature, or by accident. These experiences became the stimuli that later affected the artists. All of these transpersonal experiences facilitated a sense of unity with something larger; they afforded an expanded sense of self.

For example, when Mary went into the church, saw her Virgin Mary, and realized she was going to pray to something she'd painted, she was overwhelmed. She felt ecstatic and connected to her son. Thus, Mary's art had facilitated a spiritual connection with her son. Myrtle provides another example of being changed by an encounter with the numinous. When she left the sanitarium, she experienced nature as "bigger than life." In that instant, Myrtle knew that she wanted to paint everything she saw; her life role as an artist was set in that moment. An NDE in an automobile accelerated Mari's personal exploration process. She realized the fragility of life, was sparked to leave her past behind her, and to begin her lifelong dream of being an artist.

Most of the artists spoke about an intensity of focus when they are painting. Dorothy notices the act of painting "brings the life force into my body." Vargiu (1977) points out that meditators and spiritual teachers over the years have stressed the importance of focused attention and conscious awareness. This highly focused attention is a doorway through which the spiritual may be touched.

Maslow (1971) linked creativity to self-actualization and compared it to moments of ecstasy. Dorothy, Myrtle, and Mary have experienced such moments in relation to their artwork: Dorothy, in her communion with nature; Myrtle, when she looked out the car window and saw the grass as exceptionally beautiful; and Mary, when she created the Virgin Mary for the church.

Almost all the artists mentioned something akin to Fox's (1983) idea that art is similar to meditation and may act as a stimulant to spiritual expansion and self-expression. Most of the artists commented how intensely they focus when painting.

When Jean, Dorothy, Helen, Mia and Mari refer to their art as something that comes through them, I am reminded of Jung (1972) who said that "creativity was an innate drive which seized a human being and made him its instrument." Jung considered the artist to be one who allowed art to flow through him or herself. Mari referred to this experience as being "tied in"; Dorothy said, "God works through me"; and, Helen and Mia spoke of simply allowing paintings to create themselves.

Perhaps, creative experiences represent a stabilizing force within our nature because they permit us to respond in a childlike and meditative manner, directing all our energies toward a singular activity. And this focusing unites our body-mind.

Art: Healing and Health

I agree with Spitz (1989) who wrote, "Makers and beholders alike can, in intense relations with art media or works of art, achieve through identification and projection a sense of the imaginary ideal, a momentary experience of an unfragmented, unconflicted self." All of the artists in this study speak in some manner of their art as something that helps them access the intact part of their being.

Jean's interactive artwork technique comes to mind as I reread Klein (1971). Klein writes: "The creative person is able to remain flexible, spontaneous, imaginative, open to new experience and awareness, appropriately aware of the demands of reality and the problems with which he is grappling, and able to evaluate successfully his productions in terms which are not inappropriately restrictive."

Early psychoanalysts may have been correct in pointing out that uncovering traumatic events was the key to recovery from neurotic illness. I feel that the image which tells and retells the story of transformation exists in art to a far greater degree than in music or writing. The visual image provides the opportunity to witness the process and follow its changing character. I like Rubin's (1987) remark, "Art's value to society consists in stimulating sublimation and influencing its direction."

I agree with Rothenberg (1982), who feels the artist attempts a reversal of censorship of unconscious material to gain understanding of some inner confusion. He believes that the artist tries to create order out of chaos, and Rothenberg thinks that creativity is one of the highest forms of adaptive mental processes. Rothenberg believes the artist willfully strives to produce socially valuable products and uses the highest mental function she or he possesses.

I noted earlier in this study that the artist can depict threatening images, conquer fears, and gain peace of mind through meeting adversaries on canvas rather than in real life. I intended to give a better idea of how the process actually works by presenting these stories; my point is that artistic creativity offers an arena in which to cope with problems. That this is so is quite evident in the stories of Mia, Jean, Mari, Helen, Saille, and Mary but, far more subtle in the stories of Dorothy and Myrtle.

Creative people need not be sick (Rothenberg, 1982). Rothenberg had noticed that symptoms function to keep unconscious processes and content out of awareness, but creative thinking operated in a reverse direction. It is interesting to contemplate that art, through the creative process—if resulting in an improved adaptation to reality—may reverse the direction of pathology. Huntoon (1949), noted, "Although many patients did not show any insights into what they had painted, their improved behavior indicated that they had worked out an unconscious conflict through their art production."

Art relieves stress by resolving unconscious issues. In the cases of Saille, Mari, Helen, and Jean, art has helped them accept the conditions of their lives by experiencing them through their own artistic symbolism. For Mia and Myrtle, challenged by physical conditions, art provides a communication means that exceeds the boundaries of verbal description.

Saille uses her art to maintain her emotional health. She speaks of her art as lifting her out of her morass. Wakefield (1995) says, "By capturing an experience, owning it, and by portraying it well, he [the artist] has lifted that experience out of the tangled morass of misunderstanding into the beauty of language by rendering it into art."

Bear (1985) commented that creative expression is a valuable coping mechanism for human beings, particularly those with debilitating and irreversible physical conditions. I agree and think of Myrtle's remark,

"My painting is keeping me alive." Dorothy used art to cope with her emotional pain.

A person in the midst of a crisis may suffer physical illness instead of the real crisis (Kast, 1991). The source of Jean's physical problems was the sexual and physical abuse by her father. Saille suffers severe back pain; do her childhood memories keep returning to put her flat on her back?

Artists may be unaware that they are dealing with unconscious material. Arasteh (1968) writes, "Happiness, in a sense, is the invisible portion of creation. In the process of actualization of the vision a kind of healthy anxiety, pain and longing impinge upon the individual." I think Mary, and perhaps Dorothy, would agree. On the other hand, artists who are aware that they are personally processing their issues are already aware of this phenomena. Only four of the artists (Jean, Helen, Mari, and Saille) in this study were aware of using their art directly as a processing tool even though most of the others were doing so.

Levy (1994) noted, "Artists are often compelled to express themselves and the failure to do so can bring about a crisis." His words capture Saille's feelings. When Saille felt that she would die if she did not get into her studio, she felt that the failure to create was damaging her health. Levy continues, "It is only through experience within the symbolic imaginal realm that there is a possibility for healing and transformation." Artistic expression may be considered an attempt at self-healing. This method allows a person to transcend conscious filters and to connect to universal consciousness directly. Here, there is no illness; a sense of wholeness exists that cannot be broken.

Trauma

Giovacchini (1984) writes, "The impact of a traumatic environment is felt from the very beginning of life, and distortions of ego development and defects occur in both presymbiotic and symbiotic phases." This unfortunate development was noted in Jean's, Saille's, Helen's and Mari's stories with the onset of abuse, and at a slightly later date in the stories of Mia and Myrtle. Mia experienced abandonment both when her grandmother died and her father began hitting her, and again when her parents divorced. It happened to Myrtle when she became so ill with tuberculosis that she was placed in a sanitarium.

Helen's and Saille's stories resonate with the words of Wadeson (1980), who wrote, "The depressed individual suffered loss and/or abandonment by the mothering person on whom he or she was totally dependent in infancy. The resultant rage was repressed for fear of further rejection or retaliation."

Cluster Illness

At least three of the artists had what I term cluster illnesses. What I mean by this term is that in a short space of time the artist experienced an unusual amount of sickness or accidents. A dog knocked down Myrtle, injuring her spine. Immediately following this accident, a lung collapsed, and she also suffered a paralyzed arm. During her recuperation she was bitten by a tick carrying Lyme disease. Although antibiotic treatment halted the disease, Myrtle had a severe infection. This cluster illness pattern repeated later in her life; she suffered two strokes, breast cancer, and underwent exploratory surgeries.

Jean gave birth to a child, gave him up for adoption, had a fire in her kitchen, and had an accident wherein a horse fell on her crushing her five lowest vertebrae. Two years later, she broke her leg and dislocated her shoulder a few months after she had a car accident that resulted in her wearing a neck brace.

In 1981, she had another cluster of physical ailments. She had a fibrous tumor removed from her uterus and underwent surgery on a disk in her lower back. In 1992, complications after foot surgery on both feet confined her to a wheelchair for two months. The following month she was in a car accident and nearly careened off a cliff.

Saille also had numerous childhood illnesses that appeared in clusters and even in her adult life her trials seem to be grouped into seasons.

Now that Jean and Myrtle have progressed through their healing process, they no longer experience severe health problems. Perhaps Kast (1991) is correct when he states that an artist need not be ill. When wounding is coupled with artistic expression at the highest level, somatization of crisis need not occur. As terrible as these illnesses and accidents are, one might wonder how much the mind has to do with creating crises. I found it interesting to hear recently that Myrtle has begun to attend Al-Anon meetings and it causes me to wonder how many of her adult illnesses were somatized crisises.

Depression

Otto Rank's (1914) idea that death is denied by a duplication of the self is evidenced in the self-portrait Saille did which shows a split in her personality down the center of her face. If one holds a mirror in the center of the face, thus doubling each side one at a time, one sees two people looking back at you: one is whole and healthy, and the other is worried and depressive.

I agree with Rank when he says some artists use their depression to tap into the reality and power and soul of death. They are accessing the Via Negativa that Matthew Fox (1983) describes. In my own experience, depression fosters my creative drive. During joyful times, my creativity appears in my cooking rather than painting. My creativity does not disappear: it simply expresses itself differently. Mari, Helen, and Jean bring to mind Vargiu's (1977) discussion of emotional catharsis as: "an explosive release of repressed, or accumulated, discordant emotional energy. . . . By the purposeful utilization of mental images and symbols we can release blocked emotional energy, transform it when released, and also develop or evoke feelings which are most in tune with our best values and goals."

I agree with Vargiu (1977) who notes, "As a result of transmuting discordant emotional energies a stable harmonic relationship can develop between emotional and creative fields." He goes on to say, and those artists who have tried this technique would agree, that this "can lead to a state of deep inner harmony, where feelings, mind and creative field are aligned with one another.

Grief

I agree with Knafo (1991) who says that artists convert passive grief and helplessness into active mastery. In regard to grief, bereaved individuals often find the use of repetition healing. We see in Mari's work the repetitious nature of her healing paintings. McIntyre (1990) also notes that many times withdrawal occurs when sadness and anger cannot be expressed. This seems to be occurring in Mari's life at this point. Although she welcomes visitors to her studio, she is quite reclusive. And, though she has done an enormous amount of personal work, some of the sadness may remain; if so, this would support McIntyre's (1990) observations. I have noticed this need to be alone also in the lives of Saille, Mary, Dorothy, Helen, and Mia.

Dissociation

Crisis and dissociation are not the same kind of phenomenon. Luchokova (1995) said: "Crisis is a stimulus that causes dissociation to activate. When a crisis occurs that is too much for the person's mind they will take it out of their present consciousness and store it away, put it in a place in their mind and seal it off. At a later time it may come back. Sometimes it will appear in a physical symptom of some kind."

Most of the abused artists became emotionally self-protective in the face of abuse. Mari said, "I don't care how hard he hits me, I'm not going to cry. I'm never going to allow him to hurt me with his behavior again." Jean "refused to cry." I remember laughing nervously when I was spanked; this provoked my father to remove his belt and hit me with it. I never did cry. That was my way of saying, "You can't hurt me, no matter how much you try."

By dissociating, we may keep our spirits intact. In my experience, spankings in response to unacceptable behavior are not as damaging as those done when the child feels the punishment is unjustified. Spankings given without malice are even more frightening because they have a sexual undercurrent to them. Ring (1992) points out: "a child who is exposed to either the threat or actuality of physical violence, sexual abuse or other severe traumas, will be strongly motivated selectively to 'tune out' those aspects of his physical world that are likely to harm him by splitting himself off from the sources of those threats, by dissociating."

Dissociation may account for the surfacing of repressed memories years later. Sometimes, this occurs at an awkward time for the person, such as when Jean was attending a play with her husband.

Dissociation may be voluntary. Myrtle intentionally dissociates from her pain when she paints by focusing on the project. She notices that when she is finished for the day she has an excruciating backache that she was not aware of until she lays down her brushes.

Tension

I was fascinated by how each artist deals with tension. Tension is inherent in accepting most commissioned artwork because as one cannot create exactly what is in another person's imagination. Hopefully, the creation meets that person's expectations.

When one creates to please others the elements of judgment and uncertainty are involved. In a conversation with Kaye Kruger (1995), it became evident to me that a high correlation between expectation and tension buildup exists. She said:

> It has something to do with controlling. The energy is taken inside of oneself and something uncomfortable happens. When an artist paints for the experience or the fun of it there is no expectation for someone else. It has more a quality of exploration and the experience is more like the energy going out of oneself. When an artist paints to please someone else, both the artist and person who will judge the work have expectations. Consequently, the artist may experience tension as discomfort.

When one paints for oneself, the element of exploration replaces that of expectation; a form of acceptance takes place. During this process, energy is released rather than built up; the experience relieves tension. This is important! It appears to be one of the key elements distinguishing sensory artists from imaginary artists. Those artists Jung termed sensory, and Maslow calls "special talent" artists, are represented in this study by Myrtle and Dorothy. Myrtle in particular feels a lot of tension while painting. She takes energy in, sometimes enough to cause a great deal of physical discomfort. In other artists such as Helen, Mari, Mary, and Jean, energy is being released as they paint. Painting for them is cathartic. These are the artists Jung terms imaginative and Maslow calls "self-actualizing" artists. During commissioned work as tension builds, it is understandable why an artist may feel discomfort. There is no release of energy (tension) until the painting is completed and delivered. Buildup versus release of tension appears to be one of the distinguishing factors in these two types of artists.

When Myrtle is painting a commissioned piece, she feels "plenty of tension. . . . If they don't like it, they don't have to pay for it. And I put my whole heart and soul into a painting and it could be a good portrait but they still may not like it." The tension begins before Myrtle picks up her paintbrush. She sits: "wondering if I can do it. I stare at that canvas. I've studied every relaxation technique I could get my hands on. When I'm halfway through and I can see it's coming out good then the tension turns more into excitement. Then the tension builds up again when it comes time for the viewing." Even when not painting on commission, Myrtle may feel somewhat tense, but this tension stems from her choice and execution of subjects: figures and animals. "This is because you have to make sure the elbows are in line with the body and that sort of thing.

It's a discipline type of painting. That's why I do encaustics in-between. With encaustics you can get wild and free. I don't notice any tension in encaustics."

Neumann (1974) discussed psychic tension as something that exists in the creative person from the very start of life—something that drives them. It is my impression he is referring to the sensory (special talent) artist. An inner drive propels Myrtle and Saille to paint. Dorothy also has this inner drive although does not appear to be as driven.

Most of the artists spoke of the magnetic tension that builds as they paint colors on canvas, thus creating a new, pleasing form. These artists would agree that they experience a sense of accomplishment when they have mastered a worthwhile, difficult, and challenging task. Great satisfaction ensues. I noticed how Dorothy's drive to improve technically with each succeeding painting has facilitated a sort of transcendence; she has stretched her skills.

Archetypal Symbols

Archetypal symbology appeared throughout the stories. Jungian psychologists tend to see works of art as reflections of archetypes, energy forms that inhabit the collective unconscious. These different archetypes emerge at different times and in different ways for every person. In this way, a work of art may reflect a painter's "archetypal stage." Examples of such work are Jean's paintings of being attacked from behind and Mary's death masks.

Fish symbolism emerged in a variety of ways. The fish is one of the most widely-employed symbols, appearing especially in religion and myth. In a Christian context the fish often symbolizes the willing sacrifice. Swimming, fish symbolize devotees or disciples living in the waters of life. Both Mari and I dreamed about swimming fish.

The pointed-oval sign of the yoni (the vesica piscis or vessel of the fish) is a worldwide symbol of the Great Mother and appears often in Mari's pictures. Also, Dorothy and Mia painted fish-related paintings: Dorothy painted people fishing, and Mia painted swordfish. Mia also expressed an interest in whales and dolphins; in Greece the latter appears on ancient tombs as the carrier of the soul across the sea to the Isles of the Blest. Saille dreamed of bottom-feeding fish with big smiles after being caught, and she had many dreams of whales. In one dream, a whale broke free and was swimming in a beautiful environment. Freedom from responsibility and financial concerns is a dominant theme in Saille's life.

Fire also emerged as symbol. Mari, Saille, and Helen burned their art in retaliation for parental abuse. Fire has both transformational qualities and is said by Dora Kalff (1971) to be a metaphor for being ready to divulge a secret. It is interesting to note that these artists all suffered abuse. Jean almost burned down her cabin.

I agree with Kris (1952), who noticed that art reveals unconscious material similarly to the way in which it is revealed in dreams. In dream states, one accesses alternate levels of reality. Mari and I have attempted to paint dream material. We have found the experience quite powerful; these paintings are more like life myths than simple works of art. When I focus intensely on these paintings, I feel a shift occur in my brain. The paintings speak to me on a less-than-entirely-conscious level. When I stare at one painting in particular, I actually think I feel some sort of cellular shift taking place within my physiological structure.

As time has passed, the messages have seemed to evolve in a spiral pattern, and levels of understanding about my life percolate to consciousness. It is difficult to explain, my other works do not engender the same response regardless of how long I focus on them. Mari has experienced the same effect and has had a strong emotional attachment to her dream paintings also.

In Mari's work we also see what Rubin (1985) refers to as repeated images. He says, "Artists often develop images which are repeated, and which seem to carry a power because they are associated with experiences of intense feeling and meaning." Rubin (1985) agrees that, "Such images are usually connected to emotionally significant experiences in the person's life." Helen used the words, "You have to feel before you can heal" in her collages until she had internalized the message. In Rubin's (1985) opinion, these archetypal reflections cannot be analyzed because the deeper meaning can only be known to the artist.

Jean, Helen, Mari, and Saille experienced what Rubin (1985) describes as the externalizing of an idea or feeling. He says, "Externalizing an idea or feeling in an image often allows the artist to become aware of something not previously conscious, that is to have an insight."

Images connect us with the collective unconscious. According to Neumann (1974), "The creative impulse springs from the collective; like every instinct it serves the will of the species and not of the individual. Thus, creative man is an instrument of the transpersonal." I do not agree that it serves the will of the species and not the individual. I think that in benevolently serving the needs of the individual, the will of the species may also be served. Collectively the artists in this study have said: "My images come to me, whether I'm looking for them or not," and "Sometimes the thing just sort of comes to you in a flash."

Abstract Versus Representational Style

I thought it curious that those artists who had experienced abuse in their lives—Jean, Mari, Saille, and Helen—tended to produce abstract rather than representational artwork. I found it interesting that these artists would be termed imaginative by Jung and self-actualizing by Maslow. None of the abstract paintings were painted by sensory artist (special talent artists). These four artists are those who release rather than build tension as they paint. At the highest level of abstraction, painting can abandon the representation of subject matter entirely and rely only on the expressive qualities inherent in shapes, textures, and color.

Also, these artists were less likely to create works that include the human form, especially faces. Some of the artists drew faces, but these likenesses were different from portraits produced by the artists who had not been abused. When artists choose abstraction, one can suppose that feelings or emotions are being strongly depicted. The artist can affect that individual's reality by using art as a substitute for valued objects, persons, or situations. This happened in Mary's case; she replaced her "lost object," her son, with abstracted representations of God, images that reflected her cultural heritage.

Creativity

Adler's (1936) thought that people produce art and other aspects of culture to compensate for personal inadequacies. Mari had a need to be perfect. She felt the emotional abandonment of her father after the death of her grandmother. However, May (1975) noted that "Compensatory trends in an individual will influence the forms his or her creating will take, but they do not explain the process of creativity itself."

Nydes (1962) correctly pointed out that, for the creative person, his or her work may serve to resolve inner turmoil. For Helen, Mari, Mary, Jean, Myrtle and me, Nydes' statement is unquestionably true.

Creativity appears to be an attempt to re-create a unity and can reduce guilt feelings following a death (Haynal, 1985). I see Mary's art as a gratifying maternal protection, a defense against a lack. As Haynal writes: "The representation is a re-presentation, in a way, a re-creation of the lost object."

Memory

When we paint, or write, or dance we must use our memory. For significant creative work to be done we need our memories; we need to be able to re-create both our personal and our archetypal past. By accessing our memories we create our own personal myth. Krippner (1984) describes myth thus: "A personal myth is a cognitive structure—a pattern of thinking and feeling—that gives meaning to the past, defines the present and provides direction for the future. It serves the functions of explaining, guiding, and sacralizing experience for the individual in a manner that is analogous to the way cultural myths once served those functions for a society."

Two Types of Artists

There appears to be two types of artistic expression. One deals with the familiar material drawn from conscious life. This art tends to be representational. The other deals with visionary or even primordial images that may transcend human understanding. Most often this art is abstracted.

Some of the artists (Myrtle, Dorothy, Mia, and Saille) in this study use their art as a coping modality, while others (Helen, Jean, Mari, Mia, Saille, and Mary) use their art expressively. Saille and Mia do both. In Maslow's (1987) opinion, coping behavior is purposive and motivated, and responds to praise or blame, reward or punishment. It is also conscious, effortful, and attempts to solve a problem. Maslow (1987) describes expressive behavior as that which tends to be unmotivated, unlearned, uncontrolled and not designed to do anything. An example of this is Mari's comment, "I just go into my studio and whatever happens is OK."

Maslow (1987) speaks of expressive art as more often not conscious and as being effortless in most instances. Such art is unmotivated; it simply mirrors some state of the organism. Mari sits or stands in front of her easel and selects colors whimsically; she does not plan the outcome.

Jung (1964) refers to the sensory type and the imaginative types of artist; these types exhibit strikingly different modes of representation. Jung's "sensory" style type is illustrated by Dorothy and Myrtle in Maslow's framework, they typify "special talent creativeness." Artists in this study who used a coping modality were most often the sensory type, and artists who used the expressive modality were most often the imaginative type of artist.

Jean, Mari, Helen, and Mary are more spontaneous artists; they approach their art with little or no planning. They give little thought or judgment to the final work until it nears completion. Jung categorized this style of painting as "imaginary" and described it as a fantasy or experience that is unrealistic, dreamlike, or abstract. Maslow termed this approach "self-actualizing creativeness." This distinction between types of art and artists is pertinent because the differences are clearly demonstrated by the artwork in this study.

Mia and Saille appear to incorporate both special talent creativeness and self-actualizing creativeness. Each artist has two distinct styles of artwork. Saille's sculpture radically differs from her paintings; and, although Mia's doodles are imaginary, her horses are sensory.

Maslow (1987) describes the underlying personality that tends to produce one or the other type of art as "coping" and "expressive." I think that the coping strategy most closely aligns with the sensory style and Maslow's special talent creativeness and the expressive mode more closely describes those artists who use the imaginary style or self-actualizing creativeness. In my opinion, the sensory artists in this study tended to employ coping as a modality in both their art and their lives whereas the imaginative artists tended to use expression. This distinction becomes less noticeable in the art and lives of those who have taken their art to the highest aspects of who they are.

Characteristics of Artists

Bachtold and Werner (1973) list some characteristics found in creative people. Mia and perhaps even Mari, exhibited the following characteristics: temperamentally independent (consequently, with less need of agreement or social support), accustomed to going their own way, and independently making and implementing decisions.

Saille, Jean, and Helen are more easily emotional and changeable.

They share a lower frustration tolerance for unsatisfactory conditions and may evade necessary reality demands.

Identity

Wakefield (1995) realized that when you see life as creation it is a lot more fulfilling. He says, "It moves us from the passive victim toward the active creator." Helen appears to be experiencing this shift now that she is beginning to connect with the idea of "giving something back." Her life is beginning to feel more purposeful, and she is at the threshold of claiming her own identity—that of the artist, rather than victim.

Erikson (1974) wrote: "A sense of identity means a sense of being at one with oneself as one grows and develops and it means a sense of affinity with a community's sense of being at one with its future as well as its history—or mythology." The growth in self-esteem as a result of being an artist is evident in each artist's life.

Dorothy and Mary capture fragments of their own historical "roots" in their work. Mary captures the Mesoamerican culture in her art and creates stories to explain her work. Dorothy painted *Moss Landing,* a pier that has been torn down for years. She says: "I like to capture a piece of history, that pier has been gone for years."

Finding One's Voice

The need to find one's voice was a common theme for Dorothy, Mari, Helen, and Jean. Dorothy sat back down in her elementary school classroom when no voice came forth. Later in life, she found her voice when she became president of the camera club. Mari bode her time as a child feeling trapped and unable to say anything for fear of being struck. Later, her voice appeared in angry screams on canvas, as did Helen's. Jean found her voice when she spoke up about a friend being fired.

Additional Stimuli

Some artists needed more to facilitate personal growth than simply art. Jean used poetry and writing; Dorothy benefited from Al-Anon; Mari's introduction to bioenergetic therapy helped unblock her creativity and stimulate the flow of her paintings. Myrtle journaled.

All of these artists suffered from adult crises and creative blocks. Jean and Mari strove to heal old abuse issues, Myrtle was recovering from severe body trauma incurred by illness. The artists realized additional stimuli were necessary to shift their immobility. The artists had reached a life crisis.

Mentor

Having a single female mentor was quite common. The mentor provided validation and may have been a model for "success." Saille refers to her aunt as "my beacon of hope. . . . Without her, I would not have survived." Mari's grandmother was really kind to her. Mari said, "I had a terrible flu, and she made me a cotton gown and made a matching one for my doll. I remember being overwhelmed by that gesture, and I totally loved my grandmother." Mary had her mother. She remembers being so proud when her mother told her aunt, "Mary knows how to paint, I'm sure she can draw you something."

Likewise, Mia's mother was a source of encouragement and protection: "When I started going to school, my mother would go to the art teachers and say, 'You are not to tell my daughter what to do, just give her paper and pencils and let her do what she does." Mia is thankful for this consideration and said, "I'm very lucky, very grateful." Helen said, "All along I had a mentor, a woman who also suffered from depression. She became the one who helped me along. I was so glad to have her." Dorothy had her sister Myrtle. "Myrtle is my mentor, confidant, promoter and supporter and beloved friend in all areas of my life." Myrtle has had "sponsors, art lovers."

Jean had no mentor as a child and coincidentally did no art. However, as an adult she has a mentor/teacher and fellow classmates who support her, and Jean's art is flourishing.

Independence

Each of the artists has a very strong, independent streak. The artists tend to be loners rather than team players. Although the artists can function in groups, they are not organizers or originators. They all have a feeling of "specialness" about them. They are interesting as people, not just as artists. The word "ordinary" cannot be applied to any of them.

Chapter 7

CONCLUSION

I am not particular how you take this, scientifically or otherwise; my simple motive is to make such suggestions as will bring strongly to mind the thought that . . . the artist in the studio must be in a highly sensitive and receptive mood, that negligence is not a characteristic of the artist, that he must not bind himself with preconceived ideas, must keep himself free in the attitude of attention, for he can never be greater than the thing before him. (Henri, 1923)

IMPACT ON MY OWN STORY

During the course of reading the transcription of each story, certain comments stuck in my mind. For example, Myrtle said, "I was very sickly as a child. I had a deep inferiority complex. Now I realize I was destined to be an artist." Her comment brought to mind how frail I was as a youngster and how inadequate I felt about being so skinny. I suffered from childhood asthma and just about every childhood illness a child could possibly get. Helen said, "I feigned illness to get attention." I also feigned sickness regularly as a child, especially after the birth of each sibling. My mother was so used to my being sick that she did not notice my pretense.

I was struck by Mari's words, "I knew my father hadn't sexually abused me, but there was always a weird sexual undercurrent in our relationship that I was very uncomfortable with. . . . My parents denied the abuse ever happened." These words penetrated me like a knife. Mia commented, "Sexual energy is trading energy, you interact. "It's like voodoo; you use the body as a conduit for the spiritual aspect." Jean's statement, "I wasn't happy as a child, too many beatings going on," touched the core of my being; I recalled the times my father would hit me with his belt. I also resonated with Jean's and Mari's saying, "I wouldn't cry, no matter how hard he hit me." I did not cry either when my father hit me—perhaps, that is why my mother never came to my

215

rescue. Saille said: "I feel I had an extremely difficult childhood—to the point where it continues to open up for me how difficult it really was; and, as I get older it seems to not be as resolved as I would like. I hope that the process of experiencing this pain will cease and acceptance takes place." Dorothy's words resonate with me: "I don't want to suffer someone else's pain." Sometimes, I feel as if I am living someone else's life. Lastly, Mary commented, "I don't know if I have any sacredness in me that big."

These statements touched me so deeply and told my own life story. They enabled me to string a thread through the random happenings of my earlier life in a way that wove the seemingly disconnected events of my life into a tapestry of mild physical abuse and a subtly incestuous relationship with my father. Writing this book has accelerated and continued my processing of my personal material.

In conclusion, I find that there is something unique in the creative experience. Art helps one heal the wounds of one's life. At some point, art becomes a transcendental, or even a divine, experience. In creating an artifact, one draws from one's wounds from life experience at the most intense level. Doing so in an active and alert manner expands one's reality beyond the painting experience.

At that time, a different perspective appears. The ego has not disappeared; it is simply less active. The experience of the divine, the transcendent, goes beyond ego concerns. The artist senses something larger. Ultimately, healing occurs when the artist accesses this feeling. The artist finds an extension from ego to God intrinsic in the creative act.

The body appears separate from the universe. Even though this is an illusion, this feeling appears to be true. The ego assumes a sense of importance and feels as if that is all there is, especially if we are deeply injured emotionally or physically. The ego appears to be more active if you are wounded and makes a person more defensive (except in severe wounding where ego defenses break down i.e., schizophrenia or autism, etc.). In wounded people, the ego gives the impulse to protect the physical organism; the wounding threatens the organism. Abused or ignored children feel as if their body is dying. As children, we need someone to protect us; the ego assumes that role. When children are abused, they feel constantly on the verge of annihilation. The ego becomes hypervigilant, reflecting, "You have to watch out."

As Rank (1932) says, one fluctuates between a fear of life and a fear of death. If life is not supported, it is threatened. In abuse cases, the ego assumes a bigger part; the ego expends attention, leaving less for the person to connect with his or her spiritual essence. So it goes until the person realizes one cannot protect him or herself satisfactorily. Then, something very different happens: either severe panic, or a look toward the spiritual essence.

A person can delve into the imagery that arises in art. That person may discover that the act of creation expands the person. Creativity and intuition connect one to the creative force of the universe.

Once the wounded artist embraces the imagery that was once so threatening, it ceases to have the initial impact. The experience of connectivity to the universe happens when one combines one's creativity, wounding, and imagery in a most intense way. The art experience creates a situation wherein issues dissolve even if unresolved.

This study supports Jung's theory that there are two distinctly different types of artists. Sensory artists paint things of nature or of some object. This is a direct representation, and their work is generally termed "realistic." Imaginative artists paint fantasy, abstract, dreamlike, or in some other way unrealistic subject matter. Maslow also described these two different types of artists and named them "special talent" artists (sensory), and "self-actualizing" artists (imaginative).

It was found that these two types of artists experience tension in very different ways through their art. The sensory artist is more likely to build-up tension during the art making process (only to be released upon completion of the work), while the imaginative artists had more of a tendency to release tension during art production. The way energy moves through the body appears to be a distinguishing factor between sensory and imaginative artists.

In this work the sensory artist was also more likely to demonstrate Maslow's concept of a coping strategy; which means a conscious effort is made to solve a problem. It is a strategy that is responsive to praise or blame, reward or punishment. On the other hand, the imaginative artist was more likely to demonstrate Maslow's concept of an expressive strategy. Maslow describes this strategy as unmotivated, simply mirroring the state of the organism. It is not designed to do anything (Maslow, 1987).

Although there is a healing and transformational aspect to painting, healing and transformation was more apparent in those artists termed imaginative (self-actualizing) creativeness than in the sensory (special talent) artists. Art has helped these expressive artists work through their limitations and to break through their self-limiting ideas that manifest either physically or emotionally.

The experience of painting appears to be a self-actualizing attempt at healing. In painting, the higher parts of the artist's personality emerged; so, the act of painting facilitated a sense of wholeness and transcendence.

This study's research methodology had was inherently healing. When one reflects on the developmental stages of one's life, one may become conscious of the meaning in his or her life. This method engenders self-reflection and can be a very valuable healing procedure. The participants synthesized their experiences and saw the wholeness of the fragmented parts of their stories. Awareness became possible.

The psychological outcomes of their artwork for these people were: increased self-worth, personal growth, and a method of communication with others. Also, art provides an access to an altered state of consciousness which may facilitate a connection to the divine.

Compiling data for this study, I realized that these artists are at different stages in the individuation process. They are learning to integrate the opposites within themselves. For example, Dorothy vacillates between believing in herself as an artist and fearing the loss of stability in her marriage should she sell her art and earn more than her husband. She says, "I feel damned if I do and damned if I don't; yet, I believe there is a higher way to do things."

Those artists who suffered abuse are conscious they were abused. Most of them are capable of loving themselves despite traumatic childhood events coming into awareness. The artists have discovered that troubling issues dissolve in creating their artwork, even though those issues are not resolved in the life experience. I want to *stress* that important point. It does not matter that their parents deny that abuse occurred. The artists' healing is not dependent on parental agreement.

They are able, through working with their own images, to release enough emotional energy around any particular issue to release its energetic charge. The artist no longer reacts to the stimuli. When this happens, a connection to spirit usually ensues. The artist experiences a sense of unity, and calm pervades the artist's being. This is the transpersonal aspect of artwork, and it happens time after time. It is *not* an anomaly.

AREAS FOR FUTURE RESEARCH

1. Why is trauma incurred at age five more devastating than trauma incurred at other times? The correlation between the age of traumatic incidents and creativity may provide an area for future research.

2. The exploration of suicidal thoughts in creative populations.

3. Further study of two types of artists: expressive artists versus special talent artists. What are the differences in healing, spirituality, and transcendence in these two groups?

4. The correlation between dissociation in relation to disease: does dissociation prevent the somatization of crisis?

5. The special properties of psychic versus physical pain: does psychic pain result in dissociation while physical pain results in crisis?

6. Explore the concept of self-identity as a victim in relation to artistic expression.

7. Examine fire and fish symbology as it relates to abuse.

8. Does a woman's creative expression positively affect her husband's health?

Item 8 occurred to me with regard to marital status. In a normal population I would have expected to find some widowed or divorced women in the older age group. As per the Bureau of Census (1994) Mary, at age 76, has only a 19.3% chance of being married. Dorothy and Myrtle, who are in their early 70s statistically have a 28% chance; yet all are married to their original mates. All of the female artists aged 40–51 are also married. Mia is the only unmarried woman in this study, and she has never been married.

I believe that the spouses' health may be benefiting since they have an unusual access to fullness and completion of their own interests, because the women, involved in their own meaningful activity, are not totally dependent on the husbands. The wives do not depend on their husbands' validation for self-esteem; the capacity to respect and relate to each other independently is fostered. With less mutual identification, psychological pressure on the spouses may be lessened, thus allowing them to relax.

IMPLICATIONS

The stories in this study remind us that artistic expression is a powerful tool. The sensate nature of the material, coupled with setting aside the ego, and allowing symbols to form, permits unconscious material to present in a more easily understood way. When our defenses are lowered, we can experience the symbolic nature of the material and understand it on a level below conscious awareness. We can integrate it into our awareness when we are capable.

The power of the symbols speak to both artist and viewer during the passage of time as the symbols evolve in nature to meet the person's unconscious needs. For the artist, a painting can represent a life myth. For the viewer, the artwork is a projective medium which allows the viewer to touch levels of universal consciousness.

Additionally, as experienced by all artists in this study, art facilitates a greater sense of self. The powerful nature of art leads one to a sense of Self, one's essence, and facilitates the individuation process. Art may be a pathway which connects us with our divine essence.

Art is also a healing modality. I observed that art brought so many of the artists in this study into a meditative state where they could access their core essence, rather than simply follow encultured patterning. Artists described reaching a level where their problems dissolved even though they were not resolved. The artists touched the place of spirit within themselves, their sense of divinity.

By reading each other's stories the artwork acted as a projective device. The artists shared their entire life experience—joys and sorrows—and better understood the context of each other's trauma. The art of the others afforded insights into their own essence; the artists realized that they participate in a universal story. It was as if the artists were sharing a discovery. The story sharing was valuable and healing. The sharing of their trauma in that their common acknowledgment of trauma shifted their experience into the collective, thus accessing another dimension of spiritual growth. Validation supports one's coming closer to one's essence by instigating an "Aha!" experience. Indeed, using a community to effect healing is powerful; healing increases geometrically.

THE FIELD OF TRANSPERSONAL PSYCHOLOGY

I contend that adding the dimension of a visual experience to the group-sharing process enables the client/artist/patient to experience an ongoing flow of insights from just one visual production. Art acts like a projective screen, changing as the mind changes.

One painting of mine has become a life-myth for me, and I am continually amazed at how many levels of awareness I experience when I stare at it. It is as if I am uncovering different and ever-deepening layers of dream material; however, my artwork is tangible and thus acts as a communicative medium. Also, my artwork is special to me, and its specialness translates into a feeling of "I'm special." My artwork brings me a certain sense of accomplishment. As deeper levels of my mind unfold, the painting assumes more value, and sense of value translates into increased self-esteem.

When complimented by friends or family members even relatively simple artwork can seem like Van Goghs to the artist because the artist is emotionally attached to the work.

Sharing life stories fosters a sense of community and is a wonderful avenue through which validation can take place. In such a group, life's trauma is mirrored and its significance in the life is recognized. Although a person may be mirrored in different ways everyday, it is unlikely that a person has ever had his or her entire life mirrored with an emphasis on its significance in one sitting. Realizing one's life has been significant can deepen one's self-awareness and enhance self-esteem.

REFERENCES

Acklin, M. (1986). Adult maturational processes and the facilitating environment. *Journal of Religion and Health, 25,* 3. 198–206.

Adler, A. (1936). The neurotic's picture of the world. *International Journal of Individual Psychology, 2,* 3–10.

Anzieu, D. (1975). Vers une metapsychologie de la creation. In: D. Anzieu, M. Mathieu, M. Besdine, E. Jaques, E. Guillaumin, & J. Guillaumin (Eds.), *Psycho-analyses du Genie Createur.* (pp. 1–30). Paris: Dunod.

Arasteh, A. R. (1968). *Creativity in the life cycle.* Leiden, Netherlands: E. J. Brill.

Arnheim, R. (1974). *Art and visual perception, a psychology of the creative eye.* London: University of California Press.

Assael, M., & Wacks, M. P. (1989). Artistic expression in spontaneous paintings of depressed patients. *Journal of Psychiatry Related Science, 26,* 4. 223–243.

Assagioli, R. (1971). *Psychosynthesis: A manual of principles and techniques.* New York: Viking Press.

Avstreih, A. K., & Brown, J. J. (1979). Some aspects of movement and art therapy as related to the analytic situation. *Psychoanalytic Review, 66,* 1. 49–68.

Bachtold, L. M., & Werner, E. E. (1973). Personality characteristics of creative women. *Perceptual and Motor Skills, 36,* 311–319.

Barron, F. (1968). *Creativity and personal freedom.* Princeton, N.J.: Nostrand Press.

Bear, B. (1985). The rehabilitative influences of creative experience. *The Journal of Creative Behavior, 19,* 3:3. 202–214.

Bergman, H. J. (1993). Joyce Carol Oates: A Theory of knowledge. *International Journal of Aging and Human Development, 36,* 4. 293–302.

Bleier, R. (Ed.). (1984). *Science and gender: A critique of biology and its theories on women.* New York: Pergamon.

Bradshaw, J. (1988). *Healing the shame that binds you.* Deerfield Beach, FL: Health Communications.

Bruner, J. S. (1962). *Toward a theory of instruction.* Cambridge, MA: Harvard University Press.

Bureau of Census (1994). *Statistical abstract.* Washington, D.C.: Government Printing Office.

Chambers, J. A. (1969). Beginning a multidimensional theory of creativity. *Psychological Reports, 25,* 779–799.

Clements, J. (1994). *Organic research.* A paper delivered in a class at the Institute of Transpersonal Psychology. Winter Quarter.

Cooper, J. C. (1978). *An illustrated encyclopaedia of traditional symbols.* London: Thames and Hudson Ltd.

Cooperstein, A. (1979). The conjoint evolution of consciousness and creativity: A developmental perspective. *Journal of Creative Behavior, 19,* 3. Third Quarter.

Csikszentmihalyi, M., & Getzels, J. W. (1973). The personality of young artists: An empirical and theoretical exploration. *British Journal of Psychology, 64,* 1. 91–104.

Csikszentmihalyi, M. (1990). *Flow: The psychology of optimal experience.* New York: Harper & Row.

Drinkwater, J. (1925). *Pilgrim of eternity.* New York: George H. Doran Company.

Dudek, S. Z. (1968). Regression and creativity. *Journal of Nervous and Mental Disease, 147,* 6. 535–547.

Eissler, K. R. (1963). *Goethe: A psychoanalytic study* (1775–1786). Detroit: Wayne State University Press.

Erikson, E. H. (1968). *Identity youth and crisis.* New York: Norton.

Erikson, E. H. (1974). *Dimensions of a new identity.* New York: Norton.

Ettling, D. (1994). *A phenomenological study of the creative arts as a pathway to embodiment in the personal transformation process of nine women.* Unpublished doctoral dissertation. Institute of Transpersonal Psychology, Palo Alto, California.

Fenichel, O. (1945). *The psychoanalytic theory of neurosis.* New York: Norton.

Ford, D. Y., & Harris, J. J. (1992). The elusive definition of creativity. *Journal of Creative Behavior, 26,* 3:3. 186–194.

Fox, M. (1978). A spirituality called compassion. *Journal of Religious Education, 73,* 284–300.

Fox, M. (1983). *Original blessing.* Santa Fe, New Mexico: Bear & Company.

Gardner, H. (1983). *Frames of mind: The theory of multiple intelligences.* New York: Basic Books.

Giorgi, A. (1975). An application of phenomenological method in psychology. In: A. Giorgi, C. Fischer, & E. Murray (Eds.), *Duquesne studies in phenomenological psychology,* (Vol. 11). Pittsburgh: Duquesne University Press.

Giorgi, A. (1989). Learning and memory from the perspective of phenomenological psychology. In R. Valle, & S. Halling, (Eds.), *Existential phenomenological perspectives in psychology: Exploring the breadth of human experience.* (pp. 99–112). New York: Plenum Press.

Giovacchini, P. L. (1984). The psychoanalytic paradox: The self as a transitional object. *Psychoanalytic Review, 71,* 1. 81–104.

Greenwell, B. (1990). *Energies of transformation.* Cupertino, California: Shakti River Press.

Griffin, D. R. (1990). *Sacred interconnections: Postmodern spirituality, political economy, and art.* State University of New York Press.

Hagman, S. (1986). Mary Huntoon: Pioneering Art Therapist. *American Journal of Art Therapy, 24,* 2. 92–96.

Hagood, S. M. (1987). A study of Jung's mandala and its relationship to art psychotherapy. *The Arts in Psychotherapy, 14,* 301–311.

Hall, C., & Nordby, V. (1972). *A primer of Jungian psychology.* New York: New American Library.

Hammer, E. (1958). *The clinical application of projective drawings.* (5th printing). Springfield, IL: Charles Thomas.

Harre, R., & Lamb, R. (Eds.). (1983). *Encyclopedic dictionary of psychology.* (p. 324). Cambridge, MA: MIT Press.

Harrera, H. (1983). *Frida: A biography of Frida Kahlo.* New York: Harper and Row.

Hatterer, L. J. (1965). *The artist in society.* New York: Grove Press.

Haynal, A. (1985). *Depression and creativity.* New York: International Universities Press.

Henri, R. (1923). *The art spirit.* Philadelphia: J. B. Littincott Company.

Hieronimus, R. (1985). Symbols: Agents through which consciousness is expressed in art. *Saybrook Review, 5,* 2. 47–54.

Huntoon, M. (1949). The creative arts as therapy. *Bulletin of the Menninger Clinic, 13,* 198–203.

Interview with Olga Luchakova, Institute of Transpersonal Psychology, Palo Alto, California, April, 1995.

Interview with Hal Zina Bennett, Institute of Transpersonal Psychology, Palo Alto, California, May, 1995.

Jaimison, K. (1984, October 8). The ups and downs of creativity. *Time.* 86–89.

Johnson, L. (1990). Creative therapies in the treatment of addictions: The art of transforming shame. *The Arts in Psychotherapy, 17,* 299–308.

Jung, C. G. (1960). The stages of life. In: *The structure and dynamics of the psyche, Collected Works* (Vol. 8). Princeton University Press. (First German edition, 1931)

Jung, C. G. (1964). *Man and his symbols.* New York: Doubleday.

Jung, C. G. (1972). *Mandala symbolism.* New Jersey: Princeton University Press.

Jung, C. G. (1973). *Mandala symbolism.* Bollingen Series, Princeton, NJ: Princeton University Press.

Junge, M. (1987). Feminine imagery and a young woman's search for identity. *The Arts in Psychotherapy, 14,* 121–133.

Kalff, D. M. (1971). *Mirror of a child's psyche.* San Francisco: Browser Press.

Kast, V. (1991). *The creative leap: Psychological transformation through crisis.* Illinois: Chiron Publications.

Klein, R. H. (1971). Creativity and psychopathology: A theoretical model. *Journal of Humanistic Psychology, 11,* 1. 40–52.

Knafo, D. (1991). Egon Schiele and Frida Kahlo: The self-portrait as mirror. *Journal of The American Academy of Psychoanalysts, 19,* 4. 630–647.

Koestler, A. (1964). *The act of creation.* New York: Dell Publishing.

Krippner, S. (1984). *Personal mythology: Inner guidance for the new age.* Paper presented at the International New Age Symposium, Zurich.

Kris, E. (1952). *Psychoanalytic explorations in art.* New York: International Universities Press.

Kruger, K. (1995). *Stress and academic learning.* Unpublished, doctoral dissertation. Union Institute: Cincinnati, Ohio.

Kubie, L. S. (1958). *Neurotic distortions of the creative process.* New York: Noonday Press.

Kvale, S. (1983). The qualitative research interview: A phenomenological and a hermeneutical mode of understanding. *Journal of Phenomenological Psychology, 14,* 2. 171–196.

Kvale, S. (1988). The 1000-page question. *Phenomenology and Pedagogy, 6,* 90–106.

Landau, E., Moaz, B. (1978). Creativity and self-actualization in the aging personality. *The American Journal of Psychotherapy, 29,* 117–127.

Lawlor, E. (1992). Creativity and change: The two-tiered creative arts therapy approach to co-dependency treatment. *The Arts in Psychotherapy, 19,* 19–27.

Levy, M. (1994). *Technicians of ecstasy.* Norfolk, Conn: Bramble Books.

Maslow, A. (1971). *The farther reaches of human nature.* New York: Viking Press.

Maslow, A. (1987). *Motivation and personality.* (Rev. ed.). New York: Harper and Row.

May, R. (1975). *The courage to create.* New York: W. W. Norton.

McIntyre, B. B. (1990). Art therapy with bereaved youth. *Journal of Palliative Care, 6,* 16–23.

McNiff, S. (1981). *The arts and psychotherapy.* Springfield: Charles C Thomas.

McNiff, S. (1992). *Art as medicine: Creating a therapy of the imagination.* Boston: Shambhala.

Melanson, G. (1985). Gesture drawing: An avenue to personal myth. *Saybrook Review, 5,* 2. 73–82.

Miller, A. (1990). *The untouched key.* New York: Doubleday Publisher.

Moon, B. L. (1990). *Existential art therapy: The canvas mirror.* Springfield, IL: Charles C Thomas.

Naumburg, M. (1987). *Dynamically oriented art therapy: Its principles and practice.* Chicago: Magnolia Street Publishers.

Neumann, E. (1974). *Art and the creative unconscious* (R. Manheim, Trans.), Princeton: Princeton University Press.

Nydes, J. (1962). Creativity and psychotherapy. In: Arasteh, A. R., (Ed.), *Creativity in the life cycle.* Leiden, Netherlands: E. J. Brill.

Oakley, A. (1981). Interviewing women: A contradiction in terms. In: *Doing feminist research.* Helen Roberts, (Ed.), London: Routledge & Kegan Paul.

Piaget, J. (1962). *The origins of intelligence in children.* New York: International Universities Press.

Polkinghorne, D. (1983). *Methodology for the human sciences.* New York: Suny Press.

Pollock, G. H. (1961). Mourning and adaptation. *International Journal of Psychoanalysis, 42,* 341–361.

Putnam, F. W. (1989). Pierre Janet and modern views of dissociation. *Journal of Traumatic Stress, 2,* 4. 413–429.

Quail, J. M., Peavy, R. V. (1994). A phenomenological research study of a client's experience in art therapy. *The Arts in Psychotherapy, 21,* 1. 45–57.

Rank, O. (1932). *Art and artist: Creative urge and personality development.* (C. F. Atkinson, Trans.). New York: Knopf.

Rank, O. (1964). *Will therapy and truth and reality.* (J. Taft, Trans.). (Originally published in 1945). New York: Knopf.

Reich, W. (1961). The psychology of the body. In R. Frager, & J. Fadiman (Eds.), *Personality and personal growth.* (p. 180). New York: Harper Collins.

Reinharz, S. (1992). *Feminist methods in social research.* New York: Oxford University Press.

Rentchnick, P. (1975). Les orpheline menent le monde: Une nouvelle theorie sur la genese de la volonte de puissance politique. *Medecin et Hygiene, 33,* 1754–64.

Ring, K. (1992). *The Omega project: Near death experiences, UFO encounters and mind at large.* New York: William Morrow & Co.

Rosenberg, H. S. (1987). Visual artists and imagery. *Imagination, Cognition, and Personality, 7,* 1. 77–91. Baywood Publishing.

Rosenberg, H. S., Epstein, Y. (1991). Alone together: Collaborative imagery in visual art-making. *Journal of Mental Imagery, 15,* 157–169.

Rothenberg, A. (1982). Janusian thinking and Nobel prize laureates. *American Journal of Psychiatry, 139,* 1. 122–124.

Rubin, J. A. (1985). Imagery in art therapy: The source, the setting, and the significance. *Journal of Mental Imagery, 9,* 4. 71–82.

Sandblom, P. (1989). *Creativity and disease.* Philadelphia: J. B. Lippincott Co.

Shapiro, B. (1985). All I have is the pain: Art therapy in an inpatient chronic pain relief unit. *American Journal of Art Therapy, 24,* 44–48.

Singer, J. (1973). *Boundaries of the soul.* New York: Doubleday.

Spitz, R. (1965). *The first year of life.* New York: International Universities Press.

Spitz, E. H. (1989). The world of art and the artful world: Some common fantasies in creativity and psychopathology. *The Arts in Psychotherapy, 16,* 243–251.

Springer, J. W. (1994). *Transpersonal perspective on dissociation, association, health and illness.* Unpublished masters thesis, Institute of Transpersonal Psychology, Palo Alto, California.

Swenson, A. B. (1991). Relationships: Art education, art therapy, and special education. *Perceptual and Motor Skills, 72,* 40–42.

Tesch, R. (1990). *Qualitative research: Analysis types and software tools.* New York: Falmer Press.

Torrance, E. P., & Hall, L., (1980). Assessing the further reaches of creative potential. *The Journal of Creative Behavior, 14,* 1. 1–11.

Uhlin, D. M. (1972). *Art for exceptional children.* Dubuque, IA: William C. Brown.

Vargiu, J. (1977). Creativity: The purposeful imagination. *Synthesis, 3,* 4. 17–53.

Wadeson, H. (1980). *Art psychotherapy.* New York: John Wiley & Sons.

Wakefield, D. (1995). The joy of creation: Contrary to the myth of the tormented artist, to be creative is to say yes to life. *Common Boundary.* p. 72.

Weismann, P. (1967). Ego functions in creativity. *Psychotherapy and Psychosomantics, 15,* 273–285.

Wylie, M., & Wylie, H. (1987). The creative relationship of internal and external determinants in the life of an artist, Edward Munch. *American Imago, 37,* 73–76.

NAME INDEX

A

Adler, A., 14, 210
Anderson, Hans Christian, 114
Anzieu, D., 17
Arasteh, A.R., 203
Arnheim, R., 8
Assael, M., 17, 25
Assagioli, R., 10
Avstreih, A.K., 25

B

Bachold, L.M., 158, 212
Barron, F., 13, 19, 27, 123
Bear, B., 11, 24, 39, 202
Bradshaw, John, 23
Brown, J.J., 25
Bruner, J.S., 15
Byron, Lord George G., 108

C

Camus, Albert, 17
Chabiel, M., 5
Chambers, J.A., 13
Clements, J., 32
Coronel, Pedro, 97
Cooper, J.C., 147, 152, 166
Cooperstein, A., 13
Csikszentmihalyi, M., 12

D

Dante, 17
Dudek, S.Z., 13, 26

E

Eissler, K.R., 16–17, 26
Epstein, Y., 10
Erikson, E.H., 23, 31, 213
Ettling, D., 8

F

Fenichel, O., 25
Ford, D.Y., 13
Fox, M., 27–28, 201, 205
Freud, S., 12, 26

G

Gardner, H., 14
Giovacchini, P.L., 17, 203
Goethe, Johann, 16–17
Greenwell, B., 13, 97
Griffin, D.R., 28

H

Hagood, S.M., 11
Hall, C., 13, 26
Hammer, E., 23
Harrera, H., 18
Harris, J.J., 13
Haynal, A., 95, 211
Henri, R., 3, 8, 15, 40, 182, 191, 215
Hieronimus, R., 21
Hugo, Victor, 17
Huntoon, M., 23, 202

J

Jaimison, K., 17
Johnson, L., 23

SUBJECT INDEX

A

Abuse, 3, 19–20, 35, 52–54, 57, 60, 65, 67, 68–69, 72–75, 138, 139, 148, 168–70, 174
  fire stories, 37, 55, 143, 147, 171, 177, 182
  unfairness, 65, 68
Anger, 5, 35, 39, 49, 65, 86–87, 129, 170, 172
Altered state, vi, 3, 12, 148, 188, 200 (*see also* Artistic expression)
  artistic flow, 12, 188
  ecstasy, vi, 188, 200
  integration of self, 12, 13, 22, 81–83, 98, 102, 144
  meditation, vi, 20, 27, 114, 189, 201
    release of judgmental attitudes toward self-expression, 28
  peak experience, 12–14
  state of unity, 12, 200
Archetypal symbols, 10, 45–46, 66, 101, 103, 208–10 (*see also* Symbolism and representation)
  categories of symbols as described by Assagioli, 10
  circular representation of self, 11
    opposite parts of personality, 11
  mandala, 10–11, 25, 28, 67, 80
Art and culture, v, 5
Art and feminism, v, 49–50
Art and healing, 4, 8, 22–30, 39, 41, 53, 57, 65–70, 86–91, 95–103, 107–8, 110–14, 117–20, 127–29, 140–47, 172–78, 220
  abuse: emotional, 35, 107, 138, 168–70
  abuse: physical, 35, 52–53, 72–75
  abuse: sexual, 35, 53–54, 67, 138, 139
  coping tool for adverse physical conditions, 24, 41, 53, 57, 107–8, 110–14, 154–56
  coping tool for co-dependency, 124, 128–29, 137–41

coping tool for grief, 95–103, 205
creative transformation of pain and conflict, 23–25, 26–27, 86–91, 160, 190, 210, 219
expression of feelings symbolically, 22–25
journaling, 54, 190
transpersonal dimension, 66–68, 89–92
vibrational healing, 160
Art as therapy: theoretical analyses by various psycho/social scientists, 8–30 (*see also* Individual entries in the name index)
Artistic expression, v–vii, 5, 8–30
  active passivity, 10
  altered state, vi, 3, 12, 148, 188
  completion of artwork, 189
  imagery, 11–12
    body-image projection in pictorial expression, 12
  impact on intimate relationships, 189
  insight process, 11
  Jung, Carl, 9–11, 25, 29, 48, 201, 207, 210, 212, 217, 219
    artist: imaginative style (individuation), 9, 210, 217, 219
      abstract or fantasy, 9, 217
      non-figurative, 9
      psychic tension and energy release, 207, 217
      spontaneous, 212
    artist: sensory style (creativeness), 9, 210, 217, 219
      psychic tension and energy buildup, 207, 217
      realistic, 9, 217
      representational, 9
      self-limiting, controlled, 212
  collective unconscious through mandala archetype, 10–11, 25, 208–10